D0843033

THE STUDY OF DIALECT

K. M. Petyt

THE STUDY OF DIALECT

An introduction to dialectology

WESTVIEW PRESS
BOULDER, COLORADO

SEP 1 '83

Bethel College Learning Resource Center

Published in 1980 in the United States of America by
Westview Press
5500 Central Avenue
Boulder, Colorado 80301

Frederick A. Praeger, Publisher
ISBN 0–86531–060–2
Library of Congress Catalog Card Number 80–51350

First published 1980 by
André Deutsch Limited
105 Great Russell Street London WC1

Copyright © 1980 by K. M. Petyt
All rights reserved

Published and distributed in India by
Clarion Books
(Indian Book Company)
GT Road, Shahdara, Delhi–110032

Printed in Great Britain by
Ebenezer Baylis & Son Ltd
The Trinity Press, Worcester, and London

Contents

🐚🐚🐚🐚🐚🐚

Preface

ⓖⓖⓖⓖⓖⓖ

Dialect is a subject which has for many years fascinated a large number of ordinary people. Many believe that the differences in speech between different areas are an attractive and important feature of local life. Some have been intrigued by dialect in literature: Hardy's use of Wessex dialect, the Yorkshire speech of Joseph in *Wuthering Heights*, Dickens's attempts to portray the speech of various parts of Britain, or the numerous other uses of dialect for characterization. Many bemoan the progressive disappearance of dialect, and attempt to preserve it through writings, recitations and societies dedicated to its use and study. Some of these people distinguish between 'true dialect' and the mere 'sloppy speech' which they claim is often heard today in areas where once there was a vigorous dialect – though how valid such a distinction is they have rarely troubled to consider. On the other hand, some people seem to regard any deviation from Standard English as *sub*standard; they sincerely believe that the speech of the lower classes is incorrect, and that the education system should seek to eradicate it. But how many have thought about what dialect is, and what the relation is between different forms of English?

Such matters have also attracted the attention of scholars of language. In Britain, for example, numerous publications have described the dialects of particular areas, and there have also been dialect dictionaries and grammars, and general treatises (such as G. L. Brook's book in this series) which deal with English dialects as a whole. But though there have been plenty of works on *dialects*, there is no readily available outline of *dialectology*, the systematic study of dialect, and its history, methods and concepts – as opposed to its findings about a particular dialect or the dialects of a particular language.

The aim of this book is to remedy this deficiency: to provide a complement and a background to the available works on dialects by surveying the development of dialectology – the changing methods and emphases of those working on dialect. It will also attempt to complement some of the standard works in its orientation: they have been historical and geographical in approach, and have concentrated mainly on rural dialects; I shall try to achieve a balance between this and the structural and social-urban approaches that have generally been relatively neglected in such works. After the first chapter, which deals with general issues, the arrangement is roughly chronological. Chapters Two and Three are devoted to what may be called 'traditional dialectology' – the study of regional differences, mainly dealing with rural speech. This is what is most commonly understood by the term 'dialectology', and it has been treated in numerous works; therefore, although it is one of the longest chapters, Chapter Two does not go into as much detail as the later ones, which handle less familiar topics. Chapter Four examines some of the criticisms that have been directed against these traditional approaches, and Chapters Five to Seven are devoted to structural and social-urban dialectology, which developed partly in response to these criticisms. Finally, Chapter Eight deals with two recent approaches to dialectal differences, which have emerged largely within general linguistics rather than dialectology itself. The notes to each chapter contain material which is not strictly necessary to the discussion, but which is of interest either as amplification of points which I have deliberately simplified or by providing further references, interesting anecdotes, and so on.

The book should be of interest both to the student and to the interested layman who wants to deepen his knowledge of the subject of dialect by learning more about the nature of differences in speech between different areas and different social groups, and the ways in which they can be described. My own particular areas of interest and expertise will be obvious from the proportion of examples drawn from the Yorkshire area of Britain, but the book is intended to be of use to anyone interested in dialect. Readers in Britain will find the majority of the examples more familiar to them, and Chapters Three and Seven have a mainly British readership in view; but attention is paid to work carried out elsewhere, especially in America, wherever this is important to the picture of the development of dialectology. Although this is in a sense a survey work, it does not pretend to be exhaustive, and the works referred to in each chapter only represent a selection made by the author. They should be sufficient to give an introduction to each aspect of the subject, and the reader who develops a particular interest can then seek out other relevant items.

My thanks are due to two of my colleagues in the Linguistic Science Department at Reading University, David Crystal and Peter Matthews, for helpful comments on the first draft of the book, and to my secretary, Joan Polkinhorne, for typing the final version. I am also grateful to Susan Clarke, a student of Typography and Graphic Communication at Reading, who was responsible for Figures vi–xi and xviii–xxviii; and to the following publishers and copyright-holders for granting me permission to reproduce material: The Institute of Dialect and Folk Life Studies, University of Leeds, for Figure ii (from *Survey of English Dialects: The Basic Material. Volume I: The Six Northern Counties and the Isle of Man*, edited by H. Orton and W. J. Halliday, published by E. J. Arnold), and for Figure xvi (from *A Word Geography of England*, by H. Orton and N. Wright, published by Seminar Press); Ringier und Co. for Figure iii (from *Sprach- und Sachatlas Italiens und der Südschweiz*, edited by K. Jaberg and J. Jud); Francke Verlag for Figure iv (from *Phonological Atlas of the Northern Region*, by E. Kolb); and Croom Helm for Figure v (from *The Linguistic Atlas of England*, edited by H. Orton, S. Sanderson and J. Widdowson), and for Figure xvii (from *The Linguistic Atlas of Scotland*, Volume I, edited by J. Y. Mather and H. H. Speitel).

CHAPTER I

Language, Dialect and Accent

🔟🔟🔟🔟🔟🔟

DIALECT AND LANGUAGE

What is 'dialect'? In popular usage the terms *dialect* and *language* are sometimes opposed to each other. Forms of speech with no corresponding written form, or those used by uneducated people, are labelled 'dialects' and contrasted with the true 'languages' of the literate and educated. Thus, for example, we often hear the speech of African or South American tribes referred to as dialects; or an English farm-worker of minimal education may be described as speaking a dialect; the educated person from any of these countries would on the other hand be said to speak a language – French, Spanish, English, or whatever. A distinction along similar lines which we shall note below, is to speak of 'Standard English' on the one hand (with the implication that this is the real 'language') and 'dialects' on the other.

A more technical distinction between the two terms is to say that dialects are the various *different forms of the same language*. Using a language thus necessarily involves using one of its dialects – whether, in the case of English, this is the dialect of Yorkshire, Berkshire, Suffolk, New York, Texas – or Standard English dialect.

However, two problems arise in relation to such a definition. First, just what do we mean by 'a different form of a language'? We can speak, for instance, of 'Yorkshire' as an obviously different form of English from 'Berkshire' – but 'Yorkshire' itself has 'different forms'. 'East Riding' differs from 'West Riding' (to take just one point, the former area mainly uses the word *steer* for what the latter calls a *bullock*) – and within each of these we can distinguish 'different forms'. Within the West Riding, there are differences between the towns of Bradford (where for example *very* is often pronounced [varɪ] and *love* is [lʊv]) and say Huddersfield (where these words are [verɪ] and [lɒv]); or between

Bradford and the nearby rural area around Haworth: in Bradford *she* is [ʃiː] and *the house* is often [ʔaʊs], while in Haworth they are [ʃuː] and [θaːs]. Moreover there is rarely any clear boundary between adjacent forms: Yorkshire speech only gradually gives way to that typical of Lancashire, Bradford speech to that of Leeds, and so on.

We can then distinguish a virtually infinite number of 'different forms' of any language, depending on just what linguistic features we focus on, and in how much detail. To take a further example, in British English some groups pronounce *look* with a long vowel, others with a short. But among the long-vowel forms we can certainly distinguish [luːk] from [lɪək] – and among those with [uː]-like vowels we could distinguish [luːk], [lɪuːk], [lɪuk], [lʊuːk] etc. And the various groups who say [lʊuːk] will differ among themselves in the way they pronounce other words; and so on.

This process leads us to the speech of smaller and smaller groups, until we ultimately reach the speech of an individual. This is called the *idiolect*, and in fact each idiolect differs in some details from every other. But somewhere we call a halt to this concentration on differences, and decide that among a certain group there is an important degree of linguistic unity – that its members speak the same *dialect*. This term then implies both difference (from other groups speaking the same language) and unity (with other individuals). For the purposes in hand we may draw this line between what we consider important and unimportant differences in various places. Sometimes we speak of 'Yorkshire dialect', thus implying that the features shared by all Yorkshire speakers in contrast to outsiders are important, and those in which they differ from each other are unimportant. At other times we speak of 'Dentdale dialect', with the 'essential' features being much more detailed. So in a sense a dialect is an abstraction, based on some set of features chosen in a way which is essentially arbitrary: we have simply decided that we are going to take note of some features and ignore others when calling something a 'different form of a language'.

The second problem which arises in connection with the definition of dialects as different forms of the same language is that of deciding *how* different two forms can be before they are held to be different languages rather than dialects. When we are dealing with related languages (such as English and German, as opposed to unrelated ones such as English and Malay), it is reasonable to maintain that the distinction between dialect and language is a 'quantitative' matter. For example, we could say that Cornish and Geordie are different in many ways, but not sufficiently different to be called different languages: they are different dialects. English and German on the other hand, though they were originally the same language and though they have a considerable similarity in sound pattern, grammar, vocabulary etc, are too different now to be called dialects of say 'Germanic' – they are separate languages.

What then are the criteria for deciding that linguistic differences should count as differences of dialect or of language? Do the Americans speak a different language from the British (as the title of H. L. Mencken's famous book *The American Language* seems to imply)? Should we speak of the 'language of Wessex', as used in Hardy's novels?

Many people hold the essential criterion to be that of *mutual intelligibility*: dialects are different but mutually intelligible forms of speech. So if two speakers, in spite of some observable differences in their speech, can understand each other, they are held to be using different dialects; if two speakers cannot understand each other, they are speaking different languages. This seems at first sight to accord with what we intuitively feel to be the distinction between dialect and language: a Geordie, a Cockney and a Cornishman obviously differ in speech, but they can understand each other for the most part, so we say they speak different dialects of the same language; but an Englishman and a German cannot understand each other, so we say they are speaking different languages. A Briton and an American can understand each other, so we say they are both speaking English, and so on.

But there are difficulties with this criterion. Mutual intelligibility is not an all-or-none matter: there are degrees of comprehension between speakers. A Lancastrian and a Yorkshireman may understand each other to a very great extent, while a Geordie and a Cornishman may at times be in some difficulty. Moreover, the intelligibility may not be the same in each direction: a Geordie may understand a speaker of Standard English perfectly, whereas the latter might frequently have problems in following the former.

Now if such variations existed only within what would generally be accepted as the same language, it might not be thought too damaging to the criterion for distinguishing between dialect and language. But this is not the case: for example, some North German dialects have a greater degree of mutual intelligibility with some Dutch dialects than they have with some South German dialects. And what is called a *dialect continuum* raises several difficulties for the mutual intelligibility criterion. This term refers to a succession of geographically-adjacent dialects, say A-B-C-D-E-F-G . . ., each mutually intelligible with its neighbours. But while each dialect can be understood by speakers of adjacent dialects, say D by C and E, and perhaps by B and F too, the extremes (A and G, say) are not mutually intelligible. At what point does one say that the lack of mutual intelligibility means that there is a difference of language rather than simply of dialect? If A can just understand C, but cannot really be said to understand D, does the language division come between C and D? But C and D may understand each other quite well, so the mutual intelligibility criterion should lead us to class these as different dialects rather than different languages. Such a dialect continuum extends from Northern France to Southern Italy: speakers of the various dialects can understand the neighbouring dialects, and others within a certain geographical proximity, but the dialects farthest removed from each other are certainly not mutually intelligible. A language-boundary, between French and Italian, is held to exist somewhere along this continuum, yet some dialects across this boundary can understand each other. Obviously then, the criterion of mutual intelligibility must in practice be either replaced or supplemented by others.

One of these supplementary criteria is based on the existence of a *standard language* or of a written form shared by a set of speakers: if two or more groups who differ in speech nevertheless regard the same form of speech (which may be different again) as a standard, or if they share a common written form, they tend to be regarded as speaking different dialects rather than different languages, whatever the degree of mutual intelligibility – provided only that the standard or written form is not totally unrelated to the one they speak. Thus the Liverpudlian and the Cockney differ in their speech, but both would in a sense regard the way the news is read on the BBC as the standard form of their language, and both would find the same written form in their local news-papers, so they are regarded as differing in dialect within the same (English) language. On the dialect continuum referred to above, speakers would be judged to use French or Italian dialects according to which standard and written forms they look to, even though some 'French' speakers and some 'Italian' speakers could understand each other. Likewise, though some dialects on opposite sides of the national border are mutually intelligible, speakers would be classed as using Dutch or German by the same criterion. Another European area where this criterion plays a part to some extent is that of Scandinavia: speakers there are judged to speak three different languages (Danish, Norwegian and Swedish) according to the standard form to which they look, even though their dialects *and* these standard forms have certain degrees of mutual intelligibility.

So far we have considered cases where different dialects look to a common standard form *and* a common written language, but there is one notable case where different forms of speech are usually referred to as dialects and where they share a written form but not a standard spoken form. In China, speakers in different parts of the country use Mandarin, Cantonese, Wu, Hakka, Fukien, or one of numerous other forms. Now many of these forms are not mutually intelligible, but partly because the speakers all read and write the same Chinese written form, they are generally referred to as the 'Chinese dialects'.

Almost certainly related to the above linguistic criterion for distinguishing 'dialect' and 'language' are certain non-linguistic ones – concerning common cultural or political allegiances, or 'the consciousness of the speakers'. In the case of the Chinese, the Scandinavians, the Dutch and the Germans, and in similar situations, the fact that there are political units involved seems more important than questions of mutual intelligibility: Cantonese and Mandarin speakers are said to use dialects of Chinese, however slight their mutual intelligibility, partly because they both belong to the Chinese nation and share the Chinese cultural and literary heritage; and on the other hand, Norwegians and Danes, who can understand each other quite well, are said to speak different languages partly because they are different nations with different cultural centres and traditions. Even when political factors are not significant, cultural considerations can lead to speakers being regarded as of different languages: speakers of Zulu and Xhosa can understand each other; they mostly cannot write, and questions of standard forms do not apply to most of them; but they 'feel' that they are different – they have different cultural heritages and they feel that they speak different languages. (It may be noted that political considerations can work in the opposite direction from that in the above examples in determining which of the terms 'language' or 'dialect' is employed. For example, among non-linguists Catalan and Yiddish have sometimes been denied the status of 'languages': because they are not the official languages of any political unit, they are referred to as 'dialects'.)

It is clear then that the definition of *dialect* as opposed to *language* depends on a number of criteria, some overlapping, and not all of them mutually consistent. When we encounter either of these terms used in what seems to be a dubious way, we should pause to consider whether they are justified in terms of *any* clear criterion.

DIALECT AND ACCENT

In many situations the term *dialect* is sufficient to describe various forms within the same language, but in the case of English in particular another term is often encountered: *accent*. And as with 'dialect' and 'language', the distinction between 'dialect' and 'accent' is not as obvious as might at first appear.

In popular usage the two terms are sometimes employed interchangeably. For instance, during the hunt for a dangerous criminal, a police spokesman referred on BBC television to his having 'a local accent or dialect'. But many people would probably feel that 'accent' is a somewhat more restricted term than 'dialect'; in fact they would almost certainly accept a distinction quite commonly made by linguists, and put forward recently in the following form:

> The term *dialect* refers, strictly speaking, to differences between kinds of language which are differences of vocabulary and grammar as well as pronunciation. The term *accent*, on the other hand, refers solely to differences of pronunciation.[1]

Thus, for example, [jan ɒn əm z ðai tʊp] 'one of them is your ram' would be said to be (Cumbrian) *dialect* because it differs from many forms of English in both grammar ('thy', 'on') and vocabulary ('yan', 'tup') as well as in pronunciation. But [redɪŋ z ə beʔə tɛʊn ðən wɪnsər] 'Reading is a better town than Windsor' is standard in terms of grammar and vocabulary but shows features of a (Berkshire) *accent* ([-ʔ-] for [-t-], [ɛʊ] for [aʊ], final [-r] pronounced).

In Britain the terms *Standard English* and *Received Pronunciation* (RP for short) are related to the above distinction. Their definition has been attempted in two different ways. On the one hand some scholars have taken Standard English and RP as 'neutral' forms, and have defined dialect and accent in terms of deviation from these. Thus:

> I have used the word *dialect* for any form of English which differs from Standard English in grammar, syntax, vocabulary, and of course in pronunciation too, though a difference in pronunciation alone is not enough to make a different dialect... Some people speak Standard English, with an accent, and some speak it without... This 'accentless' pronunciation ... I shall refer to as RP.[2]

On the other hand, those who would accept our earlier definition of dialects as the various different forms of a language would say that Standard English is just one dialect of English and RP is just one accent of English, but that these particular forms have a special status because of their social prestige (and note that while Standard English can be pronounced with other accents, RP is virtually always used only with Standard English). Whichever of these two positions we adopt, it is clear that Standard English is a matter of dialect, whereas RP is one of accent.

It could be concluded from the above definitions that all matters of pronunciation are matters of accent, whereas grammar and/or vocabulary must also be involved before we speak of dialect.[3] But what is meant by 'pronunciation'?

Pronunciation is a non-technical term. More exact would be *phonetics*, referring to the actual sounds involved in speech, or *phonology*, the system of functionally-distinct sound-units in any form of speech; 'pronunciation' could be taken to refer to both of these or only to the first. Does 'accent' then cover just phonetics, or both phonetics and phonology?

Certainly those differences which involve only phonetics[4] would be accepted as matters of accent. For example, the difference between [kɑːt] *cart* in some Southern British speech and [kaːt], with a vowel produced with the tongue further forward, as in some Northern forms, could be described as a difference of accent. So could that between [kæt] *cat*, as in RP, and [kat], with the tongue lower in the mouth, as in some regional forms; or that between RP [rəʊd] *road* and [roːd], with a long vowel rather than a diphthong, in some parts of the North; or that between RP [rəʊd] *rowed* and [rɔʊd], with a wider diphthong, from some Northerners; and so on.

But in fact these last two pairs of examples, though they may strike us first as merely differences of sound (phonetics), also involve differences in the systems of contrasting sound-units (phonology): in RP, *road* and *rowed* are not distinguished in pronunciation, [rəʊd] being used for both, but in parts of the North [roːd] and [rɔʊd] are unambiguously *road* and *rowed*. So whereas RP has only one contrastive unit or *phoneme* /əʊ/ as the vowel in both these words, in the North there are two, /oː/ and /ɔʊ/, which can perform a distinguishing role between several pairs of words – other examples being *nose – knows* and *groan – grown*.

A similar situation exists with pairs such as *wait – weight*, *strait – straight*, *spate – Speight*, and *ate – eight*: each pair (except the last, for some people) is pronounced alike in RP, but in parts of the North they are distinguished as [weːt] – [wɛɪt], and so on. Here again is a situation where some people in the North have more phonemes, /eː/ and /ɛɪ/, than RP-speakers who have only /eɪ/. But again, though phonology rather than simply phonetics is thus involved, these pronunciation differences would certainly be accepted as matters of accent. And several other more familiar examples of pronunciation differences which are usually accepted as accent do involve differences in phoneme system rather than simply in phonetics. For instance, areas which 'drop *h*' differ from those where *h* is sounded in that the latter have a phoneme /h/ which the former do not. Again, the difference between the Southerner and the Northerner in their pronunciation of words such as *cup, but, love, mother* etc, involves a difference in the number of vowel phonemes between the speech of these areas: in the North there is only one phoneme /ʊ/ which occurs in both the set *full, good, put, soot* etc and the set *cull, flood, but, cup* etc, whereas in the South only the former set have /ʊ/, the latter having /ʌ/. It is therefore possible in the South to distinguish pairs such as *put – putt, look – luck* and so on as [pʊt] – [pʌt] etc.

Another difference of pronunciation which would probably be called simply accent is that between Berkshire [kaːr] *car*, [kaːrd] *card* etc and RP [kaː], [kaːd].[5] Here again phonology is involved rather than just phonetics: words of the set involved contain an extra phoneme (/r/) in Berkshire as compared with RP. But this example is rather different from those discussed above. They concerned differences between the *numbers of phonemes* in the systems of particular areas e.g. Northern /eː/ + /ɛɪ/ vs. RP /eɪ/; Northern /ʊ/ vs. Southern /ʊ/ + /ʌ/; and so on. But in the present case both Berkshire and RP do have an /r/ phoneme which is used at times in an identical way (both, for example say [red] *red* and [tʃerɪ] *cherry*). It is simply that the permitted combinations or *distribution* of this phoneme differs: in RP it does not occur as the last phoneme of a word or before another consonant, whereas in Berkshire it may. Another accent difference of the same type is that between areas (particularly in the North) which pronounce *pinch, bench* as [pɪnʃ], [benʃ], with a *sh* sound at the end, and those where the same words are [pɪntʃ], [bentʃ], with a *ch*. Now both areas have both the /tʃ/ phoneme, as in [tʃɜːtʃ] *church*, and the /ʃ/ phoneme, as in [ʃɪp] *ship* and [dɪʃ] *dish*; but in combination with a preceding /n/ the one allows only /ʃ/, the other only /tʃ/. These pronunciation differences, then, involve phonology as well as phonetics, but would certainly be accepted as 'accent' rather than 'dialect'.

Yet another set of examples of what would almost certainly be called 'accent' differences also involve the phoneme system. Most Northerners pronounce the set of words including *laugh, bath, pass, dance* with the short vowel phoneme they would use in *cat*, whereas most Southerners employ the long vowel which they would have in *cart*. Now this is not a difference in the number of phonemes in the systems of these different areas (as with say *cut – put*: North [kʊt], [pʊt] – South [kʌt], [pʊt]), for both areas have both a short /a/ phoneme (in *cat, bad, back, lap* etc) and the long /aː/ phoneme (in *cart, card, bark, barge* etc). Nor is it a matter of which phonemes can occur in which combinations (as is say [pɪnʃ] vs. [pɪntʃ]):[6] in the North one can hear both short and long vowels in similar combinations e.g. [laðə] *lather* – [fɑːðə] *father*, [fastə] *faster* – [mɑːstə] *master*;[7] so too in the South e.g. [gas] *gas* – [grɑːs] *grass*, [ekspand] *expand* – [dɪmɑːnd] *demand*, [kant] *cant* – [plɑːnt] *plant*, and so on. It is simply the case that in certain particular words Northerners use one phoneme, Southerners the other. A further example of the same type, which would also be classed by most people as simply accent, concerns whether one says *walking, running*, etc or *walkin, runnin*. Again it is not a matter of some speakers having more phonemes than some others: both sets of speakers would distinguish *singers*, with the /ŋ/ phoneme, from *sinners*, with /n/. Nor is it a matter of different permitted combinations: word-finally, both /ɪŋ/ and /ɪn/ can occur from both sets of speakers, as in [kɪŋ] *king* which is distinct from [kin] *kin*. It is simply that in this particular grammatical segment (the *-ing* of participles, gerunds etc) some people have /ŋ/ and some have /n/.[8]

It is beginning to look as if *both* aspects of pronunciation, phonetics (sounds) and phonology (phonemes, or distinctive sound-units), are considered to be merely matters of accent rather than of dialect. But would we accept differences between say an RP speaker who said [rɒŋ] *wrong*, [spiːk] *speak*, [laɪt] *light*, [kɑːf] *calf*, and a rural dweller from West Yorkshire who pronounced the same words as [raŋ], [spɛɪk], [liːt], [kɔːf], as being only differences of accent? If the latter said [wɪəz mɪ kɔɪt] *where's my coat?* or [ðəz ə fɛɪt təniːt] *there's a fight tonight*, is he differing only in accent from RP [wɛəz maɪ kəʊt] [ðəz ə faɪt tənaɪt]? Would we not describe him as speaking a different dialect? But note that no vocabulary or grammatical differences exist in these examples; they differ only in pronunciation (though of course speakers who produced such West Yorkshire forms would almost certainly have *some* differences in vocabulary and grammar elsewhere). It will be recalled that the definitions of accent and dialect we are discussing seem to say that differences in pronunciation are not sufficient for us to speak of dialect: these constitute accent, whereas dialect must also involve differences of vocabulary and/or grammar. But it seems probable that many people would feel that certain differences of pronunciation, such as those in the 'where's my coat?' type of example, are too great to be counted as just accent: a person who says [wɪəz mɪ kɔɪt] is speaking a different *dialect* from one who says [wɛəz maɪ kəʊt]. But where is the line to be drawn between those differences of pronunciation that are only accent and those which are dialect?

A solution to this problem was suggested over twenty years ago by workers on the *Linguistic Survey of Scotland*,[9] but for some reason it does not seem to be well known. The distinction suggested (somewhat amplified here, and adapted to our above examples) is that differences of accent are limited to the following types of situation, others being matters of dialect:

A. Phonetic differences e.g. [kɑːt] vs. [kaːt] *cart*; [kæt] vs. [kat] *cat*;

B. Phonological differences where there is some regular and predictable correspondence between two forms of speech. This may involve: i.e. So B. joined to I. II. and III.

I. differences between two systems in terms of numbers of phonemes. For instance we say that many Northerners have only the /ʊ/ phoneme where Southerners have /ʊ/ and /ʌ/. But the differences are regular and predictable in the sense that we can state that in virtually all words where the Southerner has /ʌ/ e.g. *cull, flood, but, cup* or /ʊ/ e.g. *full, good, put, soot* the Northerner will have /ʊ/. Similarly with 'h-droppers' there is predictability in that words beginning with either /h/ or a vowel in RP will regularly begin with a vowel in these other forms. With our other examples above it was a case of some Northerners having *more* phonemes than RP, but the regularity of correspondence still exists: words with /ɛɪ/ e.g. *straight, weight* or with /eː/ e.g. *strait, wait* in the North will all have /eɪ/ in RP; and words with /ɔʊ/ e.g. *rowed, grown, knows*[10] or with /oː/ e.g. *road, groan, nose* in the North will have /əʊ/ in RP. The regularities are always more precisely statable in one direction (e.g. RP /ʊ/ and /ʌ/ both = Northern /ʊ/) than the other (Northern /ʊ/ corresponds to either /ʊ/ or /ʌ/ in RP), but the fact that there is regularity presumably means that people can readily 'translate' in most cases, and so they regard these differences as just accent.

II. differences between two systems in terms of their permitted combinations of phonemes. For example, between Berkshire [kɑːr], [kɑːrd] and RP [kɑː], [kɑːd] there is predictability in that word-finally or before another consonant Berkshire /r/ regularly corresponds to RP /ø/ (zero). Similarly, with words like *pinch, bench* there is predictability in that /n+ʃ/ in one form regularly corresponds to /n+tʃ/ in the other. Again the regularity is presumably at least partly responsible for these differences being generally accepted as simply accent.[11]

III. differences in terms of which phoneme occurs in which particular word. With the North/South difference in pronunciation of *laugh, bath, pass, dance* etc there is a considerable degree of predictability: before /f/ *laugh, quaff,* /s/ *pass, grass,* /θ/ *bath, path,* /ft/ *craft, daft,* /st/ *past, last,* /θt/ *bathed* (i.e. 'gave a bath'), /ns/ *dance, chance,* /nʃ~ntʃ/ *branch, ranch,* /nt/ *plant, grant,* /nd/ *demand, command,* /mp/ *sample, example,* the North will usually have a short vowel, the South a long one. Speakers from these different areas can no doubt automatically 'translate' between the corresponding forms, and the Northerner who tries to speak with an RP-like accent may perhaps subconsciously formulate a simple rule such as 'before /f,s,θ/ or before these consonants or /n/ plus another consonant, or before /mp/, /a/ has to be lengthened'. The exceptions are only a fairly small minority,[12] and the usually regular correspondence of short to long vowel probably accounts for the fact that this would generally be accepted as simply a matter of accent rather than one of dialect.

The examples we have discussed so far seem to support the method suggested by the *Linguistic Survey of Scotland* for distinguishing between accent and dialect, in that these are cases which most people would probably class as accent, and they do indeed show a regularity of correspondence.

Now consider the following differences in pronunciation between an RP-speaker and one from a rural area of West Yorkshire:

	night	fight	mice	find	neither	me	beat	speak
RP	———	aɪ	———		aɪ ~ iː	———	iː	———
W. Yks.	iː	ɛɪ	aɪ	ɪ	ɔː	iː	ɪə	ɛɪ

In these cases there is no clear regularity of correspondence. Although these are not isolated examples of the correspondences in question (for instance, *light, sight* also have /iː/ in West Yorkshire corresponding to RP/aɪ/; *right* has /ɛɪ/; *sky* has /aɪ/;

blind has /ɪ/; *either* has /ɔ:/; *see* has /i:/; *squeak* has /ɪə/; *steal* has /ɛɪ/; and so on), one cannot predict that say /i:/ will be the regular West Yorkshire pronunciation corresponding to RP/aɪ/, or vice versa – as is quite obvious from others among this set of examples. This is unlike the case of say RP/ʌ/, which is virtually always /ʊ/ in West Yorkshire; the latter, because of its regularity, would be classed as a difference of accent, while [niːt], [fɛɪt], [fɪnd] etc, would be considered a different dialect from RP.

By the same reasoning, someone saying [wɪəz mɪ kɔɪt] for 'where's my coat?' would be regarded as speaking a different dialect from someone who said [wɛəz maɪ kəʊt], whereas someone who said [wɛəz mɪ koːt] would simply have a different accent, because the differences between [ɛə] and [eə], and between [əʊ] and [oː] show a predictable correspondence: [oː] in West Yorkshire *boat, both, go, hope, load* etc will regularly correspond to [əʊ] in RP, and some (mainly older) people regularly have a somewhat closer diphthong [eə] corresponding to RP [ɛə].

The distinction between dialect and accent we have been discussing does not appear to be widely known. But it seems intuitively correct: some differences of phonology, for example [liːt] corresponding to RP [laɪt] *light*, seem too extreme[13] to be regarded as just accent. These, like differences in vocabulary and grammar (for example, saying [ðaz ə gɔːmləs lad] 'thou is a gaumless lad' for 'you are a stupid boy') are matters of dialect, whereas other more regular differences of pronunciation like [ɪl], [enrɪ] vs. [hɪl], [henrɪ] etc, or [paθ], [gras] vs. [pɑːθ], [grɑːs] etc, are accepted as accent.

This method of distinguishing dialect and accent could probably be employed wherever both terms are in use. In the case of British English, the same reasoning can be applied to the distinction between Standard English and RP. The usual definition of these, as examined above, makes Standard English a matter of vocabulary and grammar and RP one of pronunciation: a person can speak Standard English with non-RP pronunciation. But just as the dialect/accent distinction as commonly drawn seems to imply that all pronunciation is a matter of accent – and this we have tried to show to be untenable – so too this Standard English/RP distinction implies that pronunciation is not involved in Standard English, but only in the question of whether something is RP or not. Now this too is surely untenable: would we wish to say that [wɪəz mɪ kɔɪt] is Standard English but just happens to have been pronounced with a non-RP accent?

That Standard English is a dialect and RP an accent, as stated by those drawing the earlier dialect/accent distinction, is quite tenable once we shift the division between accent and dialect as we have suggested above. Dialect is now held to involve vocabulary, grammar and non-predictable phonological differences; regular phonological correspondences are accent. Similarly, Standard English could be held to involve vocabulary, grammar and *some* phonology: throughout the English-speaking world, a great deal of the phonological system is shared. Some variation is possible, say whether *h* or postvocalic-*r* is pronounced or not, or [paθ ~ pɑ:θ], [kʌt ~ kʊt], or [kæt ~ kat] etc – provided this is in a regular and predictable correspondence the speakers can be regarded as speaking Standard English but using various different accents. If however the correspondences are not regular, as in say [wɪəz mɪ kɔɪt], the speaker would be regarded as using a non-standard dialect of English, whether or not he also differed in vocabulary and/or grammar. On this basis a speaker from New York who said [pæ:s hɜ:ɹ ðə kɔ:fɪ] 'pass her the coffee' would be said to differ only in accent, not dialect, from a British speaker who used RP[pɑ:s hɜ: ðə kɒfɪ]: there are no grammar or vocabulary differences, and such phonetic/phonological differences as occur are in a regular correspondence.

OTHER RELEVANT TERMINOLOGY

We have now discussed the definitions of the most important terms for the study of dialect: language, dialect and accent. But a number of others will also be met with in the literature, and it would be well to examine, though more briefly, their use in dialectology and related areas.

The term *patois* is sometimes used as more or less equivalent to *dialect*, but certain differences can be deduced. Firstly, patois seems almost always to refer to a rural form of speech; dialect too has most commonly been used in this way, but particularly in recent years it is also possible to speak of 'urban dialects'. Secondly, patois, if used in connection with social differences, usually refers only to the speech of the lower strata of society; dialect can be used of any class e.g. 'middle-class dialect', 'upper-working-class dialect' etc. Thirdly, when the two terms are used alongside one another, patois generally refers to the speech of a smaller unit than dialect; thus 'dialect' may be used for the characteristics of whole provinces or regions, 'patois' for those of villages or other small communities.

Vernacular is used both popularly and in a technical sense. 'To use the vernacular' is of course usually a phrase conveying one's apology for employing an apt but rather more earthy expression than would normally be socially acceptable in that particular situation. More strictly 'the vernacular' refers to the speech of a particular country or region. As a technical term of linguistics, a vernacular is a form of speech transmitted from parent to child as a primary medium of communication i.e. a form acquired as a native language; it can be used with reference either to the speech of an individual or to that of a particular locality.

Any dialect is likely to be the vernacular of some group of speakers, though some 'common' or 'standard' forms (see below) may not be. In Britain, Standard English is the vernacular of many speakers, but for others it is a secondary acquisition; in some other countries, for example a number in Africa, it is a standard without being the vernacular of any but a comparatively small number.

The Greek term *koinē* is sometimes used in preference to its English translation 'common' ('common tongue/dialect/language' etc). It originated in the fact that whereas all the city-states of ancient Greece had their own dialects, in the late classical period that of Athens (Attic) came to be used in wider communication as a 'common dialect' (*koinē dialektē*). 'Koinē' has thus come to refer to a form of speech shared by people of different vernaculars – though for some of them the koinē itself may be their vernacular. For example, in parts of India Hindi serves as a koinē for many people; some of them speak it as their vernacular, but many are native speakers of one of the many other languages of India and turn to Hindi as a means of wider communication. In the Roman Empire, Vulgar Latin served as a koinē; people in Britain and Western Europe used Celtic or Germanic vernaculars, while in the Eastern half of the Empire Greek and Semitic languages were native, but Latin was widely used as a common language throughout the Empire. The term koinē may also be used of a common form used for more restricted purposes; for example, Latin was the koinē of scholarship in Europe for many centuries, and is still that of the Roman Catholic church.

The above examples of koinēs are of 'common languages'; these are usually picked up by their speakers who acquire what proficiency they can by practice, but in some cases they are promoted by education. In modern times, particularly in Western states, education and the mass media and a stratified society have led to the growth of another type of koinē, the 'common dialect': one dialect of the national language is transmitted in a more precisely codified and standardized form than was possible in earlier times. A koinē codified and standardized in this way under the authority of a state is termed its *standard language*.

Until recently a standard language was generally transmitted in written rather than spoken form, so the standardization was largely in terms of vocabulary and grammar. Nowadays, broadcasting and films have probably led to a degree of standardization in phonology also. In our discussion of Standard English we suggested that this involves *some* aspects of phonology as well as vocabulary and grammar: certain 'regular' differences of phonology are permitted within Standard English, other less predictable correspondences leading us to regard them as non-standard.

A koinē, including a standard language, may or may not be a dialect of the same language as the vernaculars of the area in which it is used. In Britain, Standard English is of course a dialect of the same language as the vernacular dialects; but Standard English is also used as a standard in other parts of the world where the vernaculars may be say African, Indian or Chinese. In India, the Hindi standard language is a form of the same language as some of the vernaculars, but others are dialects of other unrelated or related languages.

Style is a very overworked term: one may hear of 'literary style', 'written style', 'prose style', 'colloquial style', 'formal style', 'conversational style' and very many others.[14] In dialectology its most common use has been in connection with what we might call 'degrees of formality' – in other words, in such expressions as 'casual style', 'formal or careful style', and so on. In this book it will be used only in this way.

Finally, the term *variety*. Two main uses of this are to be observed in the literature of dialectology. The older one is for a smaller unit than a dialect; thus, just as languages comprise dialects, so dialects in turn comprise varieties, and sometimes these are said to have subvarieties.[15] The more recent use of 'variety' is as a neutral term for 'any form of language considered for some purpose as a single entity'. It is neutral in the sense that it can refer to any form more precisely described by one of the terms discussed above: thus in this sense a dialect of any sort is a variety e.g. Lancashire, or Middle-Class Bristol; so too is a patois e.g. Dentdale; or a koinē e.g. Standard English; or a particular style e.g. colloquial Standard English; and so on. 'Variety' is then used for any form that for the purposes of the discussion in hand is being treated as a single unit, its 'internal' variations being ignored.[16] In future we shall employ this term in preference to 'form of a language' which we have used hitherto (the term 'form' can be a very ambiguous one anyway, having various possible technical uses within linguistics in addition to its non-technical ones).

REGIONAL DIALECTS AND SOCIAL DIALECTS

Though 'dialect' has most commonly been employed to refer to regional differences within a language (e.g. Northern and Southern dialects; Yorkshire, Lancashire and Northumberland dialects; or, applying to finer distinctions, West Yorkshire and East Yorkshire dialects; or even Bradford, Halifax and Huddersfield dialects; and so on), it has also in more recent years been used in reference to the social dimension of linguistic difference.

For instance, three people from the *same* geographical area in West Yorkshire may pronounce the sentence 'I'm going home to Huddersfield' in quite different ways, e.g.:

    I. [aɪm gəʊɪŋ heʊm tʊ hʌdəsfiːld]
    II. [am goːɪn hoːm tə hʊdəsfiːld]
    III. [am gʊɪn ʊəm/wɒm tə ʊdəsfɪld]

The person using the first form would almost certainly be of a fairly high social status, and the one using the third of a low status; the second form is probably the commonest in the area and would be employed by most people of medium status. The three forms can be described as exemplifying different *social dialects*.

But are such matters properly the concern of dialectology? Laymen sometimes claim that certain varieties are 'not really dialect'. Many of them deplore the fact that in areas where 'true dialect' once flourished all that can be heard today is just 'sloppy speech'. For example, the latter label would be given by some people in West Yorkshire to [wɪ geʔɪn ʊz bʊks bak ɒf əv ʔ tiːtʃə ʔəde:] 'we're getting our books back from the teacher today'; the 'genuine' dialect version would be held to be, say, [wɪ getɪn wə buːks bak θrə tːɛɪtʃə tədeː].

This objection to treating social variation as dialectology I would not accept. Any variety of language is constantly changing; in the case of a regional dialect some changes (e.g. [buːk] to [bʊk], [tɛɪtʃ] to [tiːtʃ]) are in the direction of the standard language; others may be in a non-standard direction (e.g. the use of the glottal stop [ʔ] for [t] – which in fact turns out most commonly to be the feature responsible for attracting the label 'sloppy'). But the variety is still a regionally-identifiable one – a dialect.

On the other hand, the linguist may say that social variation is the province of *sociolinguistics* rather than dialectology. But this too I would reject. It could be maintained that dialectology is a branch of sociolinguistics – but not that the former must confine itself to regional differences, for regional and social variation are obviously intertwined. The three above examples illustrate the fact that speech becomes more markedly regional towards the lower end of the social scale. The speaker of the first form is employing the regionally-neutral RP; that of the second would be judged to have a West Yorkshire accent; that of the third would probably be a dialect-speaker who could be localized as coming from the Huddersfield area.

In Britain the speech of the highest social classes tends to show little difference between one region and another. The reasons for this probably include their greater geographical mobility, and particularly the fact that these groups tend to send their children to boarding-schools, often away from the home area, where features of regional speech are likely to disappear and an RP accent to be acquired. Lower down the social scale people are more likely to remain in their home areas and to receive their education in local schools, often from teachers who themselves have certain regional features in their speech, and so they have local accents. The lowest classes, especially in rural areas, tend to be the least mobile and are least likely to acquire even Standard English; they often speak with marked regional accents and are the most likely section of the population to use regional dialect.

It has been suggested that the regional and social dialect situation in Britain can be represented diagrammatically by a triangle (see Figure *i*), where the vertical dimension stands for class and the horizontal one for region.[17] At the base there is a considerable degree of regional differentiation, widest among the agricultural and unskilled industrial worker-class; but as one moves up the social scale regional variation diminishes, until at the apex, the highest class, there is virtually none at all. The version of this diagram given here attempts also to express the fact that in respect of dialect (as defined above i.e. matters of vocabulary, grammar and some phonology) there is a larger section of the social hierarchy which uses the non-regional Standard English than with accent (i.e. phonetics and other areas of phonology), where only the highest group tends to use the 'neutral' RP.

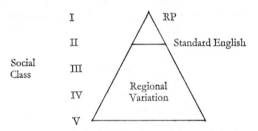

Figure i. The relation between regional variation and social class in Britain.

Having distinguished between regional and social dialects, this is a convenient place to separate two terms that have sometimes been used as if they were interchangeable: *dialectology* and *linguistic geography* (or sometimes 'dialect geography').

Dialectology has been defined as 'the study of permanent linguistic varieties within a language community'.[18] The term 'permanent' does not imply that these varieties are not continually subject to linguistic change; rather it refers to characteristics such as those relating to a speaker's regional or social provenance, which are relatively permanent in comparison with 'transient' features which depend on the immediate situation in which an utterance occurs. The latter include such characteristics as those of 'register' (broadly, the social role being performed e.g. 'scientific', 'religious', 'civil-service' etc), 'style' (the formality level adopted e.g. 'colloquial', 'formal' etc), and 'mode' (the medium employed: 'spoken' or 'written'). Transient varieties would generally be held to be the proper sphere of *stylistics* rather than of dialectology, but we shall see in Chapters Six and Seven that in recent years variation in formality has been included in the scope of social dialect study: in this area, then, dialectology and stylistics overlap.

The essential point is that 'dialectology' is a wider subject than the study of regional varieties. But the fact that until relatively recently the social dimension was relatively neglected in favour of the geographical has left many people with the impression that dialectology is *only* concerned with geographical differences. 'Linguistic geography' is properly a sub-division of dialectology: it *is* concerned with the regional distribution of linguistic varieties and their particular elements. Usually its goals are to show up such distributions on maps and also to establish the causes of particular geographical distributions.

DIALECTALIZATION AND STANDARDIZATION

Finally in this introductory chapter, we should consider something of the historical side of dialects and their peculiarities – their origins and diffusion, and, in some cases, their decay. It must be realized, however, that what follows is a very simplified account of what in reality are very often complex processes of development.

Let us start by imagining a large more-or-less unilingual area, say Gaul in the fifth century AD, when the Romans had spread the Latin language throughout the country. Now this language has continually to be transmitted from one generation to the next, and in the course of this various innovations in phonetics or grammar or vocabulary will arise. The language-system may be inaccurately apprehended by children acquiring it, for example, or some people (mainly the younger generation) may start certain new fashions of speech. These innovations will differ from place to place; most of them will quickly be rejected – for instance, as the older speakers correct or ridicule the younger –

and they will therefore have no permanent effect on the language. Others, for various reasons, will be adopted and will pass on in 'waves' of change (see p. 191 below) from speaker to speaker and place to place until they have effected a change over the whole area. Others will also be adopted, but for various reasons (see p. 63 below) their spread will only embrace a part of the whole area. These last are the crucial ones for the development of dialect differences: the region where a particular innovation has been adopted will differ in respect of this feature from the rest of the language area. After countless instances of these processes occurring over several centuries, the formerly linguistically-unified area will be a network of places differing in speech to varying extents. Neighbouring points will tend to resemble each other most, since they are most likely to have been affected by the same waves of innovation, but it is quite possible that speakers from the extreme points will not be able to understand each other. In the case of Gaul we find that the result has been that the area has become divided into that of French and that of Provençal, and that within each of these there are numerous differences of speech embracing larger or smaller areas and leading us to speak of French dialects and Provençal dialects, of varying degrees of fineness depending on how many and which features we consider important for the purpose in hand.

Thus a basic factor in *dialectalization* is time: language is transmitted from one generation to the next, and in the course of time various innovations creep in. A secondary factor is distance: some of these changes do not spread over the whole linguistic area.

Let us go a little further into the mechanisms of this process by considering a point made by the Swiss linguist Ferdinand de Saussure, in the part of his course[19] in which he examined geographical diversity in language. He held that in human society there are always two opposing forces simultaneously at work: 'parochialism' and the 'pressure of communication'. The former keeps members of a group faithful to its own traditions: the latter forces them to interact and adapt. If unchecked, parochialism would in time, as local innovations arise, create considerable differences within a large area. But the pressure of communication limits the effects of parochialism; it brings outsiders into contact with the community and sends its members out to other communities. It is thus a unifying force which counteracts the splintering effect of parochialism.

The relevance of this to language is obvious. Our speech habits are largely acquired in childhood, when our circle of acquaintance is limited and features peculiar to this limited circle (which have arisen through the innovations which creep in as a language is transmitted from one generation to the next) tend to be acquired – and possibly clung to, as they may be regarded as a sort of 'badge of membership'. This parochialism in language is an important factor in dialectalization: it is a diversifying force, helping to split a unified language into dialects. If these diverge far enough, they may become separate languages with their own dialects: thus the spoken Latin of the Roman Empire gradually fragmented into French, Spanish, Portuguese, Italian and Rumanian dialects.

The ultimate effect of parochialism would be an infinite number of different idiolects; but the opposing force, the pressure to communicate, is acting simultaneously. Its effects are both negative, in that it checks the splintering produced by parochialism by wiping out some innovations, and positive, in that it promotes unity by adopting and spreading others. In fact, though dialects are from one point of view a product of divergence, they can be seen from another as one of convergence: individuals could have become more and more different, but a dialect represents some sort of unity among a group who need to communicate regularly. Thus Saussure speaks of 'the two forces reduced to one' in, for example, a situation where parochialism creates an opposition, say between the north and the south of an area, but the pressure to communicate creates a degree of solidarity within each region. We may conclude that within a language-area the features shared by various groups are due to the pressure of communication, whereas those which typify particular groups are due to parochialism.

If a society is relatively homogeneous (i.e. with few important social or political divisions) the various dialects which have developed may exist alongside each other on an equal basis. This situation exists today in some countries and did so in Western Europe up to the Middle Ages; all varieties of language were equally acceptable, and each person spoke – and wrote – in his native dialect. But just as in ancient Greece, where each city-state had formerly used its own dialect in both spoken and written forms until wider communication led to the dialect of Athens being adopted as the common dialect, so in many other countries improved communications, a more unified nation and a more developed civilization have resulted in one of the dialects becoming the vehicle for everything that affects the nation as a whole. The dialect which comes to play this role is that of a dominant social, economic, cultural, or political group – that of the upper class, the capital, or the court, for example. This dialect has acquired its predominance for reasons that are non-linguistic, but often it soon begins to enjoy a linguistic prestige: it serves as a standard against which the usage of other groups is measured, and speakers of other dialects begin to feel inferior about their vernacular variety and attempt to use the more prestigious dialect, at least in some of their activities, while their native dialect, if retained at all, is reserved for more intimate situations. The local dialects may thus begin to have connotations of lower social or cultural status, and to be used mainly by groups of this status.

Such a 'standard language' (see p. 26 above) usually originates as the dialect of a particular region; but it may develop away from this, for two reasons. Firstly, while retaining its basic character as a dialect of that part of the country, it may, as it is more and more widely used, acquire some features from the dialects of other areas. Secondly, the popular speech of the region where the standard has arisen continues to adopt innovations, not all of which find their way into the standard language. Thus in Britain, Standard English originated in the South East (probably Essex, but later it was adopted in London), but while it is still basically a Southern variety, it has now acquired certain features from other regions; and on the other hand the dialects of Essex and that of London (Cockney) have developed into varieties quite distinct from it.

Once established, a standard language may become actually or virtually obligatory in many areas of activity, such as the law courts, the government, official ceremonies, and so on. It therefore usually becomes the medium or at least an object of education, with the result that the *non-standard* dialects, though in no way inferior as linguistic systems, frequently come to be regarded as *substandard* and incorrect.

When one dialect has become the standard variety of an area, the effects of this on the speakers may be of three broad kinds. Some will, unconsciously or deliberately, abandon the variety of their region in favour of the standard: such people are more likely to be those enjoying or desirous of obtaining a relatively high social status. A few others will be unaffected, and will continue to use the regional variety: these are most likely to be people of a relatively low status and limited contacts, the agricultural worker being the commonest example. In fact the number in this category is often smaller than might appear at first, for many people who do continue to use a regional variety also develop another form, showing a number of modifications in the direction of the standard, which they use for communication outside their local circles. Finally, the majority will continue to use a variety that is identifiable as typical of their region, but which has undergone various changes which make it more similar to the standard.

Let us examine a particular instance of this last situation, based on the author's work on the speech of the industrial towns of West Yorkshire,[20] the traditional regional dialects of which area are well described in the literature.[21] With a random sample of over one hundred speakers, in which all social classes and age-groups were represented, it was found that to a large extent the features which, by our earlier definition, would be described as 'dialect' have disappeared. In vocabulary, few items in common usage are regionally specific; the vast majority would be accepted as Standard English. In grammar, a fair number of non-standard features were observed, but they were far fewer than the traditional dialect grammars described as existing in the area; most of them only occurred a few times during the survey; and most of them were now restricted to the working classes. In phonology, cases of unpredictable correspondence (such as Yorkshire [niːt], [fɛɪt], [fɪnd], [nɔːðə] etc corresponding to RP [naɪt], [faɪt], [faɪnd], [naɪðə]) are now rare, the incidence of most phonemes being either as in RP or in a regular correspondence with this. It can therefore be concluded that most people in the area speak varieties of English approaching Standard English (as we have earlier defined this: see p. 24).

But the majority of speakers can be, and have been, identified by outsiders as coming from the Yorkshire region. For though in dialect they have largely come into line with Standard English, in accent they certainly do not use RP. It would seem that it is Standard English rather than RP which has exercised the greater influence on the traditional speech of the area; for besides vocabulary and grammar, in those aspects of phonology which we have defined as being matters of Standard English, regional features have been or are being eliminated; but in the matter of accent, which is the province of RP, regional features are still widespread. In the case of detailed phonetics, Yorkshire [aː], [a], [ɛ̞ː], [ɔ̞ː] etc as compared to RP [ɑː], [æ], [eɪ], [əʊ] etc in words such as *cart*, *cat*, *late*, *boat* and so on, are still common. In terms of the number of phonemes in a speaker's system, the absence of /ʌ/ and /h/ (resulting in *putt* and *put*, and *hedge* and *edge*, which are distinct in RP, sounding alike with many speakers in the area), and the presence of /ɛɪ/ besides /eː/, and of /ɔʊ/ besides /oː/ (with the result that *weight* and *wait*, and *rowed* and *road*, which are identical in RP, are kept distinct by many speakers) are also quite common. In the matter of the particular phoneme occurring in particular words, a short vowel (corresponding to a long one in RP) is almost universal in words of the *laugh*, *bath*, *pass*, *dance* set, and a long /uː/ (corresponding to short /ʊ/ in RP) is still frequently heard in words spelled '-ook', e.g. *took*, *look*, *cook*, *book*, though this is now mainly confined to the older generation. Of course RP, as the prestige accent, does have some influence: some people do have [eɪ] in *late*, [əʊ] or [oʊ] in *boat*, [ɑː] in *cart*, and so on – and a considerable number attempt to introduce /ʌ/ and /h/ into their systems at least on some occasions,[22] but the majority retain sufficient accent features to be readily localized.

The conclusions reached on the basis of the above survey were that the sections of the community leading the modification of local dialect are the middle classes, with the working classes being more retentive of local features but still having made considerable changes from the 'traditional' situation; that often the women in any class may be 'ahead of' the men in such modifications; and that local features which would be classed as 'dialect' i.e. vocabulary, grammar and unpredictable phonological correspondences, which are often the object of overt pressure within the education system, give way more readily to the influence of the standard variety than those which are 'accent', which are apparently not so frequently made the object of attention in the ordinary schools.

This chapter has largely been concerned with the definition of terms. This is a necessary preliminary to the remaining chapters, which will deal with the various approaches adopted in the last century or so to the study and description of dialects. We have also considered briefly the growth and decay of dialects, and have seen that many differences of language originate as differences of dialect, and that even where the increasing prestige of a standard language leads to the disappearance of many dialect features, regional features of accent may persist for much longer. Because there is this historical continuity of development between the status of dialect and language (and probably, at an earlier stage, between accent and dialect too), and also a continuity between the use of dialect and accent, as non-standard features come under pressure from a standard language, it is not surprising that there should not be an obvious division between these terms in their definition and use. I have tried to point out the difficulties in this area. The language/dialect division involves many factors, some of them too sensitive for a scholar's definition, however soundly-based, to have much influence – so I have simply stated the issues. In the case of dialect and accent, however, I have argued in favour of what seems to be the most satisfactory distinction between them.

CHAPTER 2

The Development of Dialectology
1800 – 1950

🔳🔳🔳🔳🔳🔳

HISTORY

Local differences in speech have attracted spasmodic attention for many centuries. In English literature, for example, comments about regional characteristics date back probably as far as the twelfth century. By the eighteenth century a number of *dialect glossaries* had appeared: these works listed the lexical peculiarities of the speech of a certain area – the words and phrases that seemed to be restricted to that locality. But it was during the nineteenth century that the study of dialect received its greatest impetus, from the development of *comparative philology*. This is the subject which deals with the history of languages and the relations between languages, and during this 'golden age' of the subject philologists did their greatest work in establishing the correspondences between different but related languages, drawing up 'family trees' of languages, and working out what changes must have occurred within each language. For instance, comparing the Latin forms *pater* and *ped-*, the Greek *patēr* and *pod-*, the Sanskrit *pitar-* and *pād-*, the German *Vater* and *Füss*, and the English *father* and *foot* (and many similar forms), they established a correspondence between [p] in the Italic, Greek and Indic languages and [f] in German and English. This not only helped to show that German and English are quite closely related (they were both assigned to a *Germanic* branch of the Indo-European 'family' of languages), but also enabled scholars to establish a *sound law* stating that the original [p] of Indo-European changed to [f] in Germanic.

To work out such correspondences and laws, philologists sought the most 'pure' data in each language, and they came to realize that dialects often preserve older and more regular forms than a standard language. For example, the existence of an /ʌ/ vowel in RP (and Southern British English generally, of course) as in *but*, *love* etc, alongside the /ʊ/ of *put*, *wolf* etc, was found to be a relatively recent development: dialects of Northern England preserve the older situation, with /ʊ/ in all these words and no /ʌ/ in their phonological systems. Similarly, some Yorkshire dialects provide examples of a dialect retaining a distinction between words which in the standard language have become homonyms: e.g. [rɛɪt] 'right' (from Old English *reht*) vs. [raɪt] 'write' (OE *wrītan*); [waːk] 'work (N)' (OE *weorc*) vs. [wɜːk] 'to work' (OE *wyrcan*); and so on. An example of the standard language showing less 'pure' and regular developments is provided by the set of words including *father*, *foot*, *five*, *vat*, *vixen*. All these words had initial [f] in Old English; some dialects retained this sound, others changed it to [v]. Standard English (and now many other dialects too) contains a mixture of both developments, presumably because it has grown up as a common variety for speakers of different dialects and so has received contributions from different areas. A more regular situation is seen for example in the dialects of Wiltshire, Dorset, Somerset, Devon and parts of adjacent counties, where all the above words begin with [v].

Because of the increased interest in dialects, we see from the early nineteenth century not only a greater number of dialect glossaries, but also the appearance of *dialect grammars*: these are not so much accounts of grammar in the usual sense as attempts to set out in detail the correspondences between the sounds and inflections of a particular dialect and those of an earlier stage of the language to which it belongs. Of course, the history of dialectology from this time could form a book in itself, so in this section we can do no more than pick out some of the most noteworthy developments.

The most important works for dialectology in modern times appeared in Germany. The first grammar which attempted to treat not just one dialect but all the dialects of an area was published in 1821 by Johann Andreas Schmeller. *The Dialects of Bavaria* gave a 'historical-geographical-grammatical presentation of the German language' in this area, and included a small map classifying the Bavarian dialects – probably the first mini-*linguistic atlas*. The first *dialect survey* of an area was carried out by an Alsatian parson, L. Liebich, who in 1873 sent a postal questionnaire to primary-school teachers in all German-speaking areas of Alsace. The questionnaire sought a large amount of information about local phonology and grammar, and Liebich wrote up his findings as a grammar of Alsatian dialects, with a number of maps; but unfortunately his work was never published.

Liebich completed his work in 1876, a year that was to be a milestone in the history of both dialectology and linguistics generally. In that year, four important events occurred, all in German-speaking areas:

I. Eduard Sievers published *Elements of Phonetics*, a pioneering work which helped to make phonetics a much more precise science, and this provided an important tool for all linguistic investigations.

II. A group of scholars who came to be called the *Neogrammarians* propounded their axiom that 'phonetic laws have no exceptions'. To illustrate: in a manner very similar to that employed by scientists in arriving at scientific 'laws' such as the law of gravity, we can on the basis of a number of observations (such as noting the correspondences referred to above between Latin *pater/ped-*, Greek *patēr/pod-*, Sanskrit *pitar-/pād-*, English *father/foot* and so on) formulate a 'law': that Latin, Greek and Sanskrit [p] corresponds to Germanic [f]; or that Indo-European [p], which is retained in Latin, Greek and Sanskrit, develops into [f] in the Germanic languages. Such a law was held by the Neogrammarians to have no exceptions i.e. every Indo-European [p] will have changed into [f] in Germanic. If we find an apparent exception, then either the law has not been formulated sufficiently precisely (e.g. [p] does not become [f] in certain environments, for example if preceded by [s] cf. Latin *spuo*: Eng *spew*), or some other explanation can be found, such as that the words are not in fact related, that there has later been an analogical new formation, or that the 'exception' word is a recent borrowing (e.g. *paternal*).

These two events were of profound importance for linguistics in general as well as for dialectology. The other two were of interest mainly to the latter:

III. A Swiss student of Sievers, Jost Winteler, published a monograph on the dialect of Kerenzen in the Canton of Glarus.

This work became the model for many other studies of the dialect of a single locality.

IV. Georg Wenker, a young schoolteacher from Düsseldorf, began work on a survey of the dialects of that area. This was to develop into the first great dialect survey, and we must consider it at some length.

Wenker started with the idea of surveying the Rhineland around Düsseldorf, but his aims rapidly became much wider. In 1877 he extended his investigation to Westphalia, and in 1879 to the rest of North and Central Germany. He began to publish a few maps in 1881, but then gave up this project in favour of a survey of the whole German empire.

Wenker carried out his investigation by post: with the aid of a government grant he sent out a questionnaire to every single village that had a school. This questionnaire comprised forty sentences,[1] containing selected phonetic and grammatical features, which the teacher was asked to 'translate' into the local dialect: e.g. 'It will stop raining in a minute, and then the weather will get better.' At that time the science of phonetics and systems of phonetic transcription were relatively undeveloped (and of course few schoolteachers would be skilled in such matters even today), so those responding had to manage as best they could with the resources of the orthography. But Wenker nevertheless received over 52,000 completed questionnaires.

Soon after beginning his work Wenker became University Librarian at Marburg (in 1898 he was given an honorary professorship). The University of Marburg became the home of the German dialect survey, and here Wenker began the task of editing and interpreting the vast amount of data he had elicited. It was far from completed when he died in 1911, and was succeeded as director of the *Linguistic Atlas of the German Empire* by Ferdinand Wrede, who had joined his staff in 1887. In 1926 linguistic maps began at last to appear; about 16,000 hand-drawn maps exist in the Atlas archives at Marburg, but only a small proportion were published before the project was discontinued in 1956.

In 1933 Wrede was succeeded as director at Marburg by Walter Mitzka. Mitzka decided that Wenker's material, which mainly concerned phonology and word-structure, should be supplemented by more lexical data. In 1939 he therefore posted a questionnaire (thus following Wenker's method of sixty years earlier) to schools in all parts of Germany and Austria. It had 200 questions, mostly concerning single words (mainly nouns for everyday things such as parts of the body, plants, trees, utensils and so on), but including 12 sentences for translation. Over 48,000 completed copies were returned, and 21 volumes of the *German Word Atlas* had been published between 1953 and 1978. To give just one example of its findings: about 300 items for 'potato' are recorded, only a third of which are variants of the standard *Kartoffel*.[2]

About twenty years after Wenker began work on the German survey, the second great national survey was started, in France. In a paper published in 1888, Gaston Paris had called for a survey of the local dialects of France to be carried out before they succumbed to the advance of Standard French. The task was accepted by a Swiss scholar called Jules Gilliéron, who had published in 1880 a linguistic atlas covering some 25 localities in the French-speaking area of Switzerland south of the Rhone. After careful planning, fieldwork for the *Atlas Linguistique de la France* was begun in 1897.

Gilliéron, unlike Wenker, used the method of on-the-spot investigation. But he did not do this actual *fieldwork* himself. He recruited Edmond Edmont who, though a grocer by trade,[3] had proved himself to be a good amateur phonetician, lexicographer and dialectologist, having published a dictionary of his native dialect: *Lexique Saint-Polois*. Gilliéron bought Edmont a bicycle, and sent him pedalling off around 639 rural localities in France and the French-speaking parts of Belgium, Switzerland and Italy. (After completing this odyssey, the indefatigable Edmont, by then aged over 60, set off again and surveyed 44 localities in Corsica for the *Atlas Linguistique de la Corse*, published in 1914.)

Edmont was equipped with a carefully-designed questionnaire. At the start this included some 1400 items, but it was eventually expanded to over 1900. The questions were so arranged as to attempt to provide a conversational framework for an interview. Usually Edmont interviewed only one *informant* in any locality, but occasionally he used two. They were predominantly male, but their ages were fairly evenly spread between 15 and 85; they were classified according to occupation and education as the 'local intellectuals' (about 200) and 'folk speakers' (about 500).

This fieldwork was done over the period 1897–1901, and publication of its findings followed remarkably swiftly by comparison with most projects of this nature: 13 volumes, including 1,920 maps, appeared between 1902 and 1910.

The work of Gilliéron and Edmont provided the model for many later dialect surveys in Europe and the United States, and we shall examine Gilliéron's principles and methods in some detail in the next section of this chapter. Of particular importance among these later surveys was the work of two of Gilliéron's students, Karl Jaberg (who in 1908 had published an interpretive introduction to the French atlas) and Jakob Jud; they refined their master's methods during their work on Italian dialects in Italy and Southern Switzerland. Using three fieldworkers, they investigated 405 localities with a questionnaire of about 2,000 items. Among other improvements in fieldwork techniques, they designed the questionnaire in such a way as to provide a more or less natural sequence of topics, so that the informant's interest was centred more on the subject matter than on linguistic usage, as it inevitably had been with the previous 'translate into local dialect' approach, and speech could thus be more natural. They also extended their investigation to urban centres and to the examination of linguistic differences between social classes. The realization that 'folk speech' is not simply to be equated with 'rural speech' was an important step forward, but unfortunately urban and social dialects were not given the attention they deserved for many more years (see Chapter Six). Jaberg and Jud were fortunate in their chief fieldworker, Paul Scheuermeier; a paper of his relating some 'Personal Observations and Experiences' whilst engaged in fieldwork is both instructive and amusing.[4] Jaberg and Jud's atlas was published in eight volumes between 1928 and 1940.

Surveys have been conducted and atlases published for most European countries and in other parts of the world too.[5] In France, recognition that Gilliéron's survey not only had a network of localities which was probably too widely-meshed but also had other shortcomings, led to a new scheme for a number of regional atlases, initiated by Albert Dauzat in 1939 with the title *Atlas Linguistique Régional de la France*. The original plan was for twelve regional surveys, but by the 1970s twenty-three (extending into non-Romance areas such as Alsace, Lorraine and the Basque country) were in various stages of production.[6] Much that was good in Gilliéron's work was retained, but various improvements were introduced: preliminary investigations were always conducted before the main survey; a lot of Gilliéron's questions were kept, but some of the less fruitful ones were discarded and other new ones introduced – and the questionnaire was divided into a general part and a part specific to the particular regions; all Gilliéron's localities were re-investigated, both as a check and to see what changes had occurred in half a century; and since even Edmont had faults, improvements in fieldwork techniques were made. In Germany too, further work on a regional basis was undertaken: before the Second World War over thirty projects aimed at collecting the vocabulary of individual areas had been started.

Dialect study in Britain will be examined in some detail in the next chapter; but here we should give some attention to work in the United States.[7] Though an American Dialect Society was formed in 1889, and a publication *Dialect Notes* (later re-named *Publications of the American Dialect Society*) was started, it was some time before a wide-scale survey was undertaken. The leading figure has been Hans Kurath, director of the project entitled *Linguistic Atlas of the United States and Canada*. But an overall survey of the territory was not undertaken; instead, work has been carried out on a regional basis. First, as 'an experimental investigation over a restricted geographical area',[8] came the *Linguistic Atlas of New England* under the direction of Kurath himself. New England was chosen because its dialects were 'primary' as compared to those of the later-settled more Western parts, and because it had more marked differences of both regional and social dialect. Fieldwork began in 1931; 416 interviews were conducted by a team of nine fieldworkers. The aims and methods of the survey were set out by Kurath in the *Handbook of the Linguistic Geography of New England* (1939); the atlas appeared in three volumes containing 734 maps published between 1939 and 1943; and other publications based on the survey material came out in the following years. The next survey, for the *Linguistic Atlas of the Middle Atlantic and South Atlantic States*, under Guy Lowman and Raven McDavid, was begun in 1933. Other regional projects (with the dates they were started) include the *Linguistic Atlases of the North Central States* (1938), the *Upper Mid-West* (1947), the *Rocky Mountain States* (1950), the *Pacific Coast* (1969),[9] and the *Gulf States* (1968). This last includes some territory already covered by E. Bagby Atwood's *Dialect Survey of Texas* (1955–1960), and the *Dialect Survey of Rural Georgia* (1968–1972).

Before beginning work, Kurath conferred at length with the directors of the Italian Survey, Jaberg and Jud, and their chief fieldworker, Scheuermeier.[10] Consequently, their attention to urban speech and to differences between social classes was systematically incorporated into the American surveys. Scholars realized that the dialect situation in America was different from that in most European countries. Partly because of the relatively short time that English has been spoken there, partly because there has been considerable geographical and social mobility, and partly because there is no one standard accepted throughout the country by a dominant social class, there is little 'real dialect' (in the generally-accepted European sense of *patois*), and little clear distinction between dialect and standard speech. On the other hand, there are markedly regional types of speech at all levels, including 'cultivated speech'. It was therefore decided that American surveys must not restrict themselves, as had most of the European ones, to the typical rural speaker with little education. The aim was not only to see geographical differences and to study the effects of movements of populations and of topography and routes of communication, but also to examine the effects on speech of the stratification of society and the relatively high degree of social mobility. So in addition to those using 'folk speech', two other educational types were examined, and within each of these three classes two age-groups were distinguished.[11]

METHODS

Let us begin by contrasting the very different approaches of the German and French surveys:

44

I. The German survey used the *indirect method* of sending questionnaires by post; the French employed the *direct method* of face-to-face investigation by a fieldworker.

II. The German questionnaires were completed by laymen, who had to make do with adapting the orthography in order to attempt to show the actual pronunciation. The orthography clearly has deficiencies when used for this purpose; at the very least some 'transcriptions' will be of doubtful interpretation. The French questionnaire was administered, and the responses taken down, by a skilled phonetician who was able to use a detailed and unambiguous phonetic transcription.

III. The German survey, with its 40 sentences, only investigated a relatively small number of items, mostly phonological, though some points of inflection and vocabulary were covered incidentally. The French questionnaire, with nearly 2,000 items, was much more comprehensive in its coverage of vocabulary, and also dealt with pronunciation. (We noted that Wenker's work had to be supplemented in the area of vocabulary by Mitzka's later survey.)[12]

IV. The raw data of the 52,000 responses in the German survey needed long and laborious interpretation, and in fact it was never completely published. The French data on the other hand could be made available without much interpretation, and was published quickly.

V. In all the above respects the French survey was superior, but in the matter of *coverage* it was far inferior to the German work. While Wenker's coverage was virtually total, Gilliéron only investigated 639 localities – one for every 830 square kilometres – which is less than a 2 per cent sample of Gilliéron's estimate of 37,000 French-speaking communities.[13] It was to remedy this deficiency that the later regional surveys of France were undertaken.[14]

It was basically the methods of the French survey that were to set the pattern for future projects, so let us consider in more detail some of Gilliéron's principles and the ways in which they have been modified in the light of later experience.

Gilliéron held that the localities to be investigated were to be fixed in advance. In fact, he seems to have chosen the points for the French survey in a fairly mechanical way – in a geometrical pattern, with one to every so many square kilometres.[15] But areas differ, in population-density, ease of communication, and so on; and even Edmont was forced to modify Gilliéron's plan as he went along. Nowadays, the localities to be investigated may be fixed in advance, but usually this is done only where a *pilot survey* has been conducted. In other cases an approximate location is decided on, but the fieldworker makes the final choice after seeing the area at first hand.

Gilliéron insisted that the direct method of investigation should be used. There are obvious advantages to on-the-spot investigation. For instance, the fieldworker can make sure that he obtains all the necessary information concerning the characteristics of the informant; he can clarify any doubtful points either in the questions themselves or in the informant's responses; and so on. But on the other hand the indirect (postal) method may be suitable for certain purposes: while it is difficult to elicit accurate phonetic information in this way, this method can, with care, be used for gathering lexical data. If the postal approach can be used, then there are very considerable advantages: it saves time, money and manpower, and so can permit a much more dense or extensive coverage; also, it makes it possible to obtain data of a 'contemporary' nature from all sources – whereas direct fieldwork can take many years to cover a comparable number of informants. Since postal questionnaires are completed by amateurs, some of the returns will be inaccurate, but most of these will be detectable because they are at odds with the more-or-less accurate majority. (In Germany some direct fieldwork was carried out in the 1890s; Wrede was able to show that the findings of these investigations coincided with those of the earlier indirect survey conducted by Wenker – and note that Wenker's work concerned the more difficult phonological, rather than lexical, material.)

A well-designed questionnaire is one of the most important factors in the success of an investigation, and Gilliéron had very rigid ideas on this subject. Some parts of his approach have now largely been abandoned: for example, he asked informants simply to translate a Standard French form into the local dialect – nearly everyone now accepts that this is usually less likely to produce a genuine and natural response than eliciting the form required in a more indirect manner (see p. 89). Other principles propounded by Gilliéron have been widely accepted: for instance, he held that comparability of response could only be guaranteed by asking every informant the same questions in precisely the same wording and the same order, and by recording the informant's first response. But even Gilliéron had to admit that a questionnaire could be improved in the light of experience (he even went so far as to say that the best questionnaire could be drawn up after the investigation had been completed!). Various problems with and omissions from the questionnaire will be discovered, and those of most surveys have gone through several versions and modifications. It is even debatable whether the same questions should be asked at every locality: it may be preferable to have a common general section of the questionnaire and a number of different 'regional' sections in which the different practices of particular parts of a country and their corresponding expressions are investigated[16] (a plan which was adopted in the later regional surveys of France). Too rigorous an adherence to Gilliéron's rules may also in other ways be contrary to the main aim of a survey, which is to discover the usual or the traditional expressions of a locality. For example, an informant may realize that his first response to a question was either a mistake or not the expression usually employed in that place.[17] So in addition to the first response, many fieldworkers nowadays would note his second thoughts, and also what are termed *incidental forms*. These are forms used by the informant but not in answer to the particular question designed to elicit such a form. For instance, if an informant (partly because the investigator has, possibly unconsciously, recently used the pronunciations [wɛə], [ðɛə] for *where*, *there*) produces the form [ðɛə] when asked to complete '. . . here and __ (there)', that will be recorded as his first response. But if at some other stage in the interview he uses the pronunciation [ðɪə], that is a relevant incidental form. Also, the questionnaire material, produced usually in a rather artificial and formal 'one word' style, may be less than natural. So a recording of spontaneous uninterrupted speech by the informant, either during or before or after the actual interview, will often yield valuable data.

Gilliéron believed that only one fieldworker should be

employed, and that he should not be a professional linguist. By using the same fieldworker throughout it is more possible to ensure uniformity of procedure in the conduct of interviews and the recording of responses (though even the same investigator has been known to 'hear' the same thing differently at different stages of a survey). And if the fieldworker is not an expert in the particular language under investigation, he may be a more objective recorder of data since he will not be 'expecting' any particular response because of his training. It is certainly true that different fieldworkers may transcribe the same particular sound in different ways because of differences either in their phonetic skills or in their training (see p. 130). The result could be that linguistic maps produced by the survey may appear to show up linguistic differences within an area when in fact the only difference was in the fieldworkers who investigated different localities. But in a large-scale operation, with a sizeable questionnaire to be administered at hundreds of locations, it is almost impossible to use only one fieldworker if the survey is to be completed within a reasonable time, so that all the data is 'contemporary'.[18] So most dialect surveys have employed a team of fieldworkers, but have sought to ensure as great a degree of uniformity as possible by giving them all the same training, and in some cases by running checks on them. Moreover, with the possibility nowadays of tape-recording the interview, the data can be checked at a later time. Experience has also shown that Gilliéron's preference for amateur fieldworkers has more disadvantages than the use of experts: even Edmont has been criticized for having allowed his greater familiarity with Northern French sounds to affect his transcription of those in the South,[19] and even more so those in Corsica. Later French surveys have decided it would be better to employ trained workers native to the particular areas.

The selection of informants, Gilliéron believed, should be according to definite criteria – of sex, age, educational and occupational status, and so on. Later surveys have differed widely in the importance they attach to this. At the one extreme is Sever Pop, in charge of the Rumanian dialect atlas, who lists sixteen criteria he followed in the choice of his informants. At the other, Paul Scheuermeier, chief fieldworker on the Italian survey, claims 'there is no infallible rule for the choice of a good informant',[20] and his directors Jaberg and Jud concluded that the fieldworker's rule must be *not* to stick to any rule. Now obviously there must be an irreducible minimum: the informant must be a native of the area (unless one is doing an intensive survey at one particular locality, in order to ascertain *all* the varieties in use in that place); he must not be deaf, senile or mentally defective; and he must be a 'natural' dialect speaker – *not*, for example, a local teacher who 'knows a lot about dialect', or an educated person who does recitations in dialect.[21] But beyond this the intuition and experience of the fieldworker can be relied on to choose the most suitable people. Edmont used only one informant in each locality; most later surveys (including those in France) have decided that two or more are preferable, since one person cannot be expected to know all the items, both domestic and professional, that are being investigated.

We may conclude from this consideration of the methods employed in the first great national surveys, and of changes adopted since then, that careful planning and training are essential if time, money, and effort are not to be wasted. But the planning should not be too rigid: to get the best out of a survey it may be necessary for the directors and the fieldworkers to use their judgement in making modifications as they go along.

Let us end this section on methodology with a brief step-by-step outline of the general approach to dialect investigation that is now common.

I. A preliminary investigation or pilot survey is often carried out, in order to gain some idea of the way usages vary over the area to be covered and to decide what sort of items are worthy of detailed investigation.

II. Two basic 'frames of reference' are then prepared:

A. a network of geographical points, the localities at which fieldwork is to be conducted, is decided upon. The density of this coverage will depend on factors such as the financial and manpower resources and the time available for the survey, how heavily populated the area is, what sort of features are being investigated, and so on.

B. a list of items to be investigated is drawn up, and these are eventually embodied in a questionnaire. These items may be of various types, and the proportions of these will vary according to whether the survey is to be primarily concerned with pronunciation, grammar, or vocabulary. The main types are:

vocabulary: the word or phrase used for a particular thing or idea. For example, a question such as 'What do you call the thing you carry water in?' may seek to determine whether *bucket* or *pail* is the word used in that area; another question might seek to discover whether a male sheep is referred to as a *ram*, a *tup*, or whatever.

semantics: what is the meaning of a particular item? For instance, does *starve* refer only to hunger, or can it be used (as in some parts of Britain, especially the North) for suffering cold?

grammar: this can be divided into *morphology* (word-structure) and *syntax* (sentence-structure). As an example of the former, a question such as 'We say "Today it snows – yesterday it also __" ' might be used to elicit *snowed* or *snew* (the older form, which survives in various parts of Britain); other questions would be devised to determine whether the usual form in the area is *dived* or *dove* (as in parts of America); *children* or *childer* (an older form[22]); and so on. In syntax, the interest is in whether people say 'those who are . . .' or 'them as is . . .'; 'you are . . .' or 'thou is . . .'; and so forth.

phonology: various types of pronunciation difference were distinguished in Chapter One, and we shall return to this matter in Chapter Five. But obviously a dialectologist is interested in whether /h/ is 'sounded' or not in *happy*, or /r/ in *card*; whether one says *follow* or *foller*, *thing* or *fing*, *nose* or *nooze*, and so on.

III. Fieldwork is then conducted. One or more trained investigators travel to the localities selected and make contact with people they consider will be the most suitable informants. With one or more interviews, at least one copy of the questionnaire is completed at each location. Until the 1950s the fieldworker usually had to note down the informant's responses in phonetic transcription. Since that time tape-recorders have become available, thus speeding up the interview, enabling it to be more spontaneous, and making it possible for the fieldworker or a more skilled member of the team to study the responses at leisure.

IV. Editing and publication, usually taking many years, then follow. The data is sorted and put in suitable order. Eventually it is published, often partly in list form and partly as maps (it would be too complex and too expensive to include all the information on maps).

FINDINGS AND INTERPRETATIONS

The findings of a dialect survey may be published in two main forms, and many surveys have employed a combination of the two. One form used is lists or tables of responses (often with superscript symbols, indicating for example where a particular form was not a 'first response': e.g. an incidental form). These may be arranged in different ways. Some follow the order of the questionnaire (which usually puts together the questions relating to a certain area e.g. the house, the weather, the body) with the responses to each question listed by locality. Some are arranged

IV.4.5   (a) COAL*

Q. What do miners get out of the ground?

R.   COAL(S)

Note 1—The i.m. forms of COAL(S) noted below mean *coal*, not *pieces of coal*.
Note 2—COAL(S) also occurs at V.3.8 and V.4.1.

1 Nb 1 køːl, °køːlz[2]   2 køːl   3 køːlz   4 køːl   5 køːl [kɔəlz[2] *coals*]   6 køːl, °køːlz[2]   7 kɔəl   8 køːl, °~[2], °køːˑl[2]   9 kǫəlz

2 Cu 1 kɔəlz   2 kǫəl   3 kwɒl   4 kwɔːl, °kɔɒl[2]   5 kɔəl   6 kɔəlz, °kwɒl[2]

3 Du 1 køˑl, °~[1]   2 køəl   3–4 kɔəl   5 kǫəl, °kɔəlz[2]   6 kǫəl

4 We 1 kʷǫəl   2 kwɔl   3–4 kɔəlz

5 La 1 kɔəl   2 kɔəlz   3–5 kɔəl   6 kɔəl ["older"], kɔɪl ["more modern"]   7 kɔɪl, °~[2] [kɔɪlaɒs[2] *coal-house*]   8 kɒɪl   9 kɒɪl [kɒɪln°uːk[1] *coal-nook* (=-*place, -store*)]   10–11 kǫːl   12–14 koːl

6 Y 1 kɔəl   2 kɔəl, °~[2]   3 kǫəl, °kɔəl[1,3,5]   4 kɔəl, °~[2]   5 kɔəl, °kɔəlz[3]   6 kɔəl   7 kɔəl, °kɔəlz   8–9 kɔəl   10 kɔəl, °~[2]   11 kɔəl   12 kɔəl, °kɔəlz   13 kɔəl   14 kɔəl, °kɔɪl[2,5]   15 kɔəl   16 kɔəl [blaklasɪz[4] *black-lasses* (=*coal*)]   17 kɔɪl, °~[3,4], °kɔəl [generally heard "in conversation, even from the best speakers"]   18 kɔəl, p. kɔɪl [pref.; wɪ kɔːl ɪt kɔɪl əmɒŋ uˑəsɛlz *we call it coal among ourselves*]   19 kɔəl, °kǫəl[1]   20 kɔːl; p. kɔəl, °~[2,3]   21 kɔɪl [kɔɪlz[5] *coals*]   22 kɔɪl   23 kɒɪl, °~[2]   24 kɔəl [kɔəlɔəl[2] *coal-hole*]   25 kɔəl, °~[4]   26 kɔɪl, °~[1]   27 kɔɪl, [kɔɪlɔɪl[2] *coal-hole*]   28 kɔəl   29 kɔɪl   30 kɔɪl, °~[3(2x)]   31 kɒɪl   32 kɔɪl   33 kɔɪl [kɔːlsɛlə[3] *coal-cellar*]   34 kɒɪl, °~[1(4x)]

Man 1 koˑəl   2 koːˑəl, °koːˑl[1]

Figure ii. Publication of findings in list form.

according to the alphabetical order of the *key word* – the concept for which the various expressions are being sought. Some group lexical, grammatical and phonological items separately; and so on. The example reproduced here (Figure *ii*) is from the *Survey of English Dialects*: responses to the question seeking local pronunciations of *coal* are arranged by county, with the various forms elicited beside the locality numbers.

The other form in which data is published, and the one which would probably be used exclusively were it not too expensive

Figure iii. Dialect map showing actual responses in phonetic transcription.

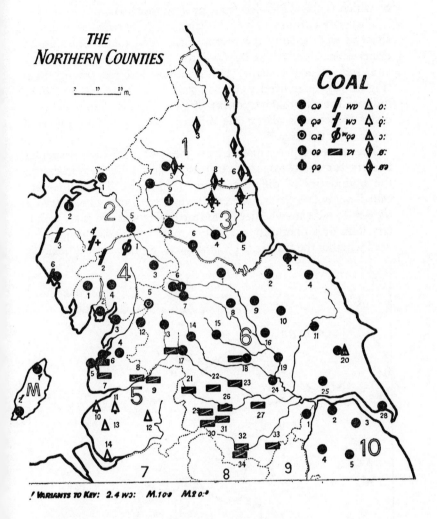

Figure iv. Dialect map employing symbols for different responses.

and often too complex to do so, is the dialect map, a collection of which is called a dialect atlas or linguistic atlas.

There are two main types of dialect map. The first attempts to show at each locality the response recorded there. This can be done either directly, as by Gilliéron and Edmont, and Jaberg and Jud, with the actual transcriptions inserted on the map (Figure *iii*), or indirectly, by using various different symbols to indicate the different responses (Figure *iv*). The latter makes it easier to see at a glance the different usages within the area covered by the map.[23]

The second type of dialect map does not mark each particular locality for some response. Instead it draws lines representing the boundaries of different usages (Figure *v*). These lines are called *isoglosses*[24] (some writers have used terms like *isolex* or *isophone* to indicate whether the feature being mapped is a vocabulary item or pronunciation, etc; but most commonly 'isogloss' is used whether the feature is phonological, grammatical or lexical).

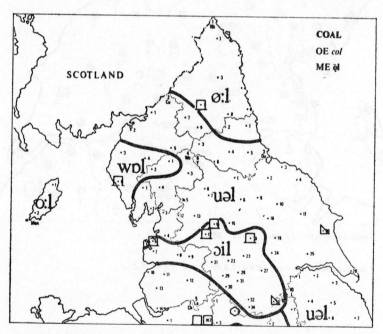

Figure v. Dialect map with isoglosses between areas with different responses.

What does an isogloss indicate? *Not* that at some particular geographical point form *x* ceases to be heard and form *y* occurs instead. There will usually be some overlap between the areas of two competing forms, and isolated examples will occur well beyond the isogloss. But the dialectologist has concluded that whereas at locality A the commoner usage is form *x*, at locality B it is form *y* which is more usual – and so he draws his isogloss to pass between these two points on the map. In many investigations even this interpretation may be too strong: the isogloss may simply mean that a particular informant or a particular type of speaker used form *x* when locality A was investigated, and so on. The majority of speakers may well not follow this pattern: this is particularly likely to be the case where a survey concentrates on elderly rural speakers. Area 1 may appear from the isogloss to use form *x*, and area 2 to use form *y* – but in fact the majority of speakers in both areas, who live in the towns, may use just one of these, or may use form *z* which is closer to that of the standard language.

These findings of a dialect survey, whether published in list form or as maps, are merely raw material. This is then available for interpretation. What sort of conclusions can be drawn from isoglosses?

Let us consider what we might have expected them to prove. Wenker appears from his writings to have been primarily interested in establishing clear dialect boundaries. But the fact that he began his work in 1876 has led many people to assume that he was seeking to provide evidence either to support or to refute the Neogrammarian axiom as formulated in that year by Osthoff and Brugmann: 'Every sound change, inasmuch as it occurs mechanically, takes place according to laws that admit no exceptions' (see p. 39 above where the usual abbreviated form of this is given). The Neogrammarians believed that this regularity would show up better in the dialects than in a standard language, which may have been subject to a mixture of influences.

In the event, the findings of dialectology – the various isoglosses emerging – did not appear to help either to establish clear dialect boundaries, as Wenker had hoped, or to prove the claims of the Neogrammarians. Indeed, Wenker's successor Wrede repeatedly used the material gathered by the German survey to argue *against* the Neogrammarian position.

The Neogrammarian view would be that a particular sound change would operate over a certain area, affecting every word whose phonological structure was such that it could undergo this change. To take a hypothetical example:[25] if it were found that in a certain part of a linguistic area [ku:t] changed to [kʊt], [fu:t] to [fʊt], [u:t] to [ʊt], [bu:t] to [bʊt], and [vu:t] to [vʊt], whereas elsewhere [ku:t], [f u:t], [u:t], [bu:t] and [vu:t] remained unchanged, we could formulate a sound law [u:t] → [ʊt] for the first area. If this were sufficiently precise, then we should expect to find that [du:t] had also changed to [dʊt], [gu:t] to [gʊt], [fu:t] to [fʊt] etc, etc, over the same area, since sound laws operate mechanically and without exception. We should therefore be able to draw an [u:t] → [ʊt] isogloss round the area where the change has occurred, thus establishing a clear dialect boundary for this feature.

But what actually emerged when dialectologists plotted the distributions of various forms was that the isoglosses for each word did not always coincide. For example, a certain village might be on the [ʊt] side of the isogloss for [k-t], [f -t], [-t] etc, but in [g-t] the [u:t] pronunciation had been retained. As Wrede stated: 'The expected congruity of the respective word boundaries, advocated so fanatically by the [Neogrammarian] theory, existed here and there, it is true, but by no means everywhere. Instead the individual lines displayed sometimes smaller, sometimes greater, deviations, so that instead of the expected boundary *lines* mostly only boundary *belts* emerged, which occasionally showed a rather precarious breadth' (my italics).

There was then a criss-crossing of isoglosses, which led to the maxim that 'every word has its own history'. And the question was asked, 'Are there such things as dialects?'.[26] The notion of dialect, as we noted earlier, involves both unity within and difference from those outside – but there appeared to be few definite boundaries. What in popular usage was called a dialect (e.g. Yorkshire) was found to share many of its supposedly characteristic features with one or more other areas (e.g. in Lancashire, Derbyshire, Lincolnshire), and was itself not linguistically uniform, being criss-crossed by isoglosses. In fact it appeared that every village had its own dialect: Figure *vi* gives a stylized picture of nine villages in the 'Swabian Dialect' area: with only ten isoglosses considered, no one of these villages is

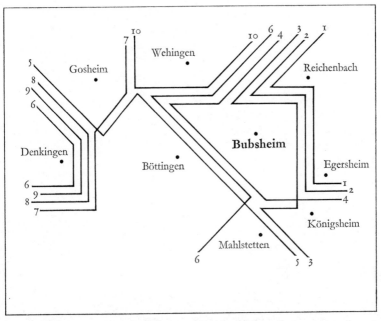

Figure vi. Idealized representation of some isoglosses around
Bubsheim in Swabia. (Based on Bloomfield, 1933.)

identical with any other. And even within a village there are
likely to be social if not geographical differences.

Even if we leave this last point aside, can anything be salvaged
from the picture of confusion and irregularity? In fact, closer
examination of isoglosses reveals two types of pattern which
suggest that there is *a certain degree of regularity* of sound change,
and that some dialect boundaries and dialect areas can be established.

In the first place, it is possible to find *bundles of isoglosses*: a
number of isoglosses for particular forms run together for at
least part of their length. Such a bundle can be taken as being of
more importance than isolated individual isoglosses and therefore
as indicating some sort of dialect boundary. An example from
France is seen in Figure *vii*, which gives the isoglosses for several
words which in Latin contained the combination of sounds [ka]
e.g. *caballus* (Fr. *cheval*) 'horse', *campus* (Fr. *champs*) 'field', *calidus*
(Fr. *chaud*) 'hot', and so on. Over the whole of Central France

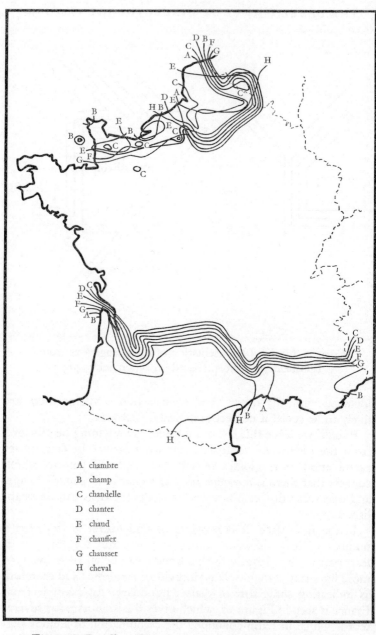

Figure vii. Bundles of isoglosses for words involving initial
[k]~[ʃ] in French. (Based on Jaberg, 1908 and on *Atlas
Linguistique de la France.*)

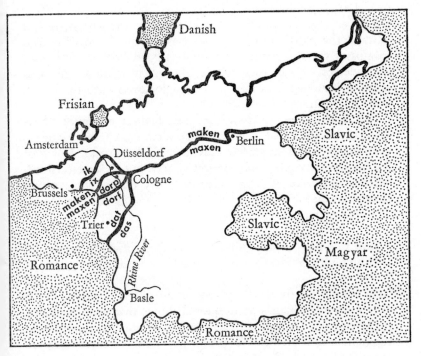

Figure viii. The Rhenish Fan.

the [k] in this environment has changed to French [ʃ], but in parts of the North and the South forms with [k] survive. The isoglosses for the particular words mapped here in few cases coincide throughout their whole length, but there are obvious signs of bundling of a number of isoglosses in both the North and the South.

Figure *viii* shows one of the most famous examples of an isogloss bundle: that running East-West across the German-speaking area and separating Low and High German. North of the bundle (Low German) the *stop* sounds [p,t,k] were retained, whereas south of it (High German) they underwent a sound change to become the corresponding *fricative* sounds [f,s,x]. Thus for example:

Low German [dorp] 'village' [dat] 'that' [makən] 'make, do'
High German [dorf]   [das]   [maxən]

This bundle clearly marks an important dialect division, but it also illustrates Wrede's point quoted above, that such isoglosses rarely coincide throughout their length. Minor 'irregularities' in the bundle as it crosses the greater part of the German area are ignored here (our map shows the precise route of only the *machen* isogloss); what is of primary interest is the fact that some thirty miles east of the Rhine the isoglosses of the bundle separate and spread out north-west and south-west in a formation that has given rise to the term 'The Rhenish Fan'. The [t/s] isogloss as in the word for 'that' is the most southerly, then that for [p/f] as in 'village', then that for [k/x]. And it is seen that the position of this last differs according to the particular word being mapped: the isogloss between [ik] and [ix] 'I' runs further north than that for [makən/maxən]. In Düsseldorf, dialect-speakers say [ix], with the [k] → [x] sound change having occurred, but [makən], with the old [k] retained.

The second type of recurrent pattern which emerges from the plotting of isoglosses is one where certain *types of area* show up. Some areas, for instance, are crossed by relatively few isoglosses but are surrounded by a number of more or less concentric ones (see Figure *ix*). These can be interpreted as being dialect centres; usually they will involve a fairly obvious centre of prestige, such as a large city, from which waves of linguistic

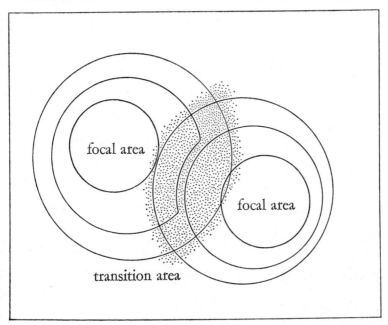

Figure ix. Idealized representation of focal and transition areas.

innovation have spread outwards. Areas of this type are called *focal areas*.

Various focal areas will send out waves of change, whose isoglosses may bundle where they meet those from another focal area, or may overlap with these. In either case there will be areas which lack sharply-defined characteristics of their own, but share characteristics with two or more adjacent areas. These are called *transition areas*. Obviously the Rhenish Fan is a transition area between those of High and Low German.

A third type of area which shows up is the converse of the focal area: a region often containing no important centre and surrounded by segments of various isoglosses from a number of centres. These regions, into which new forms have not yet penetrated, are called *relic areas*. They are often found in isolated regions such as mountains or secluded valleys, or on the edge of language areas.[27] If we look again at Figure *vii* and at the shaded areas in Figure *x*, we notice that the [ʃ] pronunciation in the common word 'horse' has spread over a wider area in France

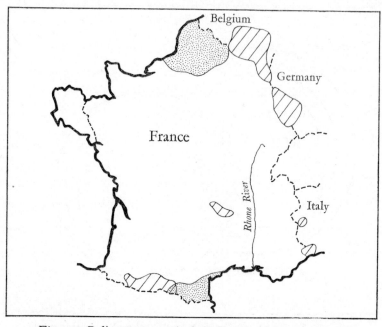

Figure x. Relic areas: survivals in France of forms of *cheval*
with initial [k] (shaded areas), and of reflexes of Latin [sk-] words
which do not have an initial vowel (hatched areas). (Based on
Jaberg, 1908.)

than it has with many other words in this set. But there are two
relic areas where the [k] pronunciation survives; both are on the
edge of the language area, and that in the south is in a mountain-
ous region. Another good example from France is seen in the
hatched areas in Figure *x*, which show up a number of relic areas
where words which in Latin began with [sk] e.g. *scola* 'school',
scala 'ladder' etc have *not* developed an initial vowel such as is
heard in Standard French *école, échelle* etc.

It is clear from our discussion of these special types of area that
there are often extra-linguistic explanations for why isoglosses
are where they are. Some surround a cultural centre, for example;
others reflect the fact that an area is difficult of access or remote
from such centres. As we shall see below, Wrede and other
members of the German school, most notably Theodor Frings,

demonstrated that not only geographical factors, but also political and cultural ones may be responsible for the position of isoglosses.

For linguistic features to spread from one area to another, there are two main prerequisites. First, there must be some sort of prestige attaching to the speech of one area which persuades speakers in another area to imitate it. Thus a focal area for linguistic change tends to be a centre of cultural, religious, economic, political or other influences. Second, there must be active communication between the two areas. Different types of geographical feature may either assist or hinder such communication. A range of mountains *may* form an effective barrier to communication; on the other hand a trade or migration route through the mountains may be the way linguistic influence spreads.[28] Similarly with rivers: a wide or swift-flowing river *may* be a barrier; but a navigable river may be a major line of communication and thus a route for linguistic innovation. It has been demonstrated that the Danube valley, for example, has been a focal area for innovation in German dialects, and that the Rhone, a great highway of commerce, has played a similar role in French. Figure *xi* shows the distribution of different expressions for 'it is necessary' in French dialects: the hatched areas use other forms (mostly derived from Latin *calet* 'it is hot'), but the white area seems to reflect a spread southward along the Rhone of forms derived from Latin *fallit* ('it deceives/is concealed', as in Standard French *il faut*).

Where dialect boundaries coincide with natural ones, it is usually found to be because there is also a cultural or political boundary at this point too. Such boundaries often coincide with linguistic difference even if there is no physical barrier. A national frontier, say that between Norway and Sweden, must have had some limiting effect on communications over a continuous geographical area, and thus have promoted dialect differences. We might expect the iron curtain separating East and West Germany today to hinder the spread of linguistic changes – though the effect of this frontier may be less than it would have been in previous centuries because people on both sides of the border can receive the others' radio and TV broadcasts. The Rhenish Fan has long been a favourite example of the way that isoglosses can reflect historical, political or cultural influences. Besides the phonological differences represented in the Fan, the

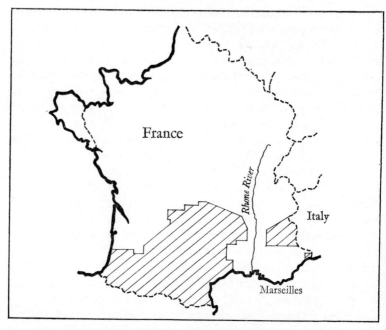

Figure xi. Spread along the Rhone of forms for *it is necessary* derived from Latin *fallit*. (Based on Jaberg, 1908.)

isogloss positions also represent lexical differences and differences in popular customs and objects: different types of bread, farm tools, house types etc. Wrede and Frings demonstrated that former political and ecclesiastical frontiers were responsible for the position of the isoglosses of the Fan. The [ik/ix] isogloss (crossing the Rhine just north of Ürdingen, and known as the *Ürdingen line*) corresponds closely to the northern boundaries of the pre-Napoleonic duchies of Jülich and Berg and of the diocese of Cologne; their *earlier* boundaries are reflected in the [makən/maxən] isogloss (crossing the Rhine just north of Benrath, and hence known as the *Benrath line*). The [dorp/dorf] isogloss reflects the southern boundary of these political and religious areas where they adjoined the diocese of Trier – and the southern boundary of the latter is marked by the [dat/das] isogloss. Frings suggests that linguistic changes travelled along the Rhine, from the southern part of Germany which was culturally dominant, to centres such as Cologne and Trier, and then outwards from these local political and ecclesiastical centres throughout the areas they administered.[29]

Scholars in another country have also been interested in the historical interpretation of the findings of dialect geography: in Italy there grew up a school of linguistics known as *Neolinguistics* – a title which was adopted to emphasize its opposition to the principles of the Neogrammarians.[30] The Neolinguists held that the Neogrammarian view of language and linguistic change was over-simplified and mechanical; their own position was that language use and change is essentially a 'spiritual, human process', an 'artistic creation', an 'expression of the spirit . . . and therefore always more or less voluntary' and 'of individual origin'. They laid great stress on the view that every word has its own history, and its own *area*, and the leading figure, Mateo Bartoli, propounded a number of *norms* (i.e. these apply 'normally' – in the majority of cases – as contrasted with the regularist doctrine of the Neogrammarians) for use in the historical interpretation of dialectology. These norms, concerning the relationship between stages of linguistic development, are supposed to enable one to determine which of two competing linguistic forms is the older, on the basis of the size and position of the areas in which they are attested. The norms are:

1. if one form is attested earlier than the other, the former is the older;
2. if one form is found in isolated areas and the other in more accessible ones, the former is the older;
3. if one is found in peripheral areas and the other in central areas, the former is the older;
4. if one is used over a larger area than the other, the former is the older;
5. if one is used in a 'later' area (e.g. a colony; a language that has borrowed it; etc), that form will tend to preserve the earlier stage of development;
6. if one is apparently obsolete or obsolescent, that is the older.

Leaving aside norms 1, 5 and 6, which are not so concerned with geography, it is obvious that norm 2 refers to what others have called relic areas, and norms 3 and 4 refer to the fact that one form may at one time have been used over a wide area, but a newer form is spreading outwards from some centre within that area.

The Neolinguistics doctrine is interesting, but it does not command much support nowadays, partly because so many exceptions can be found to these norms. They do hold in many cases: for example, we know from other evidence that *r*-pronunciation after a vowel (i.e. in words such as *car*, *card* etc) was formerly Standard in England; now it occurs only in peripheral areas in the West and North, with the newer *r*-less form in the central area, as the third norm states.[31] But many examples could be interpreted as exceptions: for instance, it could be held that what we know to be the older situation, of having only the vowel /ʊ/ in both *but*, *love* etc and *put*, *wolf* etc occurs in the *central* parts of Britain (the Midlands and the North of England), while the newer /ʌ/-/ʊ/ contrast is only found in the peripheral areas (the South and Scotland).[32]

Whereas the German school of dialectology concentrated on the extra-linguistic correlations of their findings, Gilliéron was more interested in intra-linguistic interpretation. He did demonstrate that new words spread out in waves from the cultural centre of Paris, but he was more concerned to discover the forces within a language-variety that lead to the spreading, changing, receding or dying-out of particular items. For instance, it was because of *phonetic attrition* (i.e. successive shortenings through sound change) that the word for 'sun' in French (originally Latin *solem*, then *sole*, then *sol*) came to be replaced in some dialects by the more substantial diminutive form (*soliculum* → *soliculu* . . . → *soleil*). Gilliéron's most interesting work in this field concerned *homonymic conflict*: he produced several papers on 'Mots en collision'. For example, through phonetic change the words for 'meat'(← Latin *carnem*) and 'dear' (← *caram*) became homonymous: *cher*; this situation was unacceptable and led to the rise of such terms for 'meat' as *viande* (← *vivendam* 'living'). Perhaps Gilliéron's best-known example of the consequences of homonymy in dialects is his article on the 'cock' and the 'cat'. In the dialects of Gascony, where final [-ll] developed into [-t] and initial [k] yielded [g] in certain cases, the Latin *gallus* 'cock' and *cattus* 'cat' both became the homonymous [gat]. The possible confusion led to the dialects of this area finding new forms for the cock, such as *faisan* (literally 'pheasant') or *vicaire* ('vicar').[33]

In this chapter we have examined the development of dialectology in the nineteenth and the first half of the twentieth centuries. Chapter Four will consider some of the alleged deficiencies of the approaches discussed here, and the following chapters will deal with the more recent studies in dialectology which seek to remedy these deficiencies. But in Chapter Three we shall examine in greater detail than has been possible so far the development of dialectology in one country, Britain.

CHAPTER 3

The Study of Regional Dialect in Britain

🐚🐚🐚🐚🐚🐚

In some countries, such as Switzerland, regional differences in speech are socially quite acceptable, and speakers of all social classes may use regional varieties without any loss of prestige. In Britain, however, Standard English has for several centuries increasingly enjoyed a favoured status, being accepted as the 'correct' or at least the 'best' form of English. The result has been that other dialects have come to be regarded as inferior, as a mark of lack of education and a lower social status. A good illustration of this occurred during the Second World War, when the actor and chat-show chairman Wilfred Pickles was employed for a time as a BBC newsreader. His Yorkshire dialect produced strong reactions; perhaps the complaint which forced the BBC to discontinue the experiment was the one from some listeners that they felt they just could not believe the news any longer!

Such a situation does not encourage the study of dialect, and dialectology in Britain has consequently not occupied a position of much scholarly prestige: there has not been as much effort devoted to the subject as it deserved; it has been regarded often as a matter for antiquarians and amateurs. Also responsible for this 'antiquarian' view of dialect has been the fact that most dialectologists have assumed that the only worthy object of study is 'genuine' or 'pure' dialect[1] – in other words, forms of speech which are a regular development from some earlier stage of the language, as far as possible unaffected by the corrupting influence of Standard English. This attitude has resulted in a neglect of the great majority of non-standard speakers (because their speech has been influenced *to some extent* by other varieties, especially Standard English), in favour of a historical approach to the study of a relatively small and diminishing number whose dialect has not been modified in this way.

Nevertheless, in spite of these unfavourable conditions, British dialectology has produced some important work, which we shall examine in this chapter as a particular example of what was discussed in general terms in Chapter Two. We shall confine ourselves to work *on* dialect. Work *in* dialect – whole books, almanacs, articles etc, or the use for literary purposes of dialogue passages in dialect – has been appearing for centuries and still flourishes in places; but our subject here is the *study* of dialect.

Chapter Two dealt with the development of dialectology in the modern era of more systematic study, dating from the late nineteenth century; we shall confine ourselves largely to the same period in our discussion of dialect study in Britain. For the time before this there are more detailed accounts available elsewhere,[2] and the remainder of this brief introductory section must suffice here.

It is clear that from about the 1300s some writers were conscious of the existence of regional differences within English, and from Chaucer's time there were signs that a Standard English was beginning to be recognized. From the 1500s dialect began to command more attention as: (a) poems, dialogues, and other small pieces written in dialect appeared more commonly; (b) a scholarly interest in dialect differences emerged in an increasing number of references to features peculiar to certain areas: for instance, Defoe (1660–1731) made the first recorded remarks on the 'Northumbrian burr' and noted several other interesting points about dialects, in his *Tour thro' the whole Island of Great Britain*; (c) there was increasing evidence of a standard English: 'London' English (though because of immigration into the capital it showed traces of the influence of other regions) became increasingly predominant among educated people. By the end of the seventeenth century it was more or less the norm for *writing*, and from the sixteenth century onwards there are a number of recorded statements to the effect that educated upper-class London and Southern speech was to be regarded as the model for *pronunciation* also.

The first treatment of English dialects in general was attempted by Alexander Gil, in his *Logonomia Anglica* published in 1619. This work (in Latin except for the examples!) tried to characterize the speech of the main dialect areas. The first attempt at an English dialect dictionary came later in the same century: *A Collection of English Words Not Generally Used* was published by the biologist John Ray FRS in 1674. From that time there was a greater recognition of dialect words in general dictionaries of English; also, dialect glossaries for particular parts of the country began to appear.

In the nineteenth century there were an increasing number of publications on dialect. Many of these were lexical in their bias: for example, those of T. Batchelor on Bedfordshire (1809), W. Carr on Craven (1824) and J. C. Atkinson on Cleveland (1868).[3] But of course the influence of comparative philology was also starting to be felt, in that work began to be historical rather than descriptive in its approach: scholars became interested in the development of dialect sounds and forms from Old and Middle English. Here we move into the modern era of dialectology, which in Britain seems to fall into two periods of more intense activity, with a rather quieter but still productive time between them.

1870–1905

The date 1870 is chosen for two reasons: first, it was in that year that a call went out for the founding of an English Dialect Society; and second, it was about that time that A. J. Ellis started on his monumental work on English dialects (eventually published in 1889). The year 1905 saw completion of the publication of the *English Dialect Dictionary*, edited by Joseph Wright.

Alexander J. Ellis

Between 1869 and 1874 Ellis published Parts i–iv of his work *On Early English Pronunciation*, in which he dealt with the phonology of English from the time of Chaucer to the present. For the final part he planned to cover present-day pronunciation in English dialects, a subject in which he had been interested for about twenty-five years. This Part v turned into a mammoth task, and did not appear until fifteen years later, when it was published virtually as a separate work (of 835 closely-printed pages) under the title *The Existing Phonology of English Dialects*.[4] This work marks an important change of emphasis in British dialectology, from vocabulary to phonology, and is the first major survey of English dialects.

Ellis states that his aim was 'to determine ... the different forms now or within the last 100 years assumed by the descendants of the same original word in passing through the mouths of uneducated people'. In other words he was concerned to produce a historical account of the phonology of non-standard speech. His 'fieldwork' was largely done by others. He justifies his decision not to do much of the necessary data-collecting himself[5] by saying that even at that time 'the peasantry' were 'bidialectal', and to an unfamiliar educated person such as himself they would probably have used their 'refined' pronunciation. So he relied largely on second-hand material, supplied by over eight hundred voluntary helpers. Notable among these are His Imperial Highness Louis L. Bonaparte, who provided a number of specimen texts and also gave Ellis his 'first conceptions of a classification of English dialects', and Thomas Hallam, a book-keeper in the Manchester, Sheffield and Lincolnshire Railway offices and a native dialect-speaker. Hallam was Ellis's most prolific source of information; his employment on the railways made it possible to cover much of the Midlands and North, and 'On arriving at a station he would inquire where he could find old and if possible illiterate peasants, whom he would "interview", gaining their confidence, and then noting their peculiarities of pronunciation in his notebooks.' From this it is quite clear that Ellis was seeking 'genuine dialect': the 'best' informants were held to be those old people least influenced by the standard language, who would be less likely to 'refine' their speech if the interviewer was not an unfamiliar and obviously educated person.

Ellis developed three 'tools of investigation' at different stages of his work. In 1873 he produced his 'comparative specimen': this was a passage of 15 sentences to be read by informants, in order to obtain 'dialect renderings of familiar words in various connections and some characteristic constructions'. A little later, because 'the comparative specimen did not contain sufficient examples of some categories, and the few examples of rather important cases were often ingeniously evaded by my informants', he prepared a 'classified word list' with 971 items. Numbers 1–712 were 'Wessex and Norse' words, with a number of examples of each vowel sound in Wessex literature or Icelandic; 713–808 were 'English', a term in fact covering any item without a known origin in Wessex or Norse, including those from foreign sources except Romance; 809–971 were items of Romance origin. To the list were appended a number of small grammatical constructions, and instructions to characterize the intonation of the speech by underlining such adjectives as 'rough, smooth, thick, thin, indistinct, clear, hesitating, glib, whining . . .' Ellis sent the list to clergymen in villages for which he wanted data: most did not return them, and many just gave equivalents for only a small proportion of the 971 items, but Ellis felt the effort had been worthwhile. In 1879 he devised a third tool, the 'dialect test'. This was a shorter reading passage containing only 76 words, 'in order to have a short specimen which contained an example of almost all the West Saxon categories' of the word list. It was accompanied by a set of hints and instructions: for example, FIND – 'Notice whether the word is like *fined* . . . or *finned*.'[6] Not all these three tools were employed at each locality investigated: in some only the dialect test was completed, for others only a partial word list was supplied, and so on. But often the combination used yielded a reasonable amount of data.

Most of the data supplied was of course in a modified orthography. It was nearly all rendered into his own phonetic transcription by Ellis himself (Hallam was one of the few of his helpers who mastered it sufficiently well to provide his material already transcribed). Ellis called this transcription 'palaeotype', a name chosen because it only used 'old' i.e. familiar letters. But these were employed in various different forms: lower case, capitals, italic, reversed, inverted, doubled etc (e.g. e, E, *e*, ə, ɥ, ee, EE, *ee*, and so on). Ellis admits that, with all the different phonetic values for the various symbols, it 'requires much careful study to understand it thoroughly and read it easily'.

Ellis published his findings for 1,145 localities, 75 of these being in Wales or Scotland. On the basis of this large amount of material he was able to classify English dialects into six major 'divisions' (Southern, Western, Eastern, Midland, Northern and Lowland), further subdivided into 42 'districts' (e.g. Eastern North Midland), each broken down into 'varieties' and in a few cases further divided into 'subvarieties' (e.g. Eastern North Midland divides into eight varieties: Huddersfield, Halifax, Keighley, Bradford, Leeds, Dewsbury, Rotherham, Sheffield. Figure *xii* shows extracts from his findings for this district (D24): page 367 gives the beginning of the comparative specimen, and page 380 shows a dialect test and part of a classified word list.) Besides this detailed classification, Ellis also found that he could draw ten 'transverse lines' (i.e. major isoglosses) across Britain: for example, the Northern limit of the [sʌm] pronunciation of *some*; the Southern limit of [sʊm], which does not coincide entirely with the preceding: the Northern limit of *r*-pronunciation; the Southern limit of *t'* for *the*; that of [huːs] for *house*; and so on.

Almost every aspect of Ellis's work has come under criticism. His 811 voluntary 'fieldworkers' must obviously have been of variable quality and reliability, and errors could have crept in by many routes. Nearly all of these helpers were educated people who did not speak dialect naturally: besides the danger, which Ellis himself had appreciated, of natural dialect speech being inhibited in such a situation, these people may often have had difficulty in identifying and recording dialect sounds, especially those quite different from anything in RP. Ellis too must have had problems in interpreting their 'transcriptions' (mostly in modified orthography, though a number managed to employ 'glossic', a much simpler form than palaeotype). His own palaeotype transcription is so fiendishly complicated that mistakes must have been made by anyone, including Ellis, who attempted to write, read, or typeset it: for instance, variations between say uɐ, uɐ, uuɐ, and so on for what most fieldworkers today would render [ʊə] are commonly found, and it seems most unlikely that they always represent some slight phonetic differences in an informant's speech.

Another obvious weakness is the coverage achieved. This is very uneven: some counties in Scotland and Wales are not represented at all (and this does not appear to have been part of a conscious policy of Ellis's to exclude areas where Celtic was commonest); between others there is no balance – for instance, only 21 localities in Devon are treated, as compared to 67 in Derbyshire. In general the North Midlands and the North are much better represented than Scotland, the South Midlands and the South (quite possibly the counties best covered are those which Thomas Hallam could most easily reach by railway!).

Evaluations of Ellis's work by later scholars vary greatly, for sometimes it seems certain that he is in error, but at others his findings are confirmed by further research. Even the same scholars

Eight Interlinear cs.

These cs. have been arranged interlinearly for ready comparison, forming a conspectus of pron. in D 24. The side numbers indicate the numbers of the varieties already explained. The notes for each version are given subsequently. As Mr. Robinson in his desire to record idioms has sometimes dealt very freely with the text, the lines do not exactly correspond, but sufficiently so to make reference from one to the other easy and rapid. The following is the meaning of the numbers of the lines.

i Huddersfield (:*u*dh*u*zf*i*l), or, according to TH., (:*u*₀dh*u*rsf*i*ld), and adjoining villages. See also the cwl. for Var. i. including Holmfirth, Marsden, Saddleworth, and Upper Cumberworth.

ii Halifax (:*ɛʋ*l*i*feks) and adjoining villages, as Ripponden. See also the parable of the Prodigal Son in the Halifax dialect in Part IV. p. 1400, in which some of the palaeotype forms are now superseded by those here used, but this will occasion no difficulty to the reader.

iii Keighley (:kiithl*ʋ*) or Lower Craven. Mid and Upper Craven belong to the N. div.

iv Bradford (:bradf*ɵ*th) and adjoining villages.

v Leeds and its district already described, country speech.

vi Dewsbury and its neighbourhood, excluding Wakefield, but including Barnsley.

vii Rotherham.

The above seven were written by CCR in Glossic.

viii Sheffield, written in 1875 by Mr. D. Parker, formerly President of the Literary and Philosophical Society, and Prof. of Hebrew at the Wesley College, both of Sheffield, who had been well acquainted with the dialect for 60 years, and had lectured upon it before his Society, in a systematic orthography, supplemented by notes and correspondence. Nevertheless in many common unaccented words there is an element of uncertainty in this conjectural pal. translation.

Of the Doncaster variety I can only give a cwl.

0. i *Huddersfield.*	wôi	:dɟoni	az no	daats.
ii *Halifax.*	wat for	:dɟoni	az no	dɛʋts.
iii *Keighley.*	wat for	:dɟúʋn	ez núʋ	daats.
iv *Bradford.*	wat for	:dɟoni	ez núʋ	daat.
v *Leeds.*	wat fóʋ	:dɟoni	ez núʋ	daats.
vi *Dewsbury.*	wot for	:dɟoni	ʋz nóoʋ	dɛʋts.
vii *Rotherham.*	wói	:dɟonʋ	ez núʋ	daats.
viii *Sheffield.*	woʼi	:dɟon	az)ʼnt nʋ	daats.

1. i	wiil, neebʋr,	ɟoo ʋn im		mʋ búʋth)ʋn)ɟo	lef
ii	wiil, neebʋr,	ɟoo ʋn im		mʋ búʋth ʋ ɟo	léɛʋf
iii	wiil, néʋbʋr,	ɟAA ʋn im		mʋ búʋth ʋn ɟo	laaf
iv	wiil, néɛʋbʋr,	ɟii ʋn im, tíu,		mʋ búʋth ʋ ɟʋ	laaf
v	wiil, néɛʋbʋr,	ɟii ʋn im ʋ óʋl, ɟi		mʋ búʋth on ɟʋ	laf
vi	wiil, neebʋr,	ɟoo ʋn im		mʋ búʋth o ɟo	leef
vii	will, neebʋr,	ɟo ʋn im ʋn ool	ɟon booth mʋ	laf
viii	wee, neebʋr,	ɟoo ʋn ii		mʋ búʋth	laf

i	ʋt dhis níuz	ʋ móin.	wúʋ	kéʋz?	dhat dhíʋ)z
ii	ʋt dhis NEʼuz	ʋ mi oon.	wúʋ	kéɛʋz?	dhet dhíʋ)z
iii	ʋt dhis níuz	ʋ móin.	wúʋ	kéeʋz?	dhat)s
iv	lâik, ʋt dhis néɛuz	ʋ mi ôʋn.	wúʋ	kéeʋz?	dhat)s
v	lâik, ʋt dhis néɛuz	ʋ mi óʋn.	úuʋ)s)t	kéeʋ?	dhat dhíʋ)z
vi	ʋt dhis níuz	ʋ máin.	wúʋ	kéeʋrz?	dhet)s
vii	at dhis níuz	ʋ móin.	wúuʋ	kéeʋrz?	dhat)s
viii	ʋt dhis níuz	ʋ moʼin.	wúʋ	kéeʋrz?	dhat)s

Figure xii. Extracts from Ellis (1889), showing a 'dialect

UPPER CUMBERWORTH (6 se.Huddersfield) dt.

pal. by TH. in 1881 from dict. of Mrs. Ann Littlewood, b. 1824, native, and 26
years resident ; here (*u*ₒ) and (u) were both heard.

1. A *see*, ladz, ɹɐ siin nâ¹ɐ ᴧ)m réit ɐbâ¹ɐt dhat lit'l las ku͘ₒmín
thrɐ)s)skóil ɹɐndɐr.

2. shu)z gu)ɐn dâ¹ɐn)t' rûɐd dhîɐr thruu)t' rᴇd' gjeet ɔn)t' lᴇft
and saad ɐ)t' rûɐd.

3. luuk ! [sii !] t' tɹaald)z gu)ɐn strᴇ'ít *u*ₒp tɐ)t' raq â¹ɐs,

4. wíɐr shu)l ap'n faand dhat druqk'n dîɐf wiz'nd ôud fᴇli ɐt
dhe ᴋᴀᴧl :tɔm.

5. wi ᴧᴧl noon ìm vári wiil.

6. wíl'nt t' óud tɹap sóín téítɟ ɐr nɔt tɐ du ít ɐgîɐn, pùɐr thíq !

7. luuk ! íz'nt ít tríuu ?

Note. Words omitted : 2. *way* (*wee*).—3. *door* (dœ'uɐr).

HUDDERSFIELD AND NEIGHBOURHOOD cwl.

For comparison characteristic words are here given for the following forms.

R CCR.'s cs. for Huddersfield, merely a few principal words.
D Words from the Huddersfield wl. of Mr. Dowse, who had been 10 years
acquainted with the dialect, as well as they could be interpreted.
T Words from the Huddersfield wl. of Mr. Tomlinson.
H Words from the carefully numbered Huddersfield wl. by Miss Mercy Hibbard,
who had lived there the first 18 years of her life.
B Holmfirth (5 s.Huddersfield) numbered wl. by Mr. Beardsell, 40 years ac-
quainted with the dialect, as well as the words could be interpreted, but the
meaning of the numbers was probably not always rightly seized.
Mh Marsden (7 sw.Huddersfield) wn. by TH. in a special visit. The verbal pl. in
-en frequent, and also in a printed specimen. Here (*u*ₒ) was heard.
Mb Marsden words from a wl. by the vicar, assisted by the schoolmaster, Mr. R.
Bamford, here (u) is assumed.
S Saddleworth words from a wl. by Mr. G. H. Adshead, 40 years acquainted
with the dialect, as well as they could be interpreted. As Saddleworth lies
between Marsden and La., I have assumed the use of (*u*ₒ).
C Upper Cumberworth (6 se.Huddersfield) wn. by TH., here (*u*ₒ) was heard.

I. WESSEX AND NORSE.

A- 3 D béɐk. 4 HT tak. 5 HT mak. 7 H sak. 10 Mb eg [this in La.].
12 B sag [this is quite La.]. 14 H droo. 16 H doon. 19 Mh teel. 20 DS
léɐm, Mb. leem, S loom. 21 R neem, D néɐm. 23 D séɐm, Mb seem. 24
Mb sheem. 31 Mb lat. 32 Mb bad [especially in (went ɐ badín) went a
bathing]. 35 H ool. 37 H kloo. A: 39 R kɐm, T kam. 40 H kúɐm.
42 Mh *u*ₒn [unaccented, said three times by the same informant]. 49 R aq.
51 Mh mâ¹n, S mɔn. 54 T want. 56 RTS wesh. A: or O: 58 MhC thrɐ.
60 HS luq. 61 TMh ɐmaq, S ɐmu*ₒq. 62 Mh s͘,t͘roq. 64 RDHT raq.
A'- 69 T nóɐ, Mh nee, H náu. 70 H táu. 72 H woo. 73 RH síuɐ,
T sóɐ. 76 DT túɐd. 77 H lúɐrd. 80 Mh a·lɐdí. 81 R leen, DHTB lo'ín,
C lôín. 84 HTC múɐr. 85 HB súɐr. 87 R tlúɐz, T klᴀᴧz. 88 HT klúɐdh.
89 RH búɐth 92 R noo. 97 H sául.
A': 101 HMb úɐk. 102 R aks. 104 H rúɐd, Mh rɐ́ɐd. 106 HT brood,
C brúɐd. 107 HB lúɐf. 108 HT doof, Mb dúuɐf. 111 H oot. 113 R wol,
Mb wɐl. 115 R wúɐm, HT wom, C wòm. 117 Mh wᴧ'n wòn. 118 TMb

---

parts of a 'comparative specimen' and a 'classified word list'.

seem to be ambivalent. For instance, Eugen Dieth (see below) found it possible to deduce from Ellis's material a number of maps showing the distribution of various forms – but in the same paper described the work as 'a tragedy . . . a huge store of information which every dialectologist consults, but, more often than not, rejects as inaccurate and wrong'.[7] And Joseph Wright in 1892 said that the inaccuracies in a dialect test specimen for the locality Wright knew best made him feel that Ellis's dialect tests as a whole were 'of doubtful phonetic and phonological value'. But in 1905, having completed his own enormous work on dialect vocabulary and grammar, Wright spoke of 'the monumental work of the late Dr. A. J. Ellis . . . which I have found invaluable for checking and supplementing my own material'.

Probably most dialectologists have been at times frustrated by Ellis, but few would agree with Dieth that he is 'more often than not . . . inaccurate and wrong'.

The English Dialect Society
The first clear call for the founding of a society came from W. A. Wright in 1870:

> It has long been my conviction that some systematic effort ought to be made for the collection and preservation of our provincial words. In a few years it will be too late. Railroads and certificated teachers are doing their work. Let each provincial word and usage of a word be recorded, with an example of its application if necessary, and a note of the place where it is so used . . .[8]

It may be noted that the emphasis was placed on 'words' – at this date, most British dialectology was lexically-based. But Ellis, who was himself to help to change this situation, used less restricted terms when he followed up Wright's call the next year:

> It is highly desirable that a complete account of our existing English language should occupy the attention of an English Dialect Society . . .[9]

There was a positive response to these proposals, and the Society was formed in 1873, with the Rev. W. W. Skeat, Professor of

Anglo-Saxon at Cambridge, as its Secretary and Director.[10] It embarked on an ambitious programme of publication, and between 1873 and 1896 put out 80 works in four series:

A. *Bibliographies*. The first, edited by Skeat, being 'A bibliographical list of the works that have been published or are known to exist in MS, illustrative of the various dialects of English' (1873).

B. *Reprinted Glossaries*. These included some very short word lists, often several grouped together in one volume – and on the other hand F. T. Elworthy's nine-hundred-page *West Somerset Word Book*. John Ray's work of 1674 (see above), edited by Skeat, was one of the first in this series.

C. *Original Glossaries*. A considerable number of volumes, of varying length and quality, relating to various parts of Britain, appeared in this largest series. Not all are purely lexical in orientation: Wright's *Windhill* (see below) was in this series.

D. *Miscellanies*. A very varied set, including some *Specimens of English Dialects*, some *Reports on Dialectal Work* by Ellis, a seven-page paper on 'George Eliot's Use of Dialect', etc.

Though Wright's famous *Windhill* grammar was published, it is clear from the published 'Aims' of the Society that it was primarily interested in vocabulary. And from the very first suggestion of forming a society the idea of a major dialect dictionary was ever-present. In 1874, the year following the founding of the Society, Skeat talked of producing some 'complete and exhaustive provincial glossary', and five years later, the Rev. A. L. Mayhew, later the treasurer of the Society, specifically proposed the project of a full dialect dictionary. Skeat replied in the next issue of the same journal,[11] showing some reluctance to embark on such a major task, but work did begin on the collecting of material, with the Rev. A. S. Palmer superintending in an informal capacity.

There was a good deal of bickering in the Society over the next few years in connection with finding a suitable editor.[12] Skeat made a first approach in 1887 to the man eventually chosen, but it was not until 1895 that a formal announcement was made that Joseph Wright was to be secretary of the Society and editor of the 'English Dialect Dictionary'.

In the following year, with the project properly launched, what later seemed an astonishing decision was taken: the Society was wound up! When the dictionary appeared, Wright wrote: 'After the Dictionary had been begun, it was no longer necessary to continue the existence of the Society, and it was accordingly brought to an end in 1896.' The members of the Society obviously felt that their work was now done. This complacent attitude resulted in Britain being one of the last countries in Europe to undertake a dialect survey of the type outlined in Chapter Two, covering phonology and grammar in addition to vocabulary; there was no longer a national focus and forum for dialectologists.

Joseph Wright

Wright grew up in the Yorkshire village of Windhill, near Bradford, speaking the local dialect. He was illiterate until his teens, and was largely self-taught. Eventually he went to Germany and trained as a philologist under the Neogrammarian influence. On his return to Britain he went to Oxford, where he was soon elected Deputy Professor of Comparative Philology. In 1892 he published through the English Dialect Society a phonological and grammatical description of his native dialect, a work which was to have tremendous influence on later dialect study. Later came several now standard texts, on Old and Middle English. Skeat had been looking for a suitable person to edit a scholarly dialect dictionary with a historical approach, and it was of Joseph Wright that he wrote to his son in 1895: 'At last, after 20 years, I have got hold of the right man.'

The aim of the *English Dialect Dictionary* (often abbreviated to *EDD*) was to detail 'the complete vocabulary of all dialect words still in use or known to have been in use during the last 200 years'. The methods of data collecting employed by Wright were as follows. First, he had available the various publications of the Dialect Society referred to above, the majority of which were glossaries. Then there was the material that had been collected by Skeat and Palmer in the years before his appointment, and of course 'the monumental work of the late Dr. A. J. Ellis'. Wright himself sent out 12,000 copies of a postal questionnaire containing some 2,400 words with instructions on how to transcribe them phonetically. He was also influential in the setting up of groups such as the Yorkshire Committee of Workers (1894) in order to collect more material. The mammoth task of collating the data from the various sources and preparing it for publication was done by Wright himself and his wife, Elizabeth Mary Wright. The criteria Wright applied for the inclusion of a usage in the dictionary were that: (a) it must have been reported to have been in use after about 1650; and (b) it must have some *written* authority, i.e. it had appeared in literature or articles or dialect writings of some sort.

The Dictionary was published in six large volumes between 1898 and 1905. The arrangement is alphabetical, and each item has its usage or usages described together with references to written sources and their date, and the county where attested. Figure *xiii* shows an extract from *EDD*.

As part of Volume VI Wright produced the *English Dialect Grammar* (*EDGr*), which also appeared as a separate publication. Wright considered this work, based on the material collected for *EDD*, to be more interesting philologically than the Dictionary itself – a sign of the changing emphasis from vocabulary to phonology and to a lesser extent grammar. About half of *EDGr* is the Index, which Wright compiled first. It is an alphabetical list of words (most of them everyday items, rather than dialectal ones), together with their various dialect pronunciations and the region where these were used. The Index contains about 16,000 forms altogether. Figure *xiv* includes the entry for *house*, for which 30 forms are listed.

From the Index Wright drew the material for the two main sections. 'Phonology' (247 pages in the separate edition of *EDGr*) gives a historical description of the development of sounds in their various combinations, from West Germanic through Old and Middle English to the modern dialects (see Figure *xiv*). 'Accidence' (42 pages) details various peculiarities of dialect grammar, mostly matters of inflectional morphology, with just a few points of syntax; Figure *xiv* also shows part of the section covering plural-formation in nouns.

With the publication of *EDD* and *EDGr* British dialectologists seem to have felt they could now relax. Skeat wrote in 1911:

PAUSE, *v.* and *sb.* n.Cy. Yks. Not. Also written pawse, pawze w.Yks.; and in form poise n.Yks. w.Yks.²⁸ Not.² [pọz, poəz, poiz.] 1. *v.* To kick. Cf. pouse.

n.Cy. (HALL.) n.Yks. FETHERSTON *Smuggins Fam.* 20; n.Yks.⁴ w.Yks. Heathcliff's pawsed his fit into t'first part o' 'T'Broad Way to Destruction'! BRONTË *Wuthering Hts.* (1847) iii; 'Did he kick you?' ' Na, but he paused me,' HAMILTON *Nugae Lit.* (1841) 343; Pawze him aht o' t'field, *Yksman.* (Aug. 1878); A'll pawse thy liver aght (J.T.F.); w.Yks.¹ He began o skirlin an gloarin, an paused baath my shins black and blue wi his iron clogs, ii. 292; w.Yks.²³⁴⁵ Not.² I'll poise yer.

2. *sb.* A kick.

Yks. I gave him a fling and a poise that sent him sprawling, FETHERSTON *Farmer*, 144. w.Yks. A gooid pawse 'at sent it flyin' aht o' t'door, *Yksman.* (1888) 223, col. 2.

PAUSTY, see Posty.

PAUSY, *adj.* n.Lin.¹ [pọ·zi.] Slightly intoxicated.

Slightly the worse for drink; said of persons who combine an amiable desire to impart information with an incapacity to call to mind all the necessary words. ' Drunk! naw he was n't what you'd call drunk, nobbud he was pausy like.'

PAUT, *v.* and *sb.* Sc. Nhb. Dur. Lakel. Yks. Lan. Chs. Der. Not. Lin. Wor. Suf. Also written pawt Sc. Lakel.² Cum.¹⁴ n.Yks.² e.Yks.¹ m.Yks.¹ w.Yks. ne.Lan.¹ Der.¹ Not.¹³ n.Lin.¹ sw.Lin.¹; pawte w.Yks.; port w.Yks. Not.³; and in forms paat Cai.¹ Nhb.¹ Cum.¹⁴; paout se.Wor.¹; pout Sc. (JAM.) N.Cy.¹ s.Wor.; powt Sc. (JAM.) Bnff.¹ n.Cy. Suf.¹ [pọt, poət, pāt.] 1. *v.* To poke or push with the hand or a stick; to stir up; to paw, handle, or finger things. Cf. pote.

Sc. To search with a rod or stick in water, or in a dark or confined place. To make a noise when searching or poking in water (JAM.). n.Cy. GROSE (1790). Nhb.¹ Divent paat on wi'd, or ye'll spoil'd. Cum. Children pawt when they make repeated attempts to get things with their hands (E.W.P.); Cum.⁴ A dog pawts at the door when it wants to get in, and children pawt when they make repeated attempts to get hold of things with their hands. n.Yks.¹; n.Yks.² Kneading with the fingers into a soft mass. n.Lin. SUTTON *Wds.* (1881); n.Lin.¹ I wish we hed n't noä cats, really, thaay're alus pawtin' at one, when one's gettin' one's meät. sw.Lin.¹ Some lasses are always pawting things about they've no business with. s.Wor. To beat down apples, PORSON *Quaint Wds.* (1875) 15.

Hence (1) **Pouting,** *vbl. sb.* the practice of spearing salmon; also used *attrib.*; (2) **Pout-net,** *sb.* a net fastened to poles by which fishermen poke the banks of rivers to force out the fish.

(1) Abd. In order to have a day or two at the ' pouting ' when the river was in condition. . . The river Dee was low enougb for ' pouting ' purposes, MICHIE *Deeside Tales* (1872) 213. (2) Sc. Their Association . . . have, . . for protecting the fry, given particular instructions... to prevent... their shameful destruction at Mill-dams and Mill-leads with Pocks or Pout-nets, *Edb. Even. Courant* (Apr. 16, 1804) (JAM.).

Figure xiii. Extract from *English Dialect Dictionary*, edited by Joseph Wright (1905).

The fulness of the vocabulary in the Dictionary, and the minuteness of the account of the phonology and accidence in the Grammar, leave nothing to desire. Certainly no other country can give so good an account of its dialects.

In the light of history this claim seems naïve, but it may be noted that no results of the German survey begun in 1876 were yet readily available, and it was another few years before publication of Gilliéron and Edmont's work was completed.

But it soon became obvious that *EDD* and *EDGr* had deficiencies. The Dictionary had aimed to include 'all dialect words', but soon after its publication letters and articles began to point out areas which were undercovered and items which should have been included. One of the reasons for omissions must have been Wright's criterion of written authority: if an item was in oral use but had never appeared in writing it would not have been included.[13]

More serious than the omissions is the vagueness of reference. It is not made clear whether items are still in use, and how common they are.[14] And the locality references are far too imprecise: usually they only give the counties where the forms have been attested (or at best something like 'SWYks') and no details are given about who the actual speakers are. No maps are drawn, so the regional distribution of forms is not immediately obvious. Wright does say in the Introduction to *EDGr* that 'those who consult it must not expect to find each and every dialect treated with that minuteness which ought to be given in a grammar dealing with one single dialect', but a clearer picture could surely have been given with an arrangement other than simply listing usages and counties.

In spite of their deficiencies, however, *EDD* and *EDGr* remain standard works of reference for anyone interested in English dialects.

1905–46

Though Wright remained as professor at Oxford until 1925, he seems to have virtually given up dialectology after the publication of the Dictionary. The reason for this may be hinted at in his Preface to *EDGr*:

§ 166. The ō in the combination ōht was shortened to o already in OE. This oh has had a twofold development in the modern dialects according as the spirant h (χ) has been absorbed or according as it or its further development has remained. The chief words belonging here are: *brought, sought, thought* pret.

1. When the spirant has been absorbed.

au occurs in *brought* s.Nhb.n.Dur.n.Cum.Wm.snw.Yks. nw. & s.Lan. n.Der., *sought* sw.Nhb. Wm. snw.Yks. em. se. & s.Lan. n.Der., *thought* sw.Nhb. n.Dur. Wm. em. se. & s.Lan.

ā in *brought* nw.Oxf. se.Ken. nw.Wil. Dor. w.Som., *sought* Brks. Dor., *thought* Brks. se.Ken. nw. & w.Wil.

à in *brought* I.Ma. s.War. w.Wil., *sought* I.Ma. s.War., *thought* I.Ma. s.War.

o in *brought* s.Lan. sw.Nhp., *thought* s.Lan. s.Stf. m.Shr.

ou in *brought* me. & s.Nhb. Dur. n. & m.Cum. Yks. Lan. nw.Lin. Lei., *sought* Nhb. Dur. Cum. Yks. n. nw. & sw.Lan. nw.Lin., *thought* Nhb. Dur. m.Cum. n.Wm. Yks. Lan. s.Stf. ne.Der. nw.Lin.

oə in *sought* Rut. ne.Nrf.

ǫ in *brought* Stf. s.Lin. Rut. Lei. m.Nhp. m.Bck. ne.Nrf. s.Sur. Sus. me.Wil. e.Som. Dev., *sought* s.Stf. Lei. s.Oxf. se.Ken. e.Dev., *thought* n.Stf. s.Lin. Rut. Lei. s.Oxf. ne.Nrf. s.Sur. Sus. me.Wil. Dor. w.Som. nw. & e.Dev.

ó in *sought* e.Suf.

óu in *brought* sw.Nhp., *thought* m.Lin.

ō in *brought* Uls. m.Lin. e.Suf. Ess., *thought* s.Lin. e.Suf. Ess.

House, 171, 172, 248, 328, 376, 379, 384—*ais* Chs., but s.Chs. +*aus, vus,* n.Stf.+*aəs,* nw.Der. +*aus,* e.Der.+*as, aus, avs, ās. as* s.Lan.+*avs, āŝ, ǣs, evs, vus,* e.Der., w.Der.+*ās. aus* nw.Yks.+*ūs,* es.Yks. n. & m. Lan., se.Lan.+*ǣs, əus,* s.Chs. +*ais, vus,* Dnb. e.Stf., em.Stf. +*avs,* wm. & s.Stf., ne.Der.+ *ās,* nw.Der. e.Der., s.Der.+ *eaus,* m.Lin.+*ous,* Lei. ne. Nhp.+*eus, vus,* m.Nhp.+*æus, eus, jaus, vus,* e. & w.War., n. Wor.+*eus,* w.Cor. *avs* ms.Lan.+*ǣs,* s.Lan. em.Stf.

e.Der. Not. *aəs* sw.Yks.+*ās, eəs, iəs,* n.Stf., n. Der. +*vus. ās* sw.Yks., ms.Yks.+*eəs,* s.Yks. s.Lan. ne. e. & w.Der. *æus* m.Nhp. *ǣs* sm. se. sw. ms. & s.Lan. *eaus* s.Der. *eus* s.Lin. Lei. ne. & m.Nhp. n. Wor. s.Pem. m.Bck. Bdf. nw. Hrt., se.Hrt.+*jeus,* Hnt. m. se. & s.Cmb., nw.Nrf. e.Suf.+*vus,* w.Suf., Ess.+*vus,* Ken. s.Sur., Sus.+*vus,* w.Som.+*eus, vuz,* e.Cor.+*vus.*

Figure xiv. Extracts from the 'phonology', 'accidence' and

2. Plurals in -n.

§ 379. The only plurals in -n in the literary language are *oxen* and the archaic form *hosen*. *Brethren, children,* and *kine* are double plurals.

The list is much longer in the dialects and comprises:

(*a*) Words which belonged to the weak declension in OE.: æʃn *ashes* Wxf. Pem. Glo. Hmp. sw.Cy.; bīn *bees* Irel. Chs.; īn *eyes* in gen. use in Sc. Irel. and Eng.; flīn *fleas* Wxf. se. & s.Wor. Shr. Hrf. Glo.; pīzn *peas* Wxf. Eng. gen. (also pīn s.Chs. from new sg. pī); tōn *toes* Wxf. s.Chs.

(*b*) Words which originally belonged to the strong or irregular declensions: brüðrən *brothers* Lei.; tʃīzn *cheeses* e.An. Dor.; klūtn *clouts* e.Yks.; vēzn *furze* Dor.; h)ɐuzn *houses* gen. in Eng. except n.Cy.; kīn *keys* Wil., līzn *pastures* Rut. (*obs.*); mɐuzn *mice* Glo. e.Suf. (*obs.*) e.Dev.; nīzn *nests* s.Chs. Rut. Lei. War. Wor. Shr. e.An.; ōkn *oaks* Hrf.; pōzn *posts* Nhp. Shr. Glo. Hnt.; riksn *rushes* sw.Cy.; ʃūn *shoes* gen. in Sc. Irel. and Eng.; sistrən *sisters* Cai.; trīn *trees* Fif. Wxf.; tɐrvn *turfs* Sc.; wopsn *wasps* Hmp.; wenʃn *wenches* Glo.

(*c*) Romance words to which the weak ending has been added: botln *bottles* sw.Dev.; klōzn *fields* Lei. m.Nhp. e.An.; feərīn *fairies* e.Lan.; plēzn *places* Midl. Shr. Hmp. sw.Cy.; primrōzn *primroses* Glo. Dev.

3. Plurals in -r.

§ 380. tʃíldə(r) *children* gen. in Irel. and Eng., almost *obs.* in Sc.; kār *calves* is occasionally heard in w.Frf. and e.Per.

euz w.Som.	*òus* n.Wm.+*ūs*.
evs s.Lan.	*ūs* se. & sw.Nhb. n. & s.Dur. ̇e.
eəs sw. & ms.Yks.	m. & w.Cum. Wm. ne. nw. e.
heus Uls.+*həus*, but Ant. *hus*.	m. & se.Yks. n. & nw.Lin.
hous I.Ma.+*vus*.	*vus* s.Lan. I.Ma. s.Chs. Flt. em.
hus Sc.+*hūs*, Ant., me.Nhb. n.	Stf. n.Der. Rut. Lei. ne. m.
Cum.+*hūs*.	& sw.Nhp. s.War. s.Wor. Shr.
hūs Sc. n. & me.Nhb., se. & sw.	n.Hrf. Oxf. nm.Brks. n.Bck.
Nhb.+*ūs*, s.Nhb., n.Dur.+*ous*,	w.Hrt. nw.& s.Nrf. e.Suf. Ess.
ūs, n.Cum., Wm.+*ūs*, but n.	Sus. Wil. Dor., but e.Dor.+*vus*,
Wm.+*òus*.	s.Som. e.Dev. e.Cor.
həus Uls.	*vus* w.Som.
iəs sw.Yks.	*ʒus* se.Lan. e.Hrf. Glo. n̑e.Nrf.
jaus m.Nhp.	sm.Hmp., e.Dor.+*vus*.
jeus se.Hrt.	*ʒús* n.Dev.+*ʒús*, sw. & s.Dev.
ous n.Dur. nw.Lan. m.Lin.	*ʒús* n.Dev.

'index' of *The English Dialect Grammar* by Joseph Wright (1905).

There can be no doubt that pure dialect speech is rapidly disappearing even in country districts, owing to the spread of education and to modern facilities for intercommunication . . . [Around London] the dialects are hopelessly mixed and are now practically worthless for philological purposes.

Wright was of the Neogrammarian school, interested in 'regular developments'. He deplored the disappearance of 'pure dialect', and probably for him the choice was the genuine article or nothing at all. He felt that with *EDD* and *EDGr* he had recorded what was left of English dialects, and that was it.

But Wright's influence continued over the next period of British dialectology, for two reasons. Firstly, his *Grammar of the Dialect of Windhill*, published by the Dialect Society in 1892, was 'the first really scientific historical grammar on an English dialect, thus marking a new era'.[15] It became the model for a considerable number of dialect monographs over the next half-century. A very thorough and systematic treatment of Wright's native dialect, *Windhill* has a long section on phonology, which traces the development of the sound system from its Old English (or French) origins, and a solid treatment of the morphology. Syntax is relatively neglected by today's standards – but until the 1950s syntax had a minor role in linguistics generally, as compared with phonology and morphology. There are also a number of illustrative 'specimens' and a large index. Though this certainly could not represent a speaker's total repertoire (as Wright seems to suggest in the Preface), it does include many everyday items rather than simply those found only in this dialect. Many writers on dialects, by concentrating on features peculiar to the area, give the impression of a much greater difference from Standard English than is actually the case. Figure *xv* gives examples from the three main sections.

Over the next half-century (in addition to various more 'amateur' studies[16]) twenty or so monographs on English dialects were published in the tradition of *Windhill*: they are primarily historical studies, and phonology is usually the most thoroughly-covered area (the earliest, Kjederqvist's study of Pewsey (1903) contained only 'Phonology' and 'Index'). But 'Accidence' – morphology – usually received some, though less, attention: in the only one of these works specifically suggested by Wright, Brilioth's *Dialect of Lorton* (1913), it occupies 35 pages as compared to the 95 given to phonology.

In keeping with Wright's Neogrammarian approach, these monographs are interested in 'genuine' forms. Their authors admit the difficulties of this task; Kjederqvist says: 'One difficulty of obtaining real dialect pronunciation is included in the fact that the peasantry throughout the country usually have two different pronunciations, one which they use to one another, and one which they use to the educated.' And Brilioth: 'The task of bringing together *genuine* and *perfectly reliable* dialect material is a most difficult and troublesome one . . . to make your helpers talk pure dialect without consciously or unconsciously mixing their conversation with forms and words derived from Standard English.'[17] But none of these dialectologists seem to have realized that in treating as 'The Dialect of—' a collection of 'genuine' forms that they had abstracted, they were in fact describing something artificial and quite unrepresentative of the actual speech of that area. Some of these works call themselves 'descriptive and historical', but the title descriptive usually means nothing more than that they are a more or less detailed description; it does not refer to the 'synchronic' viewpoint – the description of a variety *as it is* – which is the meaning of the term 'descriptive linguistics'. Their viewpoint is 'diachronic': they give a historical account. Just one author, however, felt that this was not all that could be desired. Helga Kökeritz, working on the speech of Suffolk which is under strong outside influence, especially from the London area, and for which there would be great difficulty in getting at 'genuine' forms, includes a truly descriptive section before going on to a historical treatment. She says: 'My intention has been to paint a true and faithful picture of the Suffolk dialect as now spoken, not to give an idealized and beautifully retouched photograph of the speech habits of very old people to the exclusion of those of the younger generation.'[18] This was an intention many years in advance of its time, as far as British dialectology is concerned.

The second reason why we could say that Wright's influence on dialectology in Britain continued even though he himself did little active work in the subject after 1905, is that he helped to see to it that the gap left by the winding-up of the English Dialect Society in 1896 was not left unfilled. The Yorkshire

§ 165. ō has become uə before r: dluə(r) (ME. glōren) *to stare*, fluə(r) *floor*, muə(r) *moor*.

§ 166. ōw has become ou: dlou *to glow*, flou *to flow*, grou *to grow*, stou *to stow*.

§ 167. ōht became oht already in OE. (Sievers, OE. Gr. § 125), and has become out in the W. dialect, cp. § 101: brout *brought*, sout *sought*, þout *thought*.

§ 168. ō has become ou in: skoup *scoop*.

§ 169. Shortenings of old ō.

(*a*) To o: blosm *blossom*, fostə(r) *foster*, foðə(r) *fodder*, kom (OE. cōm) *came*, soft *soft*, šod *shod*, tof *tough*.

(*b*) To u: bruðə(r) *brother*, dluv *glove*, duz *dost, does*, mundə *Monday*, munþ *month*, muðə(r) *mother*, sluf (OE. slōg) *slough*, tuðə(r) *the other*, uðə(r) *other*.

§ 170. ō has become e in wednzdə (OE. wōdnes-dæg) *Wednesday*.

ŭ.

§ 171. ū has generally become ā: ā *how*, āl *owl*, āmivə(r) *however*, ās *house*, āt *out*, bā *to bow*, bān (O. Icel. būenn, lit. *bound*; generally used in the sense of *going*, as wiə(r) tə bān? *where art thou going?* am bān dān tloin *I am going down the lane*), brā *brow*, brān *brown*, bāt (OE. būtan, be-ūtan) *without*, ə-bāt *about*, dān *down*, dāst *dust*, dlāmi (not the same word as *gloomy* which is dliumi § 164) *sad, downcast*, drāzi *drowsy*, fāl *foul, ugly*, kā *cow*, krād *crowd*, lād *loud*, lās *louse*, mās *mouse*, māþ *mouth*, nā *now*, rām *room*, rāst *rust*, prād *proud*, sāk *to suck*, sāþ *south*, slām (OE. slūma) *slumber*, sprāt (cp. ME. sprūtə, M. Low Germ. sprūte) *to sprout*, šrād *shroud*, tān *town*,

Figure xv. Extracts from *A Grammar of the Dialect of Windhill*, by Joseph Wright (1892).

6. Relative.

§ 356. The relative pronoun is expressed either by **et** for all genders and numbers, or by **ue** for the masc. and fem., **wot** for the neuter. **et** is invariably used when the antecedent is expressed; in other cases we always use **ue**, **wot**. Thus: **im et sed suez reɒ** *he who said so is wrong*, **tman et i soe jestede** *the man whom I saw yesterday*, **tlas et i gav e pund e aplz tul ez etn em oel** *the lass to whom I gave a pound of apples has eaten them all*, **tkoilz et te bout dān i Windil e vari guid** *the coals which thou boughtest down in Windhill are very good*, **did je sī ð̌em et did it?** *did you see those who did it?* **ð̌em men et te so(e) i trued wer on trant** *those men whom thou sawest in the road were on the spree.*

a no(e) uez dunt *I know who has done it*, **we no(e) uez it iz** *we know whose it is*, **a noe wot te sez** *I know what thou sayest*, **a ken** or **kɒ ges ue ð̌az bīn wi** *I can guess with whom thou hast been*, **a duent belīv wot e sez** *I don't believe what he says*; but **a duent belīv e wēd (et) i sez** *I don't believe a word (that) he says.*

Committee of Workers, set up in 1894 at Wright's suggestion in order to collect material for *EDD*, grew into the Yorkshire Dialect Society, founded in 1897. This was the first of several regional dialect societies – others include the Scottish Dialect Committee (1907), the Lakeland Dialect Society (1939) and the Lancashire Dialect Society (1951) – which have provided a focus for both scholars and laymen. Such societies act as a link between the academic study of dialect and its use in prose and poetry: the still-flourishing *Transactions of the Yorkshire Dialect Society*, for example, includes articles *on* dialect, mainly but by no means exclusively those of Yorkshire, and reprints and original pieces *in* dialect. The meetings and the other publications of the societies reflect a similar diversity of interest.

1946–80

In 1946 Eugen Dieth, Professor of English at Zürich, drew attention to the fact that Britain was one of the few blanks on a map of Europe showing which countries had published, or at least begun work on, a linguistic atlas.[19] True, there had been the great works of Ellis and Wright, and many studies of particular areas, but no survey of the types pioneered in Germany and France which could result in a set of maps and tables giving a clear picture of the regional distribution of different forms. Dieth's challenge was accepted: within a few years work began in the Universities of Leeds and Edinburgh on dialect surveys of England and Scotland.

The Survey of English Dialects (SED)
An old friend of Dieth, Harold Orton, Professor of English Language at Leeds, became his joint-director of the *Survey of English Dialects*. It had originally been their intention to produce an atlas of regional speech for the whole of Britain, but when the Scottish survey was started in 1949 the project was restricted to England. In his 1946 paper Dieth had written:

The historical enquiry is not the only one; there are many phenomena in dialectal speech which are well worth recording and investigating although they cannot be traced back to Alfred the Great. . . It is the aim and object of dialect geography, by making a simultaneous synchronic record of what people say at a given time, to reveal all the trends and forces at work.

This sounds promising: the use of the term 'synchronic' and the statement that the historical viewpoint is not everything might have seemed to suggest that *SED* would have as much in common with modern structural linguistics as with comparative philology, with its legacy in British dialectology of a concern with the reflection in 'genuine dialect' of earlier stages in the history of English.

But the actual aims of *SED* were in fact very 'traditional': it chose to concentrate on the oldest generation of rural speakers i.e. those most likely to produce 'genuine dialect'.[20] The preferred informants were over sixty, male (since various studies have suggested that men are less likely to have modified their speech) and agricultural workers: this group is the least mobile, and farming is the most widespread industry and can therefore yield comparable material for the whole country.

A network of 311 localities was decided on, with the general aim of finding points with preferably 400–500 inhabitants and not more than about 15 miles apart. The questionnaire passed through five versions between Orton and Dieth's first effort in 1947 and the time it was published in 1952.[21] There are a total of 1,322 questions in nine 'books': each book, with its questions around a particular subject following on fairly naturally (e.g. I The farm; III Animals; VI The human body; VII Numbers, time and weather), took about two hours of interview time. The questions are of five main types: (1) 'naming', the greatest number e.g. 'What do you call this?'; (2) 'completing' e.g. 'You boil water in a__'; (3) 'talking' (not many) e.g. 'What do you make from milk?'; (4) 'converting' e.g. 'I haven't seen it'; 'he__seen it'; (5) 'reverse' (only a few) e.g. 'What do you separate fields by?' (ditch, dike, hedge, etc). If the informant says 'ditch', ask 'What do you mean by "dike"?'; if 'dike', ask '. . . "ditch"?'. Of course none of these suggests to the informant the actual form to be elicited. Orton (1960, 1962) claims that the questionnaire is 'linguistically comprehensive': it aims 'to reveal the distinctive lexical, phonological, morphological and syntactic features of all the main English dialects.' But in fact there is a lexical and historical bias: all questions are assumed to yield phonetic data, but 730 are primarily designed to elicit lexical information, 387 are phonological, 128 morphological and 77 syntactic. And the phonological questions are geared more towards finding the historical descendants of Middle English sounds than to establishing the present-day 'system' at each locality.

The fieldwork was carried out between 1948 and 1961 by a total of nine fieldworkers; all had been given phonetic training at Leeds. The highest number of localities (118) was investigated by Stanley Ellis between 1951 and 1958. The fieldworkers made the final choice of locality and informants (usually 2 or 3), and administered the questionnaire in a number of interview sessions, keeping to the precise form and order of questions, in accordance with Gilliéron's principles. They took down the informants' responses in an impressionistic transcription; they were specifically briefed not to 'normalize' or 'edit' in any way, but to treat each response individually. They also noted 'incidental material' of interest, and at the end of the interview tape-recorded a stretch of free conversation from the 'best' informant at any locality.

The findings of *SED* were published first in list form: in 1962 Orton produced a brief introduction together with the questionnaire, and the first volume of *Basic Material*, which gives lists of responses to every question, by county and locality (see Chapter Two, Figure *ii*); Volume 1 (1962-3) gives the material for 'The Six Northern Counties and the Isle of Man'; Volume 2 (1969-71) that for 'The West Midland Counties'; Volume 3 (1969-71) that for 'The East Midland Counties and East Anglia'; and Volume 4 (1967-8) that for 'The Southern Counties'. Each volume is in three parts, covering Books I-III, IV-VI and VII-IX of the questionnaire. It had been intended to publish four companion volumes of incidental material, but this has not yet happened.

Dieth died in 1956, before the publication of any of the findings of the survey he had called for. He had been working on a set of maps, and this work was taken over by his former research assistant, Eduard Kolb, Professor of English at Basel, who produced the first cartographical results of *SED*:[22] *Phonological Atlas of the Northern Region* (1966). Though this is a beautifully produced volume, with clear maps of the type marking each locality with different symbols for the various pronunciations recorded (see Chapter Two, Figure *iv*), it is not 'phonological' except in a historical sense. It simply reproduces cartographically some of the *phonetic* data from *Basic Material*, selected so as to show the modern dialect forms of Middle English phonemes.

Shortly before his death in 1975, Orton, in collaboration with Natalia Wright, produced *A Word Geography of England* (1974). This set of over two hundred maps examines the regional distribution of various historical categories of words: those derived from Old English, Scandinavian, Anglo-Norman, Celtic, Dutch and Low German, and other sources. The maps are of the isogloss type, with the innovation that various symbols are employed to indicate the occurrence of forms on the 'wrong' side of the isogloss enclosing the area where they appear to be the normal expression: e.g. Figure *xvi*. In some cases it was found impracticable to display every form elicited in responses or incidental material; clarity was retained by mapping only a few items at a time, with the result that sometimes several maps have to be devoted to one 'key word'. Some more lexical maps are included in the *Linguistic Atlas of England* published in 1978, almost exactly thirty years after *SED* began fieldwork. But of its 474 maps the largest number are phonological (249); 83 are morphological, 65 lexical and 9 syntactic. They are of very much the same type as those of Orton and Wright: an isogloss is drawn round the area where a particular form predominates, with a special symbol indicating the occurrence of this form at any locality outside this area (and a small × at any locality showing that the usual form for the area was *not* recorded there). The phonological maps differ slightly from those for other types of feature, in that while in the latter different forms are referred to simply by number (see Figure *xvi*), the different vowels and diphthongs are directly shown (see Chapter Two, Figure *v*).

It is not difficult to criticize *SED* on various grounds. Any project taking thirty years is almost bound to appear antiquated in design and orientation by the time it actually appears in print, and it is perhaps unfair to judge it in the light of developments that have taken place in the intervening years. The fact that it records the speech of only a small and unrepresentative sample of the population of England, almost entirely ignoring urban

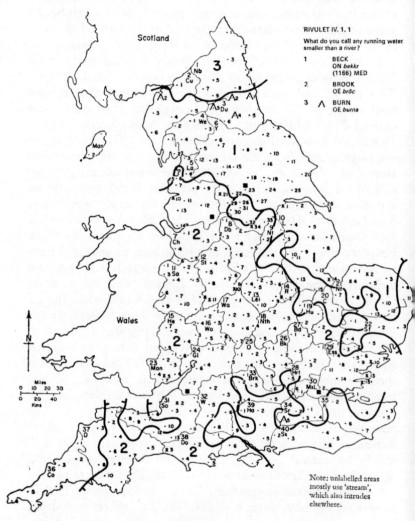

Figure xvi. Map 39 of *A Word Geography of England*.

areas, and that it gives relatively little attention to variation, especially between dialect and Standard English forms, makes it a target for some of the criticisms that were directed against 'traditional' dialectology in the 1950s (see Chapter Four); but its designers (working in the late 1940s) could perhaps be forgiven for not having taken these matters into consideration. But its bias towards vocabulary and phonetics at the expense of grammar and of phonology in its modern sense, its total neglect of intonation, and its historical orientation at a time when linguists had generally come to accept the primary importance of the synchronic viewpoint and the notion of structure, are more legitimate complaints. Moreover, its traditional fieldwork approach, with several different fieldworkers using impressionistic transcriptions, leads to variations in the amount of detail shown and in the interpretation of different sounds[23] – there are quite probably some 'isofieldworkers' disguised as isoglosses.

But the achievements of *SED* are considerable. The 'basic material' and the tape recordings are a permanent record of dialect speech in the mid-twentieth century, which can be reinterpreted from time to time according to one's interests or theoretical persuasions.[24]

A collection of detailed studies based largely on *SED* material was published in 1972 under the editorship of Martyn Wakelin, a former *SED* worker, who also made much use of *SED* findings in a book entitled *English Dialects* (see Wakelin 1972*a* and 1972*b*). Other scholars are making use of the *SED* material in particular projects, and there are definite plans for publishing a number of gramophone records with accompanying transcriptions, for a dictionary, and for putting all the *SED* data onto computer for later processing. There are still hopes that the incidental material will be published, and that further fieldwork can be done – on the towns, and on a sample of the localities visited thirty years ago.

The Linguistic Survey of Scotland (LSS)

Dialectology in Scotland did not begin with *LSS*. In 1873 Sir James Murray had published his *Dialect of the Southern Counties of Scotland*, in which he had made clear that 'the vowel system of the dialect is not the same as the English vowel system'. He also gave a grouping of dialects into North East, Central, and Southern, which he displayed on a simple map. In order to 'show the exact value of the sounds . . . and their relation to English sounds', Murray employed both Ellis's palaeotype transcription and the work of another Scot, Alexander Melville Bell, who had devised a 'Visible Speech Alphabet' which attempted to show the actual position of the vocal organs during the production of a particular sound. But little more had been done by 1909, when William Grant, later to become the first editor of the *Scottish National Dictionary*, published a pamphlet with the title 'What still remains to be done for Scottish dialects'.

A Scottish Dialect Committee had been formed just before this, in 1907, with the aims of: (1) gathering words, meanings and usages not yet recorded in any dictionary; (2) providing an exact description of the pronunciation of Scottish words; (3) dividing the country into dialect areas according to pronunciation differences. Four numbers of *Transactions* of the Committee were published between 1914 and 1921, but then its financial resources were exhausted and little more was achieved.

The project of dialect investigation in Scotland was next raised in 1936 by a pupil of Gilliéron, John Orr, who was Professor of French Language and Romance Linguistics at Edinburgh. In a *Memorandum* Orr set out the tasks of a survey, taking as a model what he considered to be the best linguistic atlas yet published, that of Jaberg and Jud (see p. 42). The war intervened. In 1946 Dieth published his paper, and *SED* was begun. Shortly afterwards, in 1949, the *Linguistic Survey of Scotland* was instituted under the joint direction of the Heads of the Departments of English Language, Phonetics, and Celtic at Edinburgh University. In 1965 *LSS* became a department in the Faculty of Arts, thus emphasizing that a linguistic investigation is not a once-for-all business, but a continuing project.

The theoretical approach of *LSS* is different from that of *SED*. Its chief workers have been linguists rather than philologists, and, in tune with the prevailing climate in linguistics in the 1940s, they designed a survey that would be 'synchronic and systematic': it would examine the situation as it is, describing items in terms of their functions and their relations to other items within the same system – rather than being concerned with the present-day reflexes of some historical situation. But of course, when the findings appear after nearly thirty years, even this approach seems somewhat dated: besides vocabulary, *LSS* has mainly concentrated on phonology, whereas linguistics is now primarily interested in grammar (especially syntax) and semantics. But the continuing nature of *LSS* is a safeguard here: it is accepted that publications will always be somewhat out of step with the times, but members of the team are aware of the 'considerable potential programme' of future tasks: the investigation of intonation, grammar, the notion of 'Standard Scots', and so on.

The scope of *LSS* is in two respects less restricted than some people might have expected. Firstly, its area: since it cannot be assumed that the isoglosses of 'Scots' features will coincide with Scotland's geographical boundaries, this extends beyond Scotland itself into the adjacent English counties of Cumberland and Northumberland, and also to the Isle of Man and Ulster.[25] Secondly, the varieties with which it is concerned: the survey is divided into two main sections, Gaelic and English, and the title 'Linguistic Survey' rather than 'Dialect Survey' emphasizes the fact that the project claims to be concerned with all forms of English spoken in its area – whether 'Scots dialect', 'Scottish accents',[26] 'Highland English' (Standard English on a Gaelic substratum), or 'Island English'. Fieldwork experiences showed that 'it is difficult to find informants who speak "pure" dialect in the sense of using consistently in all situations and all contexts all the maximally deviant features from Standard English': informants are often in fact constantly switching between a number of varieties at their command, and *LSS* is interested in all such varieties. 'Pure' dialect is regarded as 'a *potential*', but not something usually realized in full.

In 1952, one of the directors of *LSS*, Angus McIntosh, set out their intentions in a little book, *Introduction to a Survey of Scottish Dialects*. It was held that different methods are appropriate to different aspects of a survey, and that it is legitimate to proceed in several stages using different techniques. Accordingly, unlike most other surveys, *LSS* has approached vocabulary and phonology as two separate tasks, and has tackled them by 'indirect' and 'direct' methods respectively.

Lexical data was gathered first, by means of postal questionnaires, which for this restricted purpose are believed to have more advantages (in terms of economy and greater coverage) than disadvantages. A first questionnaire, with 211 questions, was sent out in 1951; a second, with 207 questions, two years later. The questions concerned such everyday areas as parts of the body, weather, time, animals, etc – and agriculture, the most widespread industry. They were sent to local schoolteachers, who were asked to pass them to a suitable informant (a middle-aged or older lifelong inhabitant of the district). The great majority of questions were lexical, though informants provided some phonological information through their use of a modified orthography, and a small number of specifically phonological, idiomatic and grammatical questions were included: for example, informants were asked to identify their own pronunciation from a list of possible rhyming words or orthographical transcriptions, or to add one if needed. About 3,000 copies of the first questionnaire were sent out; 1,774 returned copies were usable. The second questionnaire was sent out to a smaller number, and 832 returns were used. The distribution of informants shows that the Lowlands and Eastern parts of Scotland were best represented: counties such as Caithness, Sutherland, Ross and Cromarty, Inverness, and Argyll are more sparsely populated, and also come more within the scope of the Gaelic section of *LSS*.

Since vocabulary was covered by the postal surveys, the 'direct' investigation by trained fieldworkers has been able to concentrate on other matters. Fieldwork began in 1955, and a total of 250 localities have been investigated. A questionnaire was employed, containing 907 phonological items and 75 morphological ones (involving systems of personal pronouns and deictics). 'Phonological' is used in the sense of modern linguistics rather than that of most other dialect surveys: the questions were designed to elicit words which would show up the 'systems' of sound-units (phonemes) and their structural relations, as well as their precise phonetic qualities. Articles published in 1957 by one of the principal researchers, J. C. Catford,[27] describe how fieldworkers sought to get at the systems of stressed vowels, unstressed vowels, consonants, consonant-groups, and so on. It had been decided that the fieldworker should work out the systems on the spot while he had access to his informant and could check his hypotheses; it was felt that subsequent phonemicization of impressionistic phonetic transcriptions was more difficult and apt to be of doubtful validity. Tape-recordings of all informants provided material for later examination of phonetic detail where required.

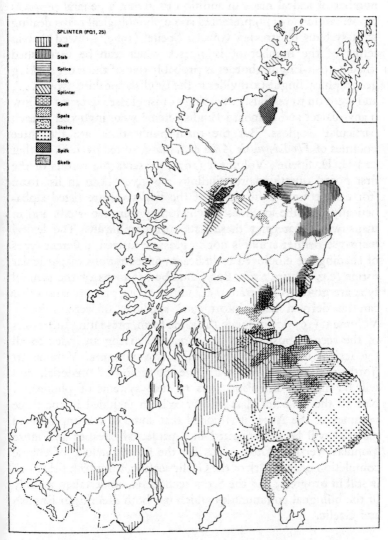

Figure xvii. Map 4 of *The Linguistic Atlas of Scotland*, Volume I.

Some findings of *LSS* were published before the bulk of the material appeared. For example, Catford (1957*a*) produced a number of lexical maps in addition to giving a general progress report, and in (1957*b*) presented some phonological maps dealing with systems of stressed vowels; Speitel (1969) showed that in terms of the number of isoglosses which can be established 'the Scottish-English border is probably one of the most striking geographical linguistic divides in the English-speaking world...', and went on to establish a typology of isoglosses in terms of how many dialect and Standard English items were involved in each particular isogloss. But the main publications are the three volumes of *The Linguistic Atlas of Scotland*, edited by J. Y. Mather and H. H. Speitel. Volume I (1975) presents the results of the first postal questionnaire: findings are given both in list form (for each county equivalents of the key-word are listed alphabetically with the localities at which they were reported), and in maps which interpret these lists cartographically. The lexical maps use neither symbols nor isoglosses: instead, different types of shading are employed to indicate concentrations of particular forms (e.g. Figure *xvii*). But a number of maps of the symbol type are given to illustrate the findings about pronunciation that can be derived from informants' spellings of certain items. Volume II (1977) is of much the same form, presenting the results of the second postal questionnaire, and giving an index to all the lexical items occurring in the two volumes. Volume III (forthcoming) will deal with the phonological material, and will be the first linguistic atlas to map systems of phonemes. Not all the collected data will have been included in the three volumes of the Atlas; it is hoped that some of the unpublished material will be incorporated in a projected cheaper and more 'popular' version. Other plans for the future include of course completion of the work of the Gaelic section, for which fieldwork is still in progress; and the Scots section has undertaken a study of the bilingual communities which use both Hebridean English and Gaelic.

Welsh Dialects

Finally, having referred to the Gaelic section of *LSS*, some account should be given of research into Britain's other Celtic language. Recent work on Welsh dialects (i.e. dialects of Welsh as opposed to English dialects spoken in Wales) has centred on the University Colleges of Cardiff and Bangor. The best-known work is that of A. R. Thomas of the Linguistics Department at Bangor.

In the 1960s Thomas published a number of papers[28] illustrating the application to Welsh of the methods of 'structural dialectology' and 'generative dialectology' (see Chapters Five and Eight). In the light of this his more recent major work, *The Linguistic Geography of Wales* (1973) looks surprisingly traditional. It is largely a work on word geography, though some phonological data was gathered and used to support the lexical findings.

The methodology of the survey by which Thomas gathered his data has points in common with both *SED* and *LSS*. Like *SED*, it was decided to concentrate on the oldest generation of speakers, and those who had as far as possible escaped the effects of formal education and the influence of other dialects (and English), and who therefore spoke 'genuine dialect'. The questionnaire resembles those of both *SED* and *LSS* in dealing with a number of everyday areas e.g. the body, the weather, the family etc, and aiming predominantly at rural and especially agricultural communities: besides agriculture being the most widespread industry, such groups are the least mobile and the most likely to speak Welsh. The questionnaire is 'archaic' in parts in seeking local terms for obsolete agricultural instruments etc.

On the other hand the approach is closer to *LSS* in its use of the indirect method of postal questionnaires for this lexical survey. At each of a network of 180 points (selected on the basis of their position relative to physical geographical features and to the main routes of communication), contact was made with a person of educated background who undertook to receive the questionnaire and to supervise its completion by a suitable informant. The number of questionnaires not returned was exceptionally low. Most questions were not designed to gather phonological data, but informants were encouraged to simulate regional pronunciation by manipulation of the Welsh orthography. Where phonological items were explicitly investigated, they were asked to select, from a set of variant orthographic forms, that which most closely reflected the local pronunciation.

Findings were published largely in map form. Thomas was able to draw conclusions about the relation of linguistic differences to geographical factors: he established six major 'speech areas', with various subdivisions. Such areas are defined by 'a unique association of a number of vocabulary items with an easily-identifiable geographical area': he found that their boundaries consistently coincided with physical geographical features. One wonders, however, how far such areas, based on lexical and often archaic material, would be reflected in the present-day phonological and phonetic situation.

This survey of some of the main dialect research which has been carried out in Britain has provided more detail on the part of the world which will be of the greatest interest to the majority of the readers of this book, and has given a more specific illustration of the approach discussed in general terms in the preceding chapter. It has emerged that, though Britain has not always been in the vanguard of the study of regional dialect, there have been notable achievements, and it is possible to extract a fairly good account of the dialect situation. Work within this tradition is continuing, but in Chapter Seven we shall look at a different type of British dialectology which has become increasingly common in recent years.

CHAPTER 4

Traditional Approaches under Fire

𝕾𝕾𝕾𝕾𝕾𝕾

By the 1950s dialect surveys had been undertaken in most European countries and in many other parts of the world, and dialectologists could feel that their subject was firmly established as an academic discipline which had yielded an impressive amount of scholarship. But its methods and assumptions were about to be subjected to serious criticisms, which challenged the soundness and relevance of its findings. These attacks came both from linguistics, of which dialectology is usually considered to be a branch, and from social science generally, within which wider context the study of language, which is an essentially social phenomenon, should have relevance.

CRITICISMS FROM LINGUISTICS

In the early days of 'modern' dialectology – in other words, in the late nineteenth and early twentieth centuries – the subject had been quite closely related to what may be termed 'mainstream linguistics'. Linguistics was then in fact still largely comparative philology, interested in the historical development of languages and the relations between them; and the study of dialect was obviously relevant to the development of linguistic differences in general and to questions such as the 'regularity of change' in particular.[1]

But from around the 1920s and 1930s the two had tended to go their separate ways. The emphasis within linguistics had shifted from *diachronic* or historical to *synchronic* or descriptive. Linguists were concerned less with the development of languages, and more with their structure at a particular point in time (usually the present). At first the leading scholars often had expertise in both these areas, but gradually the philologist or 'historical linguist' came to be a specialist among linguists, the majority of whom had less interest and training in the historical-comparative area: linguistics had generally become synonymous with 'descriptive linguistics'. Thus, in the linguistics departments of British universities the historical linguist in some cases is seen as an optional extra; in others, he can find no place at all, and is accommodated within the department of English – or French, German, Slavic, or other foreign languages – and is regarded by the new 'mainstream linguists' as rather old-fashioned and sometimes as out-of-touch with linguistics proper.

Though there was no inevitability about this, dialectology often continued to be associated with the historical rather than the descriptive side of linguistics. Furthermore the dialectologist, like the historical linguist, either was considered to be on the fringe of a linguistics department, or was to be found outside it – in the department of English language, for instance. This was less the case in America (though even there comparatively few dialectologists have been leading linguists), than in Britain where, for example, only one or two people associated with *SED* have held posts in linguistics – the majority have been employed as specialists in English language.

Two lines of criticism from within linguistics of the traditional approach in dialectology came to light in the 1950s.

A. *Structuralism*

One of the differences between dialectology and mainstream linguistics can be described in terms of a dichotomy drawn by the 'father of modern linguistics', Ferdinand de Saussure: that between *substance* and *form*. Dialectology had continued to be primarily concerned with substance, the actual details of how people speak – whereas linguistics had come to be more interested in form, the abstract structures and systems underlying this substance.

Let us restrict ourselves to the area of sounds for an illustration. Dialectology was still mainly concerned with *phonetics*, the impressionistic differences of sound between the speech of two areas: e.g. do speakers say [ket], [kęt], [kêt], or [kɛt]? Linguistics on the other hand had become more interested in *phonemics*, the systems of structurally important differences of sound: e.g. do some speakers treat [ket] as 'different from' [kɛt]?; is [kɛt], whatever the detailed transcription of its vowel, interpreted by speakers as 'different from' [kæt], [kåt], [kat] or whatever?; and so on.

To take a more familiar actual example from English. A dialectologist might note that in one area *man* is pronounced [mæn], in another [mɛn], and in another [man]; he draws isoglosses around the areas of each pronunciation. He might also find that *cup* is pronounced [kʌp] in one area, [kap] in another, [kʊp] in another, and so on; again he draws his isoglosses. He might find that *bath* is [bɑːθ] in one area, [båːθ] in another, [baθ] in another; he draws more isoglosses. Having completed his maps, he may then turn his interests to showing why the isoglosses are located as they are.[2]

A structural linguist is interested in these phonetic differences, but he is more concerned with their consequences for the phoneme-system of each dialect, and in these terms he would not see all isoglosses as of equal importance. Those between [mæn], [mɛn] and [man] he would find involve a difference merely in phonetics: in each area the form in question unambiguously represents *man*, and is phonetically distinct from some other form (possibly different in each area) corresponding to *men*. In all areas then, there is a phonemic contrast between /ʌ/ and /ɛ/ (or whatever symbols we decide to use), but it just happens that in one area the phoneme /ʌ/ is represented by, or *realized as*, [æ], in another [ɛ], in another [a]; and /ɛ/ may similarly have various realizations. This the linguist would regard as a relatively 'low-level' difference.

But the isoglosses involved in the pronunciation of *cup* are a different matter. The investigator will find that in some areas, those which say [kʌp] or [kap], the vowel is the same as that in *blood* or *putt*; in others, those which say [kʊp], it is the same as in these two words and also the same as that in *good* or *put*. Further investigation will show that *good* and *put* are pronounced with more or less the same [ʊ] sound in all areas; but that since the vowels of *blood*, *putt*, *cup* etc may be [ʌ], [a] or [ʊ] in different areas, it happens that in some areas [pʊt] is unambiguously *put*, while in others it could be *put* or *putt*. The interpretation of all this in phonemic terms is that in some areas there is a phonemic contrast between /ʊ/ and /ʌ/, as in *put – putt* (it just happens that /ʌ/ may be realized phonetically as [ʌ] or [a]), whereas in others the phonemic system does not contain /ʌ/, and therefore the above contrast is not present. The isoglosses for *cup*, then, involve a difference in phonemes, between /ʊ/ and /ʌ/, as well as one of phonetics, between [ʌ] and [a]. (In everyday terms, this means that there can be problems of understanding between people who have /ʌ/ in their systems and those who do not: a Cockney woman who went to live in Yorkshire on getting married asked the grocer for *butter*; she pronounced this with the London realization of /ʌ/, instead of with /ʊ/ as is usual in Yorkshire where the /ʌ/ – /ʊ/ contrast does not exist for most people; she was misunderstood as wanting *batter* (the closest-sounding word), and was told to make it herself.)[3]

The isoglosses concerning the pronunciation of *bath* turn out to be a different matter again. Further examination of data will show that it is not, like the case of *man*, merely a difference of phonetics, and that neither is it, as with *cup*, a difference in the number of phonemes in the systems of various areas. Rather, it will emerge that all areas have a short vowel phoneme we may call /ʌ/, which occurs in words including *cat* and *man*, and they also have a long vowel phoneme we may represent as /ʌː/, which occurs in words such as *cart* or *barn*. Now in certain particular words like *bath*, *grass*, *laugh* etc, it will be found that some areas have their /ʌ/ phoneme, and so pronounce [baθ] (or whatever other sound is their realization of this phoneme), while others have /ʌː/, and so pronounce [bɑːθ], [bâːθ], or whatever their realization of this phoneme. So in the case of *bath* the isoglosses are produced not just by a difference in phonetics (which is the reason for the difference between [bɑːθ] and [bâːθ]), and not at all as a result of there being a different *number* of phonemes in the systems of different areas; the difference between [bɑːθ ∼ bâːθ] and [baθ] is a matter of areas differing in whether they use their long or their short vowel phoneme in this particular word.

These familiar examples have been discussed in order to help the reader understand a rather more difficult hypothetical case examined in a famous article that challenged dialectology on the issue of structuralism: Uriel Weinreich, 'Is a Structural Dialectology Possible?' (1954). This paper will be examined in more detail in the next chapter; here let us just concern ourselves with his point that the maps produced by a dialectologist using the traditional approach and by a structuralist might look very different.

Suppose that over a linguistic area there is a geographical difference between speakers who pronounce a particular word as [san] and those who say [sɒn] for the same word.[4] A traditional dialectologist might map this as Figure *xviii* which looks fairly straightforward. But a structuralist will be interested in the function of these items within the total sound-systems at the various localities in the area covered by the map; this may lead him to draw several isoglosses, of which the traditional one may not be the most important. For instance:

1. There may be a difference between dialects which make a phonemic distinction between long and short vowels and those where length is not significant. So in one area, labelled 1 in Figure *xix*, [san] may realize /ă/, which could contrast with say [saːn] with /aː/, whereas in another (labelled 2), [san] simply has /a/ there being no /ă/ – /aː/ contrast. Similarly [sɒn] might represent /ŏ/ (as contrasting with /oː/, area 5), or /o/, area 4. This difference we have represented by the isogloss_____; it is a matter of difference in the number of phonemes in the systems at various localities (as is [kʌp] – [kʊp] in our English example).

2. There may be a difference between dialects in terms of which of two phonemes they happen to use in this particular word (as in our *bath* example). Thus while all may have '/ʌ/' and '/o/' phonemes, in one region (areas 1–3) /ʌ/ occurs in this particular word, while another (areas 4–5) has /o/. This difference we may represent by the isogloss_____.

3. Finally, within the area using the phoneme /a/, there may be a difference between dialects which represent /a/ by [a] and those which represent it by a vowel sound produced further back in the mouth and with some lip-rounding i.e. [ɒ]. This is a difference of phonetics (like [mæn], [man] etc), and we can represent it by the ...... isogloss. It just happens that this [ɒ] realization of /a/ in the area labelled 3 is phonetically identical with the [ɒ] realization of /o/ in area 4 and of /ŏ/ in area 5: it is an example of a different phonemic situation underlying a similarity at the phonetic level.

The resulting map thus shows a far more complex and interesting situation than the traditional map suggested. There is indeed a difference between dialects which say [san] and those which

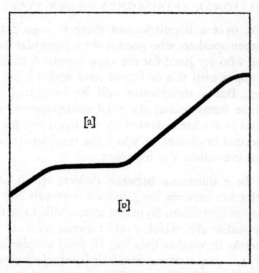

Figure xviii. Map such as might be produced by a 'traditional' dialectologist concerned simply with phonetic differences between areas.

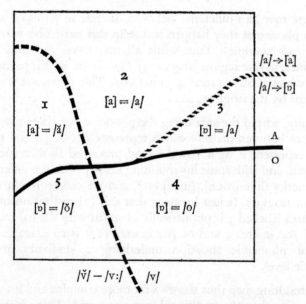

Figure xix. Map such as a 'structuralist' might produce: the phoneme system in different areas assumes greater importance than phonetics.

say [sɒn], but it is important to see that [san] may represent /săn/ (area 1) or /san/ (area 2), and that [sɒn] may represent /sŏn/ (area 5), /son/ (area 4), or even /san/ (area 3).

Both the phonetic and the phonemic points of view should be considered in the *description* of a dialect situation, and both may be important in the *history* of dialect differences. For instance, a simple phonetic change of [ʊ] to [ʌ] in certain words in parts of Britain led eventually to a new phonemic contrast of /ʊ/ – /ʌ/ in some English dialects. On the other hand, *structural pressures* within a phonemic system may be as important as geographical or political factors in determining whether dialects undergo certain phonetic changes: for instance, if a dialect had a vowel system ${}^i{}_e{}_a{}^u$, it would not be surprising to find 'symmetry' being created through either the /e/ vowel disappearing by *merger* of its word-set with /i/ or /a/, or an /o/ vowel developing through the *split* of /u/ or /a/ or both.

The call for 'structural dialectology' stressed that both viewpoints had a place, and we shall devote Chapter Five to this subject.

B. *Variation*

This line of criticism was not in fact directed originally against dialectology in particular, but against linguistics as a whole. But since it certainly applies to dialectology, and helped to lead to a different type of dialectology, we shall discuss it here.

In London, one speaker may pronounce 'half a pint of bitter' as [hɑːf ə paɪnt əv bɪtə], while another may say [ɑːf ə paɪnʔ ə bɪʔə]. In other words, some people 'sound *h* and *t*' while others 'drop them': there is variation in these respects – some speakers do one thing, some another. Moreover, it may happen that the first of our two speakers occasionally 'drops an *h*' or uses a glottal stop for /t/, or that the second sounds the odd [h] or [t]: in other words, *individuals* vary in respect of certain features as well as the community as a whole. It seems probable that nowadays there is more variation of this sort, since regional varieties are constantly under some influence from the standard language; the result in London, for example, is that speakers show varying proportions of those features which are standard and those which are Cockney, the local variety (such as absence of the /h/ phoneme and the use of the glottal stop as a realization of

/t/ in certain environments). But variation is most probably not a recent phenomenon: it seems quite likely that all sorts of linguistic changes start out as occasional uses, then become commoner, and eventually more or less universal – in other words, a period of variation occurs between the stage when the earlier feature is usual and that when the later one has ousted it.

Until quite recently, when faced with variation, linguists in general and dialectologists in particular have adopted one of two attitudes.[5] On the one hand, some have in effect pretended it does not exist: they have simply ignored it, and their description of a variety has been of what they regard as the normal or 'traditional' system. A linguist describing Standard English and RP will describe the standard system; the fact that an RP-speaker may occasionally drop an *h* or use a glottal stop in a non-standard way is ignored. Similarly, a dialectologist describing Cockney will not include /h/ in the consonant system, and of /t/ he will say that at the beginning of a word it is realized as [t] but word-finally and between vowels it is realized as a glottal stop [ʔ]; the occasional use of /h/, or of [t] in the environments just referred to, is ignored – these features are not part of the 'genuine dialect'. Most works entitled *The Dialect of* — have been of this sort: they have described the 'extreme' system, and ignored variation between this and 'non-genuine' *variants*.

On the other hand, within 'mainstream linguistics' the existence of variation has sometimes been recognized, at various *levels*. For example, at the level of phonetics, it has been observed that in some varieties of English the /ɑ:/ vowel in words such as *car, rather* etc may vary between a fairly front [a̤:] and a back [ɑ:], and certain points between; at the level of phonemes, *economics* may begin either with /i:/ or with /e/, and *with* may be pronounced with final /ð/ or /θ/; at the level of grammar, words like *none* or *neither* may in some contexts be followed by either a singular or a plural verb form; and so on. The term *free variation* has been applied to phenomena at all levels, to describe such a fluctuation between variants which seems to have no discernible pattern.[6]

In the 1950s both these approaches were challenged. The first (as employed by dialectologists: describing the 'extreme' system as *The Dialect of* —) was attacked not so much on the grounds that it ignored variation as on those of whether such a form of speech could be said to be representative of the population of the area (see below), though criticisms of the inadequacy of the way it treated variation apply at least as strongly here. But the use of the term 'free variation' by some dialectologists and by most linguists was criticized in an important paper by J. L. Fischer: 'Social influences on the choice of a linguistic variant' (1958). He pointed out that 'free variation' is really only a label, not an explanation; yet having given something this label has the effect of excluding the problem from further enquiry.

Fischer examined a particular instance of variation in English which is widespread: pronunciation of the participle or gerund form -*ing* varies between [ɪŋ] and [ɪn]. (In popular parlance, the '*g*' may be sounded or dropped. Phonetically, there is no [g] in either variant: it is variation between articulating the final nasal consonant against the soft palate or against the teeth-ridge.) Observing a group of children, Fischer found a situation such as would generally have been described as widespread 'free variation' between [ɪŋ] and [ɪn]. But instead of leaving it at that, he examined this variation *quantitatively*, i.e. in terms of the numbers of uses of each variant by each speaker. He found that the proportions of each variant correlated with a number of non-linguistic factors. For instance:

sex: boys generally used more [ɪn] variants than girls;

personality: e.g. 'model' boys used fewer [ɪn] variants than 'typical' boys;

socio-economic status: higher proportions of [ɪn] variants were used by children from lower down the social scale;

formality: the proportion of [ɪn] variants increased in less formal contexts e.g. more [ɪn] forms occurred in play periods than in the classroom; in interview situations, more [ɪn] occurred as the atmosphere became more relaxed; there were more [ɪn] variants in 'less educated' words such as *punchin, chewin*, as compared with *criticizing, reading* etc.

So, Fischer concluded, much of what had previously been labelled 'free variation' is seen *not* to be free: it is in fact 'socially conditioned variation'. Over the following years this point was taken up by a number of sociolinguists and dialectologists (see Chapters Six and Seven), and a number of 'models' for describing variation have been proposed (see Chapter Eight, II). It was realized that not only must variation be described if a true picture of a dialect or language is to be presented, but also that the social correlations of the use of particular variants may be very important for linguistic change.

CRITICISMS FROM SOCIAL SCIENCE

Population surveys have been increasingly employed this century in order to investigate opinions and practices, and social scientists have developed and refined survey methodology to a point where it has become a specialist subject. In 1956 an important paper by Glenna R. Pickford, 'American Linguistic Geography: a Sociological Appraisal', severely criticized dialectologists for not having made proper use of this expertise in the design and conduct of dialect surveys – with the result that their efforts have been to varying extents misdirected and their findings of doubtful value.

A social scientist such as Pickford would criticize 'traditional dialectology' on the two main grounds of deficiencies in the 'reliability' and in the 'validity' of the findings.

A. *Deficiencies in the 'reliability' of the findings*
Reliability concerns the question of whether a survey produces a representative and unbiased picture of the population under investigation. For results to be *representative* it is necessary that the sample of the population which is examined should contain the same proportions of people in all the different categories as are present in the total population. For example, if the population of an area under investigation contains 6,000 women and 4,500 men, a sample containing 60 women and 45 men would be representative as far as sex is concerned (though it might not be in respect of age-groups, social class, and so on); a sample with 75 women and 30 men would be *biased* towards women.

We have already introduced the term *sample*. Because it is usually impracticable to investigate every member of the population, a sample of some size is usually taken. Broadly, there are two main methods of sampling. First, *judgement samples*: selection of subjects is by human judgement. (A particular type of judgement sample is a *quota sample*, where one attempts to find informants in each of a number of predetermined categories.) Second, *random samples* (the American term is *probability sample*), where each member of the population has a calculable non-zero probability of being selected. (A refinement of this is the *stratified sample*, where the population is first divided into strata according to factors relevant to the survey topic, and a random sample is then taken from each stratum. There are other specialized varieties of random sample which we shall not go into.) Note that 'random' is not synonymous with 'haphazard': a human selector may be haphazard but will hardly ever be random – he will tend however unconsciously to favour some types within the population; truly random selection is by the use of a lottery or random numbers. It is generally accepted that a random sample of some sort must be employed if a representative selection is to be obtained.

We have seen that up to this period dialectologists had largely, and often exclusively, been concerned with the geographical dimension of linguistic variation: they were interested in the regional distribution of linguistic features. Moreover, they were often preoccupied with 'genuine dialect', which reflects regular historical developments 'uncorrupted' by contact with other forms of speech; this had usually resulted in a concentration on rural speakers, and generally those of little formal education, low social status and limited mobility. Let us take *SED* as a particular example: the sample on which its findings were based was largely made up of rural dwellers, usually agricultural workers, preferably men, and over the age of sixty. The survey was mainly carried out in the 1950s. Now the 1951 census of the United Kingdom revealed that only about 4 per cent of the working population was employed in agriculture (a figure which has continued to fall); and of course those over sixty and who had not travelled far would not even be representative of this small group. Yet it was from this very small section of the population that *SED* drew the great majority of its informants. So the findings of *SED* cannot possibly be representative of the British population: it is based on a judgement sample which is deliberately biased towards a certain group within the population.

The study of the sort of speakers *SED* investigated is a legitimate academic pursuit. They represent a type of speech which is almost certainly disappearing, and a record of this is valuable and interesting. But it is *not* legitimate to say that this is a 'survey of English dialects': it is a survey of the dialects of a particular type of speaker. While its results are of value to some people, they will be less valuable to a much wider range of social scientists who would have been interested in findings about the general population. Modern developed countries such as Britain are predominantly urban rather than rural, and group affiliations such as social class or politics or religion, and factors such as urbanization, probably account for speech patterns to just as great an extent as geographical location.

Pickford's criticisms were in fact aimed at American rather than British dialectology, and one might have thought the American surveys were less vulnerable to this sort of attack. They selected speakers of three different educational groups, and of two age-groups within each of these; and the locations were not so exclusively rural: towns and cities made up about one-fifth of them. But the 'classes' of speakers investigated are considered naïve, for several reasons: the criteria on which they are based are not objective – they depend on the fieldworker's assessment and sometimes are obviously circular (e.g. the age-groups are 'A. Aged and/or regarded by the fieldworker as old-fashioned; B. Middle-aged or younger, and/or regarded by the fieldworker as more modern.' There is the obvious possibility that the field-worker will decide a speaker is 'old-fashioned' or 'modern' at least partly on the basis of his speech – so statements will be made about the speech of certain groups within the population when these groups have in fact been established on the basis of their speech!); the three social classes are largely based on education, which sociologists would maintain is only one of the factors relevant to social class; and these social classes are not represented in the same proportions as in the population as a whole. In other words, the major American surveys suffer from many of the faults typical of judgement samples.

So far we have looked at surveys which are primarily interested in linguistic geography – in other words, those concerned with the regional distribution of features, and mainly concentrating on rural areas. But there have been British and American studies of the speech of towns; and since the majority of the population is urban, surely their results must be more representative? Unfortunately, no.

In Britain, *SED* had said: 'We deliberately ignored the towns

. . . though they should certainly be studied by somebody soon',[7] and members of the Leeds school have expressed their intention of investigating urban speech after completing their rural work: their aim is to work with labourers and artisans native to their respective towns, thus providing data comparable to that obtained by rural work. But this too would be an unrepresentative sample; those classed as 'labourers' by, say, the Registrar General may make up less than 15 per cent of a town's population, and even the whole 'working class' is by no means the total urban population. Urban work actually carried out in Britain was until recently subject to this sort of criticism. For example, Eva Sivertsen published in 1960 a book entitled *Cockney Phonology*; now even if 'a Cockney' is taken, as it justifiably may be, to mean something much more restricted than 'a Londoner', of whom there are several million, Sivertsen's sample is by no means representative of Cockneys: she studied only a restricted selection (working-class, minimal education and social contacts), and in fact for intensive study she concentrated on just four old ladies from Bethnal Green! The approach of Viereck in his work on the dialect of Gateshead-upon-Tyne[8] is similar: in spite of a chapter on the population of the town (over 100,000), and how it divides into social classes, age and sex groups, and so on, his main informants were twelve men, with an average age of seventy-six, most of them resident in old peoples' homes and formerly manual workers. An analysis of the speech of such people is not without interest, but a social scientist would certainly say that it should not purport to describe 'The Dialect of Gateshead'.

American urban dialect work was, until the mid-1960s, little better. One of the earliest such studies was that of David De Camp on San Francisco, begun in 1952. He selected 25 informants, all long-time residents, of three education-based classes, making sure to include one Negro and one Jew in each group. Leaving aside the question of whether a sample of 25 is large enough for a city the size of San Francisco, and the fact already mentioned that education is not considered by sociologists to be the only factor in social class, it is clear that the method of informant-selection is unsound: it suffers from 'hand-picking', chains of contact, and considerations of availability and willingness to co-operate – it is a judgement sample, with the attendant deficiencies in terms of reliability.

So an important sociological criticism of dialectology concerns the reliability of its findings. For results to be representative they must be based on surveys using sound sampling-methods, and samples of an appropriate size (another technical matter, which we have not gone into here). Dialectologists had concentrated on rural dwellers and particular age-groups and social classes (and the whole notion of social class had generally been treated very naïvely too); their samples were judgement samples – in fact they were largely handpicked. The results of such methods are heavily biased towards certain sections of a population.

B. *Deficiencies in the 'validity' of the findings*
Whereas *reliability* is a matter of whether findings are representative of the total population, *validity* concerns firstly the problem of asking the right questions and secondly that of how to draw out this information. In other words, validity is a matter of survey-methods, questionnaire-design, interview-techniques, and so on. In these areas social scientists have developed expertise, but until recently dialectologists have rarely made use of this expertise in their surveys.

Survey-methods may have been wasteful of time and resources. For example, most major surveys have employed only the 'direct' method, of interviewing informants. Some sorts of information, for instance in the lexical and semantic areas, could have been gathered by 'indirect' postal methods, providing the questionnaire was carefully designed. Not only would this have been more economical, it would also have (a) made it possible to reach a larger number of informants in the time available; (b) allowed actual interviews to be much shorter (see below) and to concentrate on matters that could only be handled in this way; and (c) thus enabled fieldworkers to have interviewed more informants in the available time.

Questionnaire-design has also been faulty. The responses to some questions used in postal surveys have been useless because the questions were badly phrased or ambiguous. With the direct method, the fieldworker can of course expand or revise his questionnaire as the work progresses; but this may cause problems with regard to the comparability of data, and the rewording of questions on the spot is a delicate matter (see below). The questionnaires used by many surveys have, for reasons outlined in the preceding paragraph, been needlessly long – sometimes requiring a week of an informant's time. This could deter many potential informants, thus increasing the problem of *non-response* which can produce a bias in the sample actually interviewed, however sound may have been the initial sampling procedure: for instance, retired people would be the most likely to be able to give up such a considerable amount of time. A lengthy questionnaire can also produce errors due to *fatigue bias*. It was reported that during one of the most recent major surveys, for example, the questionnaire could take up to nine days to administer; perhaps not surprisingly, in the course of this interrogation two informants went deaf and one died (we are not told how many went mad).

Interview-technique is a matter of skill and training. Many dialectologists would not be regarded by social scientists as having been properly trained as interviewers, and so either they may have failed to draw out the right responses, or if they 'suggested' a response or reworded a question in a way that made the informant feel he had somehow failed, this could have invalidated not only that particular response but possibly also the whole interview, since the relationship between interviewer and informant would have been changed. Some surveys have undertaken some training of interviewers; this could of course help to eliminate these faults. But on the other hand, if the training itself was faulty through not having been carried out by experts, it could introduce mass bias.

These criticisms of dialectology by social scientists – that its methods were antiquated, that it had failed to make use of expertise developed in related disciplines, and that as a result its findings were of dubious reliability and validity – were in part responsible for the fact that some dialectologists began to turn their attention to social and urban dialects, and to conduct their investigations along different lines (see Chapters Six and Seven).

'Long-term research projects cannot escape the risk of becoming antiquated in design before their completion.'[9] The dialect surveys of England and Scotland, and many others including most of the American ones, were started before the criticisms we have discussed in this chapter were published;[10] so it is not really fair to judge them in terms of these criticisms when the atlases actually see the light, often many years later. Of course, their findings are by no means worthless: they are of interest to many people, even though structural linguists, sociologists and others would have preferred something different. But from the 1950s, though some traditionalists have carried on as before, we begin to see different kinds of dialectology being undertaken. The remaining chapters of this book will concentrate on these more recent approaches; rather more detailed examination of some of the individual works involved is justified, partly because these approaches have as yet received less attention in books about dialect than has traditional dialectology, and partly because with more recent work it is less easy to decide which are the most important studies and developments.

CHAPTER 5

Structural Dialectology

🙚🙚🙚🙚🙚🙚

Between the speech of different parts of a country there may be very many phonetic differences. In England, for example, where some people say [kʌt] for *cut*, others will say [kʊt]; where some have [kɑːt] for *cart*, others will have [kaːt]; some say [ɪntʃ] for *inch*, others [ɪnʃ]; some pronounce *book* as [bʊk], others as [buːk]; and so on. We can draw isoglosses around the areas where each pronunciation is used, and this is of course what traditional dialectologists have been accustomed to do. But what results from this kind of mapping is often a network of different isoglosses, with not many of them running together throughout their length. In this sort of situation how are we to say where the important dialect divisions lie?

Sometimes it has been possible to offer a solution by pointing to bundles of isoglosses (see p. 57): though few isoglosses follow an identical course right across a country, a number more or less coincide for some distance, and so it can be concluded that this is an important dialect boundary. But quite often in such situations of a network of isoglosses, dialectologists have had to resort to *external* criteria in deciding about dialect areas; in other words, they have based their decisions, at least in part, on non-linguistic factors such as political divisions or cultural differences, because their linguistic data did not seem to offer an answer.

But perhaps some isoglosses are more important than others, and mark the important divisions? The Russian linguist Prince Nikolai Trubetzkoy was the first to bring fresh light to this problem from the structural viewpoint of modern linguistics. In a paper published in 1931, he pointed out that not all differences of pronunciation are alike in their relation to the sound-systems of the dialects concerned. In particular, it is possible to distinguish between *phonetic* and *phonological* differences. Phonetic differences can be gradual (e.g. *cat* may vary gradually in pronunciation

[kat], [kåt], [kɐt] . . .) and there may be 'transitional' sounds (e.g. [kæt] is transitional between a more [a]-like and a more [ɛ]-like vowel). But phonology is a more clear-cut matter: a dialect either does or does not make a particular phonemic distinction. For example, whatever the phonetic details involved, either *put* and *putt* are pronounced differently in a certain dialect, and it is possible for a hearer to distinguish which is which, or they are pronounced alike.

In more detail, Trubetzkoy held there to be three main types of sound difference. Each has subdivisions, but we shall only refer to these in the case of the first of his three types. The three are:

I. Differences of *phonological system*, subdivided into:

A. differences of *inventory*. For example, the difference within England between [kʌt] and [kʊt] relates to the absence in the North of the /ʌ/ phoneme: dialects of the North and the South differ in their inventory of phonemes. A similar example is the case of *weight* and *wait* referred to in Chapter One: in parts of the North there is an extra phoneme in the inventory, with the result that these two words are distinguished as /wɛɪt/ – /weːt/, while in other parts of the country both contain the same /eɪ/ phoneme and so they are not distinguished in pronunciation.

B. differences of *distribution*.[1] For instance, the [ntʃ] – [nʃ] difference referred to above arises from the fact that while all areas have both the phonemes /tʃ/ and /ʃ/ in their inventories (both have /tʃ/ in *chip* and /ʃ/ in *ship*, for example), they are differently distributed: in other words, the rules about what combinations of phonemes they can occur in are different. In some dialects, after /n/ only /tʃ/ occurs, so words like *inch*, *branch*, *bench*, *lunch* etc are pronounced with [ntʃ]; in others, only /n+ʃ/ occurs, so these same words have [nʃ]. The differences between [kɑː] and [kɑːr] for *car*, and [kɑːd] and [kɑːrd] for *card* are also a matter of distribution: all the dialects have the phoneme /r/ (for example, in *red*), but in some it cannot occur at the end of a word or before another consonant, while in others it does occur in these environments.

II. Differences in the *phonetic realization of phonemes*.
The difference between dialects which say [kɑːt] for *cart* and those which have [kaːt] occurs because while all of them have a

phoneme we could call /ʌ:/ in their inventories, and its rules of distribution may be the same, the way this phoneme is pronounced or *realized* is different. In some areas it is usually pronounced further back in the mouth than in others, which have a front vowel. The difference in the pronunciation of *man* referred to earlier is also a matter of realization: nearly all British dialects have a short /ʌ/ phoneme, but some pronounce it as a more open vowel, giving [man] rather than [mæn], where the tongue is slightly more raised.

III. Differences in the *incidence of phonemes*.[2]
The [lʊk] – [lu:k] difference in the pronunciation of *look* is an example of this type. All the areas in question have both the /ʊ/ and the /u:/ phonemes in their inventories; in most of them they occur in *good* and *boot* respectively. Moreover the difference is not a matter of distribution: /lu:k/ does occur, as the word *Luke*, even in areas which have /lʊk/ for *look*; and /lʊk/ occurs, as the word *luck*, in areas where *look* is /lu:k/; so clearly it is not a matter of different rules of combination. It is simply a matter of which of the two phonemes happens to occur in this particular word, and because of differing historical developments it is /u:/ that occurs in parts of the North of England, and /ʊ/ elsewhere: the *incidence* of these two phonemes is different. The *bath* example discussed in the last chapter is another case of different incidence. Both North and South have /ʌ/ and /ʌ:/ (or /a/ and /ɑ:/, to use the symbols we have employed elsewhere) in their inventories, with no major difference in rules of distribution, but it just happens that in the South it is /ʌ:/ which occurs in words like *bath*, *grass*, *laugh* and about a hundred others, while in the North the same set of words has /ʌ/.[3]

When comparing areas and deciding what are the important dialect divisions, Trubetzkoy held that a recognition of these different types of difference, and a decision as to which is most important, could make one's task much less complex.

There is little evidence that this important contribution from a member of what is known as the Prague School of Linguistics made any real impression on dialectologists or on 'mainstream linguists' over the following twenty years.[4] Not until the 1950s was recognition given to the notion of *structural dialectology* – an approach which examines dialect features in relation to their place in the systems of their dialects.

The notion is generally associated not with Trubetzkoy, but with a series of articles initiated by the paper by Uriel Weinreich referred to in Chapter Four: 'Is a Structural Dialectology Possible?' (1954).[5] From this paper we can draw two main points, both of which were taken up in the following years. The first is essentially that made by Trubetzkoy: that not all phonetic differences between dialects are of the same nature. Whereas traditional dialectology had simply recorded all differences between geographical areas, and treated them essentially as of equal importance, structural dialectology must distinguish various types of phonetic difference according to their effects on the phonological structure of their particular dialects.[6]

Let us briefly digress, in order to explore a little further the general point about structural relations in language. The main tenet of structural linguistics is that any variety of language is a *system*; the items within this system are defined not in terms of anything outside the system, but by their mutual oppositions and functions in relation to one another. To take a simple example: in English there are two main types of 'p-sound', an aspirated $[p^h]$ and an unaspirated $[p]$, and one 'b-sound', unaspirated $[b]$. These same sounds can be heard in several other languages, for example various forms of Chinese or Gaelic. So at first sight, defining their sound-systems in terms of *external* criteria – general phonetics – it might appear that English, Chinese and Gaelic are alike, in that they all have three labial stop consonants $[p^h]$, $[p]$, $[b]$. But when we examine the functions of these consonants *within* each particular language we see that there is a great difference between English on the one hand and Chinese or Gaelic on the other. In English, 'p-sounds' and 'b-sounds' are opposed to each other: they perform a contrastive function, say between *pan, nap* and *ban, nab*. But $[p^h]$ and $[p]$ are never opposed to one another: they never make a contrast between two words, and in fact they are *complementary* to one another – one (p^h) occurring initially e.g. $[p^han]$, the other (p) in other positions e.g. $[nap]$. So the difference between $[p^h]$ and $[p]$ is not important; most English speakers are not even aware that it exists; we say that $[p^h]$ and $[p]$ are just different phonetic realizations of the one phoneme /p/. But the difference between /p/ and /b/ *is* important, and we therefore say they are separate phonemes. In Chinese or Gaelic it is the difference between aspirated and unaspirated consonants that is important: in Cantonese, for example, [pʰɑ:] pronounced on a mid-level tone means 'afraid', while [pɑ:] on the same tone means 'greed'. Since they obviously perform a contrastive function, /pʰ/ and /p/ are classed as separate phonemes. On the other hand, if a [b] occurs, a Cantonese speaker would not treat it as different from [p]: the two sounds are never in opposition; they never perform a contrastive function between words, so they are classed as just different phonetic realizations of the phoneme /p/. Looking at the *internal* relations between the terms has thus led us to see a major difference between the systems of English and Cantonese, which would not have shown up simply from studying the phonetics: in English the system is /p/ ([pʰ] + [p]) versus /b/, while in Cantonese it is /pʰ/ versus /p/ ([p] + [b]).

'Structural dialectology' must therefore not simply compare the phonetic elements of two dialects; rather, it should look first at the structural relations – the oppositions and complementarities – within each dialect, and see the function of these phonetic elements within their own systems. Only then should it go on to compare one system and its elements with another. When this is done, the conclusions reached may be quite different from those of traditional dialectology, as Weinreich demonstrated with the example outlined in the preceding chapter (p. 105). It was shown that when one considers the functions and oppositions within the sound systems at various localities, a mere phonetic isogloss between certain areas which have [san] and others which have [sɒn] is of less importance than the phonemic iso-glosses between:

> *dialect 1*, which has /săn/, realized phonetically as [san];
> *dialects 2 and 3*, which have /san/, realized as [san] and [sɒn] respectively;
> *dialect 4*, which has /son/, realized as [sɒn]; and
> *dialect 5*, which has /sŏn/, realized as [sɒn].

The second major point in Weinreich's paper concerns the

comparison of the different systems, after they have been established for various dialects on the basis of the internal relations between their elements. Strictly speaking, if a system is defined solely by such internal relations of elements, it is not possible to compare two separate systems because no element in one can be identified with any element in another – each element exists only through its place in its own system. But where the systems in question are dialects of the same language, there are presumably some similarities in the functions of some elements. Weinreich suggested that some 'higher level' system could be constructed, which would embody both the similarities and the differences between the individual systems.

This higher-level system, or *diasystem*, could be expressed in formulaic terms, and Weinreich suggested one or two examples. For instance, suppose dialect 1 and dialect 2 had identical short vowel inventories, this could be expressed thus:

$$^{1,2}//i{\approx}e{\approx}a{\approx}o{\approx}u//$$

where the double slash and tilde indicate that more than one system is being described. On the other hand, if the two dialects had different sets of front vowels (dialect 1 having three such vowels, dialect 2 four), we could write:

$$^{1,2}//\frac{/1/i{\sim}e{\sim}a/}{/2/i{\sim}e{\sim}\varepsilon{\sim}a/}\ {\approx}o{\approx}u//$$

Here the single slash and tilde are used when describing just one of the systems. Similar formulae can of course be devised to include long vowels, diphthongs, etc.

Weinreich also referred to the possibilities of including in a diasystem what he called 'phonic' and 'distribution' differences. The former term corresponds to the later *realization* that we have adopted: the latter was unfortunately used ambiguously for some time, but it is clear that Weinreich was referring to what Trubetzkoy called 'etymological distribution', or, in later terms, *incidence*. In the latter area Weinreich foresaw a problem: how was one to express the fact that whereas two dialects had the same inventory, say,

$$^{1,2}//{\ldots}{\approx}o{\approx}u{\approx}{\ldots}//$$

in certain particular words dialect 1 had /o/ but dialect 2 had /u/?

Though Weinreich did not feel that the external viewpoint in dialectology was irrelevant (it was still of interest to consider what factors may have led to an isogloss being located where it was, or to see what correlations might exist between linguistic and non-linguistic boundaries), he thought that with the development of a structural approach such as he had suggested new possibilities opened up for distinguishing major dialect boundaries from less important ones, for the classification of dialects, and so on. In the decade following the publication of his article, a number of papers took up Weinreich's ideas and explored them further. We shall look briefly at some of the main points in just a few of the more important contributions to this debate.

Taking up Weinreich's first point, about 'different types of pronunciation differences' between areas, Edward Stankiewicz (1957) suggested that these distinctions might help to provide an answer to two opposing problems for dialectologists. The first, that of defining *discreteness* – in other words, of deciding which among a more or less continuous network of isoglosses are the important divisions between dialects – was a problem, as we have seen, for traditional dialectology. It had often been tackled in a fairly arbitrary way or with the help of extra-linguistic criteria. The opposite problem is that of defining *continuity*, or similarity between separate systems. This is the problem for structural dialectology: how is one to compare systems which are defined in terms of their own internal relations?

Stankiewicz suggested that if dialects were classified on the basis of their phonemic inventories, this would provide an objective way of tackling the discreteness problem. Dialects either do or do not make the same phonemic distinctions (whether or not the phonetic realizations of the phonemes involved are identical), and dialect divisions can be drawn on this basis. The opposite problem of continuity can be handled at least in part through examination of phonetic realization: one measure of similarity between different phoneme systems is the extent to which they use the same phonetics. We saw for instance in Figure *xix* that though different dialects may have different vowel phonemes in /san/, /son/, /sŏn/, they all have the phonetic realization [sɒn].

In 1959 G. R. Cochrane's paper on Australian vowels concentrated more on Weinreich's second point, the diasystem. He held that a proper description of a *speech community* (such as that of British English speakers, or even that of all English speakers) demanded the setting-up of such a higher-level system which embraced several partially-different systems. This was necessary because, he claimed, a diasystem is not just a linguist's construction, but a symbol of what actually happens when members of the community who have different systems converse with one another. In other words, Cochrane was claiming that a diasystem has some sort of reality as a means by which speakers 'translate' between their partially different systems as they converse.

Having made this general point, Cochrane set about clarifying and expanding on Weinreich's suggestions about diasystems. He made clear for example that it was essential to distinguish between the four main types of pronunciation difference we have referred to. One must be especially careful to keep comparison at the phonemic level (he used the term 'diaphonemic comparison', referring to matters of inventory) separate from that at the phonetic level ('diaphonic comparison', matters of realization). For instance, if two dialects had differences in their inventories of back vowels, but their front vowels differed only in realization, writing a diasystem such as

$$^{1,2}//i \approx \frac{1/\varepsilon \sim a/}{2/e \sim æ/} \approx a \approx \frac{1/ɔ \sim o/}{2/o/} \approx u//$$

would be to confuse these two levels of comparison. Better to deal with inventory first, say as

$$^{1,2}//i \approx E \approx A \approx a \approx \frac{1/ɔ \sim o/}{2/o/} \approx u//$$

and then handle the more superficial differences separately. Cochrane also suggested that the diasystem could be used to express differences of distribution, in the sense of the combinatorial possibilities of phonemes. For example, a German dialect might only permit /s + t/ at the beginning of words where Standard German has /ʃ + t/; this could obviously be written:

$$^{1,2}//\frac{1\#\int t}{2\#st} \approx ...//$$

Similarly, the difference between English dialects in their pronunciation of words spelled with '-nch':

$$^{1,2}//... \approx \frac{1 \; \mathrm{ntʃ}}{2 \; \mathrm{nʃ}} \approx ...//$$

Finally, Cochrane addressed the problem of what he called 'lexical correspondences' (what Trubetzkoy had termed 'etymological distribution', Weinreich simply 'distribution', and for which we are employing the unambiguous 'incidence'). He pointed out that the question of sameness or difference between two varieties could not be handled simply in terms of inventory, distribution and realization: two varieties could have identical inventories of phonemes, with identical phonetic realizations and identical combinatorial possibilities, and yet they could sound very different because of differences in which phoneme occurs in which particular words. For instance, ignoring other matters, Northern and Southern British English are identical in their inventories of open vowels:

$$^{N,S}//... \approx a \approx ɑː \approx ...//$$

but these two vowels are only partly shared in terms of incidence:

$$\mathrm{N}/\mathrm{kat, \; baθ, \; kɑːt}/ \; \mathrm{but} \; ^{S}/\mathrm{kat, \; bɑːθ, \; kɑːt}/$$

The difficulty of handling incidence was a major problem with the notion of a diasystem for W. G. Moulton. A scholar of German with expertise in both modern linguistics and philology, Moulton had taken a particular interest in the recent major dialect survey of Swiss German, directed by Hotzenköcherle. This had been a project on traditional lines, and its records were in an impressionistic phonetic transcription. Moulton attempted to interpret the findings of the survey in terms of structural linguistics.

Besides other findings, such as confirming Weinreich's point that dialect divisions drawn on the basis of phonetics often do not correspond with those established on phonemic grounds, but also claiming that there are grounds for believing that the boundaries between phonemic systems are *not* always clear-cut, Moulton made two noteworthy points in an article about Swiss vowel systems published in 1960. First, he found that the question of incidence causes considerable difficulties for the notion of the diasystem. As has already been pointed out (see note 3), if the incidence of phonemes in particular words is not considered, a diasystem could be set up for quite unrelated varieties – for separate languages, in other words – since they could be very similar or even possibly identical in terms of their inventory, distribution and realization of phonemes. Yet this had hardly been what the diasystem was intended for: it was surely supposed to summarize the similarities and differences between related dialects, and incidence is a part of this.

To illustrate the problem, Moulton took two particular Swiss dialects, of localities about fifty miles apart, Luzern and Appenzell. If incidence were not considered, a diasystem could be set up which would suggest that there was no systemic difference between the two dialects in terms of their short vowels:

$$^{\text{LU,AP}} // i \approx e \approx \varepsilon \approx æ \approx a \approx ɔ \approx o \approx u \approx ü \approx ö \approx ɔ̈ //$$

But native speakers would certainly not accept that the two have identical vowel systems (and neither would traditional dialect-ologists or historical linguists), for they certainly do not sound alike. The reason is that different phonemes occur in the 'same' word (just as in English all dialects have /a/ and /ɑ:/, but differ in which occurs in *bath* etc); in other words, the incidence is different. It is, of course, a matter of history: Luzern and Appenzell both have /ɛ/ phonemes, for example, which are the same phonologically and phonetically – but not historically: they have developed from different origins, and their different word-sets reflect this. Yet if we were to attempt to build incidence into the diasystem, say by indicating with a subscript symbol beside each vowel just what set of words this phoneme occurs in, then we should find that only one of the eleven short vowels has identical incidence:[7]

$$|| \frac{^{\text{LU}}/i_0 \sim e_1 \sim \varepsilon_2 \sim æ_{3,4}/}{^{\text{AP}}/i_{0,1} \sim e_{1,2} \sim \varepsilon_3 \sim æ_4/} \approx a_4 \approx \frac{^{\text{LU}}/ɔ_2 \sim o_1 \sim u_0 \sim ü_0 \sim ö_1 \sim ɔ̈_2/}{^{\text{AP}}/ɔ_2 \sim o_{1,2} \sim u_{0,1} \sim ü_{0,1} \sim ö_{1,2} \sim ɔ̈_2/} ||$$

But this seems even less satisfactory: here are two dialects which are geographically quite close to each other, and which are certainly mutually intelligible, but the diasystem suggests a very considerable difference since they only have one 'diaphoneme' totally in common. Moulton concluded that the diasystem may be a useful concept when comparing phonemic systems where relationship is not a concern – but this is just not dialectology.

The other important point made by Moulton was that the structural viewpoint is very enlightening when considering historical developments in dialects. If the vowel system for Middle High German (twelfth to fifteenth centuries AD) is set out, it appears to have a 'hole' in it; in other words, it looks asymmetrical:

$$
\begin{array}{ccc}
\text{i} & \text{ü} & \text{u} \\
\text{e} & \text{ö} & \text{o} \\
\text{ë} & & \\
\text{ä} & & \text{a} \\
\end{array}
$$

But nearly all the modern dialects in the area Moulton examined have removed this asymmetry, in one of three ways. In the West and Centre /ë/ and /ä/ have merged as [æ] (i.e. the number of front vowels has been reduced), resulting in system (*a*). In Northern dialects /ë/ and /ä/ merged as [ɛ], and later /o/ split into [o] and [ɔ] (i.e. the number of front vowels was reduced, and that of back vowels increased); there was also a split in the central vowels – the result was the 'triangular' system (*b*). In the East there was also an increase in the numbers of back and central vowels, producing system (*c*):

$$
(a)\begin{array}{ccc}
\text{i} & \text{ü} & \text{u} \\
\text{e} & \text{ö} & \text{o} \\
\text{æ} & & \text{a} \\
\end{array}
\qquad
(b)\begin{array}{ccc}
\text{i} & \text{ü} & \text{u} \\
\text{e} & \text{ö} & \text{o} \\
\text{ɛ} & \text{ɵ} & \text{ɔ} \\
& \text{a} & \\
\end{array}
\qquad
(c)\begin{array}{ccc}
\text{i} & \text{ü} & \text{u} \\
\text{e} & \text{ö} & \text{o} \\
\text{ɛ} & \text{ɵ} & \text{ɔ} \\
\text{æ} & & \text{a} \\
\end{array}
$$

Some people may think that to talk of the 'symmetry' of systems in this way is simply to be carried away by patterns the linguist himself has created. But Moulton claims that the developments in the North show that these systems are *not* just a linguist's toy, but represent some sort of reality. Otherwise, after the merger of /ë/ and /ä/ it would have been perfectly possible just to *draw* a symmetrical pattern:

$$
\begin{array}{ccc}
\text{i} & \text{ü} & \text{u} \\
\text{e} & \text{ö} & \text{o} \\
\text{ɛ} & & \text{a} \\
\end{array}
$$

But phonetically [ɛ] and [a] cannot be considered a front and back 'pair' – and the fact that speakers did not 'feel' them to be such is proved, in Moulton's opinion, by the later split of /o/, giving a vowel /ɔ/ which really does match /ɛ/ in phonetic terms, and produces the 'truly' symmetrical system (b).

In 1964 Ernst Pulgram returned to the question of the diasystem, in an attempt to see whether the views of Weinreich and Moulton were irreconcilable. In essence, a diasystem is intended to be a class or grouping of dialects. What are the criteria for membership of such a class? The decision is not easy: if we say that the dialects must be mutually intelligible, or that they must be dialects of the same language, we run into the problems of deciding just what is 'the same language' that we discussed in Chapter One – with the attendant difficulties over chains of mutually intelligible dialects, with non-intelligibility between the extremes and with conventionally-accepted language boundaries at some point between speakers who *can* understand each other. But a line must be drawn somewhere to the process of including more and more dialects in a diasystem, and so the linguist should be conscious of some purpose in his setting up of diasystems: it should be of some use, and it becomes progressively less useful as its membership becomes more and more diverse. A grouping of dialect A and dialect B in a diasystem (like putting together an apple and an orange in a fruit bowl) may make some sense; but to group together unrelated varieties in a diasystem, though technically possible, may be of no more value than grouping together a fruit, a worm and a motor car, which have no more in common than that they are physical objects.

Pulgram held that Weinreich's purpose was to show up equivalences and differences in function between elements of two or more systems; Moulton's purpose seems to be to determine which forms are related and to what degree, and to establish boundaries. In other words, the two are not really at odds; they are simply interested in different things when doing dialectology. Moulton is concerned with the description and circumscription of classes of varieties; Weinriech *starts* from this point, and is interested in structural comparisons between the classes thus established. Both pursuits are of value. And the concept of the diasystem can play a useful part for each of them: Weinreich's use of the diasystem is clear; for Moulton, the juxtaposition of the two possible ways of writing a diasystem for the dialects of Luzern and Appenzell should itself be interesting and instructive about the nature of dialect and dialect differences.

At this point let us leave the debate about structural dialectology initiated by Weinreich. The movement did continue, and nowadays many dialectologists have a structural orientation; whether or not they try to write diasystems, they recognize that not all phonetic differences are of the same type and have the same effect on the phonological system.[8]

But how really new is the structural viewpoint in dialectology? Several years before Weinreich's paper, the *Linguistic Survey of Scotland* had started work, and they consciously set out to gather information about phonological systems rather than just phonetics. Volume III of the *Linguistic Atlas of Scotland* will present some of their findings, but over twenty years earlier J. C. Catford (1957*b*) had described how *LSS* sought material on five phonological systems (stressed and unstressed vowels, initial and final consonants, and consonant clusters),[9] and showed how dialects could be classified initially as having 8, 9 or 10 stressed vowels, and then subdivided according to what vowels they were in each case.

But structural dialectology may in a sense go back much earlier than this. In fact, it may only be in relatively recent times that most dialectologists have not behaved, however unconsciously, like structuralists when dealing with particular dialects. In a different article on structural dialectology from that referred to above,[10] Moulton pointed out that scholars in the days before phonetics was such a detailed and technical subject tended to act like structuralists in that they noted only phonemic rather than phonetic differences between sounds. This was not always the case, but from an examination of, say, descriptions before 1900 of British dialects, it might well be concluded that it is much easier to deduce a picture of the phonemic system from the works of 'amateurs' than from those burdened by a more detailed knowledge of phonetics, such as A. J. Ellis.

Paradoxical as it may appear, scholars may have become *less* reliable because they became more skilled in phonetics and attempted to be more 'scientific' in their transcriptions. The problem starts with a misconception on the part of those requiring fieldworkers to employ a very detailed and precise transcription and not to 'edit' or 'normalize' in any way: they assume that a fieldworker can act like a tape-recorder – that he can write down exactly what he hears; that he just records raw data. But in fact no transcription, however detailed, is just a record: it involves some 'processing', in that the writer has to decide just what symbols and modifying marks to employ. Moreover, it has been demonstrated that such processing and transcription is not objective: it tends to reflect the worker's training and background. Even highly-trained phoneticians show considerable variation; in fact, their differences can even indicate in what school of phonetics they were trained![11]

Of course, the older scholars also 'processed' their material as they transcribed it. But they processed not into the categories of general phonetics (i.e. categories not specific to any particular languages), but according to the internal relations of the dialect under investigation. Some of them were native speakers or at least knew the dialect well, and so realized, consciously or unconsciously, that some differences were unimportant. Others deliberately asked their informants such questions as whether form x really was different from form y, or whether form x rhymed with form z, and so on. These methods tended to yield a phonemic description, whereas the 'scientific' approach – which attempted to treat informants simply as talking machines answering a fixed set of questions, and fieldworkers as recording machines obtaining an objective record – produced results which at best required a lot of editing and analysis, and at worst were simply inaccurate.

In an article entitled 'The phonemes of a dialectal area, perceived by phoneticians and by the speakers themselves' (1965), K. Ringgaard contrasts the results of a direct survey by trained phoneticians with those of a postal survey which sent a questionnaire to five hundred native speakers. His conclusion was that the detailed transcriptions of the phoneticians gave little clear information about the phoneme system; in fact, they revealed more about the fieldworkers themselves and their native pronunciations. The dialect speakers, on the other hand, responding as best they could with the orthography, produced a much clearer picture of the phonemic contrasts over the area. Not every advance is progress!

In this chapter we have examined the response by dialectology to one of the lines of criticism discussed in Chapter Four: that dialectologists were concerned with phonetic detail, rather than with the more illuminating structural viewpoint that 'mainstream linguistics' had adopted. In the next two chapters we turn to the new approaches that developed at least partly in response to the other criticisms voiced in the 1950s.

CHAPTER 6

Social and Urban Dialectology I:
the United States

𝕾𝕾𝕾𝕾𝕾𝕾

We noted that in addition to the criticisms of traditional dialect-ology which came from modern structural linguistics, and which led to the development of structural dialectology, there were also criticisms in the 1950s from social scientists, which were directed against various deficiencies in methodology, and especially against the bias towards a small and unrepresentative section of the population. In the period since then the study of the speech of different social groups within the same area, and that of urban as well as rural communities, has become much more prominent. America led the way in this development, and this chapter will be devoted to 'pioneering' studies carried out in the United States.

As we saw in Chapter Two, even before the criticisms referred to were voiced, American dialectologists had decided that there must be a social dimension to their studies. This was because although there was on the one hand no nationally-recognized standard form of speech, and on the other little 'real' dialect in the sense of extreme regional differences of the type found in some European countries, there were *some* regional differences at *all* levels of society – among the 'cultivated' as well as the 'uncultivated'. This was clearly a different situation from that in, say, Britain, where a standard dialect (Standard English) was usual among all middle- and upper-class speakers, from whatever region, and the higher classes also used a standard accent (RP), but at the lower social levels there were very different regional dialects, which attracted almost all the attentions of dialectologists. So the various American dialect surveys looked at three educational types, and at two different age-groups within each of these. They also paid some attention to the speech of urban areas: whereas most European surveys concentrated on rural speech, about one-fifth of the communities investigated in the American surveys were towns or cities.

But the attitude of many American scholars of the pre-1960s period is perhaps hinted at in the words of one of their leading dialectologists, Raven McDavid. In an article published in 1948, which describes one of the earliest dialect studies with an emphasis on social differences, he said: 'A social analysis proved necessary because the data proved too complicated to be explained by merely a geographical statement or a statement of settlement history.' This suggests that the social viewpoint was a secondary one, only resorted to because a straightforward geographical approach was found to be inadequate.

Nevertheless, McDavid's work is an interesting early example of a study taking account of social factors. Working on the speech of South Carolina, he examined the phenomenon of 'postvocalic-r pronunciation'. (Whether r is pronounced or not after a vowel, either word-finally (e.g. car) or before another consonant (e.g. card) is a topic which keeps recurring in American studies.) South Carolina was generally considered to be an area where r was not pronounced in such environments. McDavid pointed out, however, that some natives of South Carolina did pronounce r, but in previous work this had been either overlooked or deliberately ignored because it did not fit into the generally-accepted geographical pattern and was therefore considered simply as aberrant. He went on to demonstrate that the r-less pronunciation was that of the old plantation-owning caste, the top social class, and so was the established 'prestige form' for the area, with certain correlations with educational status, age, urban centres, and so on. But on the other hand there were some signs that r-pronunciation was starting to gain respectability.

An early study of an urban community was that of G. N. Putnam and E. M. O'Herne, published in 1955. They investigated a group of generally low social status, the Negro dwellers in a Washington slum alley. They concentrated mainly on phonology, examining the phonemes in some detail; with morphology, syntax and lexicon they merely noted the peculiarities as compared to more generally-accepted forms. But of greater interest is the fact that they introduced certain innovations which, though fairly unrefined at that stage, were to assume more importance in future studies of this type. Firstly, they attempted a more objective assessment of social class than had been employed in previous studies, which tended to depend on a fieldworker's personal impressions of a speaker's status. Secondly, they showed some awareness of the principles of sampling, though they do not appear to have put these into practice in their own selection of informants. Thirdly, they tried to test the hypothesis that speech serves as a marker of social class. This they did by playing tape-recordings of various speakers to subjects who were asked to perform certain judgements about them. The speakers were twelve Negroes from different 'positions on the prestige continuum', who retold in their own words an Aesop fable that had just been narrated to them. A total of 70 'judges' produced assessments that were very largely in accord with the speakers' objective status.

There are some fairly obvious criticisms of this experiment. For instance, it could be held that the judgements were based not simply on speech (as they might have been if all speakers had reproduced an identical passage) but on language in general, which also revealed their levels of intelligence and education. For the recording of free narrative (the speaker's own version of a fable), while obviating the disadvantage of the less literate being more likely to betray themselves if asked to read a set passage, made it even more probable that the more intelligent and better educated would show up through their sentence-construction, vocabulary, memory for detail, and so on – so the result that the judges' assessments were generally 'correct' is not so remarkable. Moreover, the judges were predominantly white women, and all of them were of high educational status (postgraduate students and teachers), and such people might well be more capable than average of assessing speakers in this way. But in spite of these deficiencies, the study was certainly a step forward in establishing the social significance of speech differences.

Another project which sought to examine differences within an urban community was that of David De Camp, working in San Francisco (published in 1958–9). With a sample of 25 long-term residents, divided into three educational classes (in each of which he deliberately included one Negro and one Jew),

De Camp concentrated on analysing the phonemes of San Francisco speech in their various phonetic realizations. But though this was one of the first urban studies with subjects of all social classes, it is disappointing, largely because it did not succeed in breaking away from the traditional approaches.[1] Leaving aside De Camp's method of selecting informants, which has been criticized in Chapter Four, two aspects of the work show this 'traditional' deficiency. Firstly, the treatment of variation: De Camp noted a good deal of 'apparently free variation', which he classified in various ways e.g. phonemic or sub-phonemic variation; variation within an informant and variation between informants; and so on. And he states that he made 'extensive counts of the relative frequency of variants for each informant and for the dialect as a whole'. But the results of this are generally labels such as 'rare', 'occasional', 'common', and so on: there are no clear conclusions about whether this 'apparently free' variation is really free. The other area in which De Camp failed to break away from traditional preoccupations is in the explanations offered for various features of San Francisco speech. He devoted much attention to its 'social and historical context' – in other words, to the different origins of the inhabitants – and attempted to label features as typical of certain parts of the United States. So his correlations and conclusions were more concerned with settlement history than with the present-day social structure.

Of more importance for the future of social dialect studies (and of dialectology, and linguistics, in general) was the paper published by J. L. Fischer in 1958. This we have already examined in Chapter Four. Let us simply recall here that Fischer established that the commonly-employed term 'free variation' was both a hindrance (since having applied this label – and it is *only* a label, not an explanation – has the effect of excluding the phenomenon from more detailed investigation), and also was in fact often inaccurate, since more careful examination of the data would probably show that variation is not free: it is 'socially conditioned', correlating with various features of the speaker and the context. The quantitative treatment of variation – counting just how many instances of each variant were produced by each particular speaker – was a great step forward from the previous informal and impressionistic approaches. So too was Fischer's suggestion that the social factors involved in variation could be important for linguistic change. For instance, the 'mass' might in a sense pursue the 'élite' linguistically, by producing more of their variants, and the élite might fly from the mass by adopting new ones. Fischer suggested that fuller investigations along these lines should be carried out with fairly large samples of a speech community.

A larger-scale investigation of this sort was carried out in the early 1960s by L. Levine and H. J. Crockett, though it was not reported in print until 1967. Their study was carried out in the North Carolina piedmont, and was concerned with postvocalic-*r*, the same feature that McDavid had earlier examined in South Carolina. It was an advance methodologically in that its sampling and fieldwork techniques were far sounder than in most previous linguistic investigations. The sample was properly designed, in accordance with the principles established by social scientists. Moreover, the subjects investigated were 'evaluated': in other words, the characteristics of both those who co-operated and those who refused to take part were examined, in order to check that the sample actually interviewed was representative of the population as a whole, in that it was not just people of a certain type who responded or people of some other type who refused. The questionnaire too was carefully designed, and the fieldworkers were trained. The reliability of these workers was checked by comparing the transcriptions of different fieldworkers, and also by examining the performance of the same worker at different stages of his work (it sometimes happens that a worker will transcribe the same thing differently at different periods, either because his hearing becomes more acute or because he is unconsciously concentrating on different features).

Levine and Crockett found considerable variation in the pronunciation or otherwise of postvocalic-*r*, and this variation they were able to correlate with both linguistic and social factors. The linguistic correlations were that *r*-pronunciation decreased according to (1) whether the syllable was stressed or unstressed; (2) whether *r* was followed by another syllable, a final consonant or cluster, or the end of the word; (3) whether the vowel preceding *r* was high central, low central, front or back. The finding that *r*-pronunciation varied according to whether the words involved were read in list form or occurred within a sentence showed that the formality of the linguistic task and the context was an important correlate. More clearly social correlates were the educational and occupational status of the speakers, their age and their sex.

Perhaps the most interesting finding was that greater formality, better education, and superior occupation correlated with both increasing *and* decreasing *r*-pronunciation. The conclusion was that there were two competing norms of correctness: the older 'Southern' *r*-less pronunciation and the newer more nationally-accepted *r*-form. Higher social status correlated with 'norm clarity' (i.e. either high or low *r*-score), while those of lower status showed intermediate *r*-scores. But the results for the different age-groups suggested that *r*-pronunciation would become the commoner form; young people (and recent arrivals in the area) were more likely than older people (and longer-term residents) to have the *r*-pronouncing norm. That this 'outside' national norm will eventually gain ascendency is also suggested by the fact that women tended to increase *r*-pronunciation in the more formal word-list style more than did men (in several studies women have been found to be more likely to lead the way in that they use the prestige form more frequently than men of the same status); and that while *r*-pronunciations both increased and decreased in the word lists as compared to sentences, there was a greater number of *r*-increases than of decreases, and the average increase was greater than the average decrease.

In the mid-1960s came the work that appeared to be a real breakthrough – that of William Labov, which, because of its influence on later work, repays examination in some detail. Though known mainly through his studies in New York City, Labov's first important work, in which he developed the approach which was to be so fruitful, was carried out not in a city, but on the little island of Martha's Vineyard, in Massachusetts. In an article entitled 'The Social Motivation of a Sound Change' (1963), Labov examined the use of centralized variants of the /aɪ/ and /aʊ/ diphthongs, i.e. their pronunciation as [ăɪ], [ăʊ] or even [əɪ], [əʊ]. Both from a comparison of the present situation with that reflected in the *Linguistic Atlas of New England* (for which the fieldwork had been done thirty years earlier) and from the fact that the older age-groups seemed to use fewer such forms than the younger, these variants appeared to be increasing in frequency. What could account for this change away from the more standard pronunciation of that part of the United States?

Labov did a quantitative study of the type Fischer had advocated. Interviewing a 1 per cent judgement sample (see p. 110) containing 69 speakers chosen to represent the apparent social groupings on the island, he classified all examples of /aɪ/ and /aʊ/ (about 3,500 and 1,500 respectively) as [aɪ], [ʌ̈ɪ], [əɪ] etc. Totals of these various forms were worked out, and expressed as proportions of the total occurrences of the diphthongs, and in this way 'average scores' for centralization were produced for various groups within the population.

From these results it was possible to draw some interesting conclusions. Centralized forms were most common among those with a 'positive orientation' towards Martha's Vineyard, i.e. those who were proud of being Vineyarders: for example, the 'older' families; those who felt their way of life to be under threat from outsiders, especially summer visitors, and were fighting to preserve it; the members of ethnic groups who associated themselves most strongly with the island; and so on. Among the younger people, those who had tried life away from Martha's Vineyard but returned, showed very marked identification with the centralizing trend; those still at school revealed considerable differences between those who intended to leave the island (little centralization) and those who wanted to remain (marked centralization).

Labov had thus not only shown that variation in the pronunciation of /aɪ/ and /aʊ/ was not 'free variation', but correlated with certain social groupings and attitudes within the population; he had also used his findings to attempt to answer an important question of linguistics: 'Why do sound changes occur?' This determination not simply to produce descriptive studies, correlations of linguistic and social differences, but also to aim to solve linguistic problems – to make theoretical advances – is an important aspect of Labov's attitude and of his contribution to the subject.

The work for which Labov is best known is reported in *The Social Stratification of English in New York City* (1966a) and in a number of articles published in the mid-1960s.[2] Seeking to find some 'structure' in an apparently very confused situation, one of his hypotheses was that linguistic variation correlates with social stratification – and a pilot survey carried out in 1962 attempted to test this in relation to postvocalic-*r*. As in several other parts of America, *r*-pronunciation appeared to be on the increase in New York, which is a traditionally *r*-less area, and Labov sought to show that this is a social differentiator in all levels of New York City speech. The pilot study was very simple, but provided fascinating results: Labov examined the speech of salespeople in three Manhattan department stores, Saks, Macy's, and Klein's, which in terms of location, advertising, prices, physical conditions and job prestige (though not wages) would be ranked in that descending order of reputation by New Yorkers. Labov asked various staff in the stores a question about the location of certain products which would elicit the reply 'Fourth floor'; pretending not to have heard properly, he then got a repetition in more deliberate form. He thus obtained data on *r* in both preconsonantal and final position, in both casual and emphatic styles, from 68 employees in Saks, 125 in Macy's and 71 in Klein's.

The amount of *r*-usage clearly reflected the relative prestige of the stores: 62 per cent of Saks employees used some *r*-forms, compared to 51 per cent of Macy's, and 20 per cent of Klein's. There were also more *r*-forms in *floor* (i.e. final position) than in *fourth* (i.e. preconsonantal), and in emphatic than in casual speech. It was also found that Negroes generally used less *r* than whites (and the larger proportions of Negro employees in Klein's and Macy's than Saks thus contributed to the overall difference), but with both whites and Negroes studied separately the three stores still remained in the same order of *r*-use. Within Macy's, three jobs of different prestige were examined, and it was found that floorwalkers, salespeople and stockboys used less *r* in that order; and in Saks there was less *r* on the ground floor than on the more select upper floors! The only unexpected finding was that while in Saks *r*-usage was more common with decreasing age (as expected), in Macy's the reverse was the case. Further examination was called for, but it seemed that in the 'better' store the younger people had come under the influence of the new trend, while in Macy's the older groups were more anxious to adopt this newer prestige form.

The pilot study had confirmed the hypothesis that speech is a stratifying feature within society, even within what might have been considered, from an occupational classification only, as a single group. Labov turned to a more elaborate examination of the speech of the Lower East Side of New York City. This was an area with a changing population, including many non-natives of New York, where a random sample would obviously pick up many 'unwanted' subjects, i.e. non-native speakers of English, recent arrivals with speech typical of other parts of America, and so on. Labov was fortunate in having access to the records of a scientifically selected sample interviewed by a social survey team only two years earlier; using the personal details available on each subject, he was able to eliminate certain unwanted groups and then to take a stratified sample (see p. 111) of the rest. He succeeded in interviewing about 120 people, who were reasonably representative of all the main sub-groups of English speakers in the population at large. To check that those who refused to be interviewed or could not be contacted at the time were not of a particular linguistic type, which would mean that the sample was biased against this type, Labov contacted almost half of them by telephone, pretending to be researching reactions to TV programmes; he concluded that these 'failures' did *not* render his actual sample unrepresentative.

Labov's sample was thus much larger and more scientifically selected than those of previous urban studies. His division of this sample into social classes was more objective too: instead of the usual impressionistic and simplistic classifications that were unacceptable to sociologists, he employed one developed by social scientists themselves. It was based on a combination of three factors: the education of the subject, his occupation and his income (or that of the chief breadwinner of the family, if different). Each of these was 'scored' on an objective four-point scale (0–3), so that informants ranged in total class scores from 0 to 9. Certain groupings of these ten classes were possible; that most frequently adopted produced five major social classes.

Labov made important innovations in interview method. The whole interview was tape-recorded, and was organized with the aim of eliciting a range of *styles*, in the sense of levels of formality. Whereas most previous dialect research had been based on individually-elicited words, Labov recognized that such responses were likely to be in a very 'artificial' careful pronunciation; other styles would be more natural, and obtaining a range of these would also help to show whether there was any general structure and direction to formality-shifts. Much of an interview between two people not previously acquainted, and based on a questionnaire, could be assumed to be in a relatively careful style of speech. A more careful style than this was elicited by getting informants to read a scripted passage; a more formal one still by asking them to read unconnected lists of words (similar to the single-word response style of traditional dialect surveys); and the most formal style of pronunciation by getting informants to read *minimal pairs* of words, such as *hedge – edge*, *coughing – coffin* etc. More interesting from the point of view of seeing the most natural patterns of speech, but obviously more difficult within the fairly artificial interview-situation, would be to move in the opposite direction along the formality-scale towards what might be called 'casual' or 'spontaneous' speech. Labov sought to obtain such data in several ways: he allowed informants to wander off the subject on to a topic where they might be more interested or involved, and so speak more naturally; he had the tape-recorder running before and after the actual questionnaire-based interview, and also when the informant broke off to speak to another member of the family or a caller, so as to obtain this 'unscripted' material; and he introduced topics which might produce a more emotional response such as would override the constraints of the rather formal situation of the interview (he asked them to describe an occasion on which they had nearly been killed, for instance). Labov recognized that the fact that situations such as these occurred during the interview was not in itself sufficient to guarantee that spontaneous speech would occur: a speaker *could* continue to use a more careful style. So he decided that before he could count certain material as 'casual style', there must be some evidence in the form of 'channel cues': changes of speed, pitch, volume, rate of breathing, or an outburst of laughter were assumed to indicate a shift to spontaneous speech.

Labov was primarily interested in variation, and to examine this he further developed the method he had begun to use in his work on Martha's Vineyard. He recognized that very many features at all levels of language show variation, but for detailed investigation he chose five phonological *variables*: postvocalic-*r*, symbolized as (r); the vowel in such words as *bad, back, bang* etc (eh); that in *dog, coffee* etc (oh); and the dental consonants in *this, the, with* etc (dh), and in *three, thing, both* etc (th). Each variable had two or more *values* (or variants): (r) was either [r] or [ø]; (eh) could be [ɑː], [aː], [æː], [æ], [ɛ²] or [ɪ²], and (oh) had a similar range of back vowels; (dh) and (th) could be pronounced as fricative [ð], [θ], affricated [dð], [tθ], or stop [d], [t]. Each variant was associated with a certain score, and the appropriate score was recorded for each occurrence of a variable in an informant's speech.

Let us take (r) as a simple example of this method. Suppose that in a certain style during interview Informant X uses 42 words where postvocalic-*r could* occur; in 26 of these he pronounces [r] (scored as 1), in 16 he does not (the [ø] variant, scoring 0). His total score is obviously 26/42 (or 61.9 per cent). This total score can be added to those of other members of the same sub-group within the population, say men of Class W (when using the same style): for instance, 26/42 + 16/30 + 41/52 + 12/29 + 51/54 = total 146/207 (or 70.53 per cent). This average score for the sub-group can then be compared with similar scores for the same group in other styles (for example, if the above score was for 'careful' or 'formal' speech, we might find that in casual speech it dropped to 123/299, or 41.1 per cent), or with those of other groups in the same style (for instance, men of Class Y in formal speech might score 142/263, or 53.96 per cent). These different scores can be set out in tables or on graphs, and certain patterns of variation may emerge.

Labov presented a large number of findings, of which we can only note a few examples. The most striking correlation which seemed to emerge was that between some linguistic differences and both social class and style. Figure *xx*, with the labels of classes and styles slightly changed, shows Labov's findings for (th), with each occurrence of [θ], [tθ], and [t] scoring 0, 1 and 2 respectively (thus someone using only [θ] variants would score 0, while someone using all [t] would score 200 per cent). It can be seen that the social classes are clearly stratified in terms of their use of non-standard variants, with the highest class (labelled I) using such in only a small percentage of cases, and the other classes following in the order of their social status, with the lowest (Class V) using very many more non-standard pronunciations.

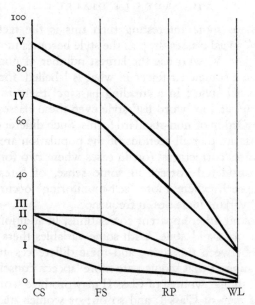

Figure xx. Class and style graph of (th) in New York City
(Based on Labov, 1966*a*).

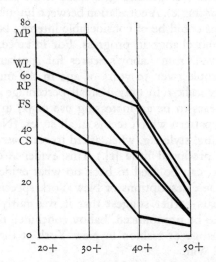

Figure xxi. Style and age-group graph of (r), for speakers in the
highest class only (Based on Labov, 1966*a*).

But perhaps more interesting than this is the fact that the scores of *all* social classes drop as the style becomes more formal. Classes IV and V, who use the largest number of non-standard variants, have somewhat fewer in what is labelled 'formal style' than in 'casual style'; in a 'reading passage' there is a further marked drop, and in 'word list' style even these classes use only a small proportion of non-standard forms. Such differences would seem to indicate that all sections of the population are aware of some norm of 'correctness' (or, in cases where two forms might both be considered correct in some sense, of 'prestige'). In styles of speech where more 'self-monitoring' occurs, use of the 'better' variant increases in frequency.

Labov found other apparent correlations, in addition to those with social class and style. With some variables there are clear differences between the sexes, and these differences are usually such as to suggest that women are more 'speech conscious' than men. For instance, women of Class II may produce scores similar to those of men of Class I, and so on; or women may show a more marked style-shift towards the use of prestige variants. Race, too, seemed to relate to linguistic differences: with some variables there were differences between speakers of Jewish, Negro or Italian background (the three main racial groups in the New York sample). A correlation between linguistic difference and age-groups could be of considerable interest, because it may indicate a sound change in progress. For instance, Figure *xxi*, which is derived from Labov's scores for speakers in Class I, shows that people over 50 years of age in the mid-1960s pronounced postvocalic-*r* in only a small percentage of instances; but there appears to be an increasing use of [r] in the younger age-groups, a pattern which recurs in all styles. (Note that even in 'minimal pairs' style e.g. when asked to read *source* – *sauce*, the over-50s still produced little [r].) This evidence of change in 'apparent time' can be used to back up what evidence we have about 'real time': descriptions of New York speech published a number of years earlier suggest that it was fairly unusual for postvocalic-*r* to be pronounced. Labov concluded that there was a linguistic change of fashion in New York at the time of the Second World War.

The fact that stylistic and social variation are so closely related – that a variant which is in all styles used most frequently by speakers who are ranked higher on an objective socio-economic scale is also the variant that is used more frequently by almost all New Yorkers in more formal styles – suggests that the majority of speakers feel that particular variants are more correct or more prestigious. Such *social evaluation* is held by sociologists to be the other side, to *social differentiation*, of the full picture of social stratification: 'the normal workings of society have produced systematic differences between certain institutions or people, and these differentiated forms have been ranked in status or prestige by general agreement.'[3] Labov therefore attempted to investigate speakers' evaluations, their conscious or unconscious feelings about New York speech in general and his special variables in particular.

Three main methods were employed. The simplest was to ask direct questions such as 'What do you think of New York City speech?'; 'Do you think that out-of-towners like New York City speech?'; 'What do you think of your own speech?'; 'Have you ever tried to change your speech?'; and so on. This was found to be the least fruitful method of investigation, as far as details were concerned: many informants expressed strong opinions in general terms, but few were able to mention specific features. It clearly emerged however that New Yorkers generally did not consider their speech to be 'good', and believed that outsiders did not like it.

Feelings about particular features of speech are probably too far 'below the surface' to be discovered by direct questioning, so Labov had two other methods of getting at an informant's opinions. A 'self-evaluation' test sought to find out how informants thought they spoke or would like to speak. Items were read by the fieldworker with a number of alternative pronunciations (e.g. *card* as [kɑːd], [kɑːrd], [kɑːᵊd]), and the informant was asked to identify his own. Labov found that there were a considerable number of cases of inaccuracy, but that these often pointed in an interesting direction. For instance, many people claimed to use an [ɾ] pronunciation where *r* occurred in postvocalic position, but in their actual performance throughout the interview they generally had *r*-less forms. Such 'over-reporting' supported the conclusion drawn from the class and style differences that [ɾ] is now the more prestigious variant.[4] Very similar to the self-evaluation test was one designed to detect 'linguistic insecurity': again, a number of words were read with alternative pronunciations, but this time the informant was asked to identify both his own pronunciation and the one he considered correct. If these differed, this was evidence of his insecurity about the way he spoke, and a further indication of which were considered to be the 'better' variants.

Labov's 'subjective evaluation' test was a development of the tape-recording experiment devised by Putnam and O'Herne (see above). He was concerned not so much with the general impression of a speaker's status as with the conscious or sub-conscious reactions hearers may have to particular variants. He had recordings of five female subjects reading a passage consisting of five paragraphs: the first was a 'zero section' (it was supposed to contain none of his main variables), then came a paragraph with a concentration of words containing (oh), then one with (eh), then (r), and finally (th) and (dh). For instance, the first sentence of the (r)-paragraph was: 'I remember where he was run over, not far from our corner'. The five zero sentences were played first, and the informant had to rate the speakers according to the sort of job he considered them fit for, from a given set of occupations in an agreed 'prestige hierarchy': TV announcer, executive secretary, factory worker . . . etc. The other paragraphs were then played over, in different orders of speakers, and after each paragraph the informant rated the speaker again. Labov could then compare the way they had scored the same speaker on the zero passage and on the paragraphs with concen-trated variables. If, for example, a speaker used all [r] variants in the (r)-paragraph, and informants tended to upgrade her from 'factory worker' to 'executive', this could be assumed to indicate a positive response to r-pronunciation; if they down-graded a speaker using [t] variants of (th), it could be taken to show that this was a castigated variant; and so on. As with the self-evaluation test, the results of this experiment tended to point to the same conclusions as the findings about variation in the sample's actual performance. Indeed, it could be concluded that the differentiation in linguistic performance and the fact that speakers are at some level conscious of different features and evaluate them, are two sides of the same coin.

We noted that Labov was not interested merely in descriptive study: he was concerned with finding answers to fundamental linguistic problems. In both his book and several of his articles based on the same research, he tackled questions such as the mechanism of linguistic change; the nature of linguistic variation and its relation to change; how far it was possible, in a situation of such widespread variation, to distinguish sound-*systems*; and so on. Though some (including Labov himself) would consider these as among his most important contributions, we shall not examine them; we have already devoted a good deal of space to Labov because he is such an important figure in recent social and urban dialectology, but these matters are more the concern of general linguistics.

Labov's work on New York provided a model for future urban surveys. A more elaborate one, carried out in Detroit under the direction of Roger Shuy, soon followed.[5] This was a much larger operation, in terms of both personnel and financial resources, but we shall not examine it in detail; let us simply note a number of additions to Labov's approach. As well as examining a number of phonological variables, the Detroit team also investigated some grammatical features: multiple negation (e.g. 'I never did nothing') and pronominal apposition (e.g. 'the other guy, he left') were handled as variables; certain larger constructions – phrases and clauses – were examined in an attempt to determine whether they had any socially-diagnostic function. They developed the notion of a distinction between 'conscious and unconscious indices': the conscious ones are features such as are drawn to speakers' attention in some way, say in schools (e.g. multiple negatives), while unconscious ones, such as vowel qualities, are not. This difference may result in differences in the nature of linguistic stratification: conscious indices tend to show a clear division between the performance of the higher social classes, who have responded more to the overt pressure on certain features, and the lower classes; with unconscious indices on the other hand there is more likely to be a gradual difference over the social scale. Other less important innovations in the Detroit study were the development of a computer-coded record of phonetic transcriptions, in order to keep a permanent record in convenient form for future use in testing new hypotheses; and an attempt to investigate some of the attitudes of teachers to linguistic matters and the possible uses of sociolinguistic studies for the teaching of English.

A sub-study within the Detroit survey by Wolfram[6] concentrated on Negro speakers, and examined four phonological and four grammatical variables. Wolfram noticed a difference, which clearly contributed to the development of the notion of conscious and unconscious indices referred to above. It was that between *sharp stratification*, where there was a considerable gap between groups with very low scores and others with quite high scores (this was more typical of grammatical variables and probably was indicative of the prestige or stigma of certain features), and *gradient stratification*, where there was a *gradual* increase or decrease of certain variants between groups (this was more usual with phonological features and probably indicated a less conscious recognition of social significances).

Another study within the same tradition (and the last we shall describe here) was another project in New York, this time conducted by a team of investigators led by Labov. The title of the main work reporting this research makes it clear that the concern was not with the whole population but with particular subgroups: *A Study of the Non-Standard English of Negro and Puerto Rican Speakers in New York City* (1968). Because of this, random sampling was not employed for the most part; instead, contacts were built up with 'natural peer groups' (i.e. gangs!) of lower-class Negroes and Puerto Ricans in the 10–17 age-range. Elicitation methods too were different: the individual interview, designed to elicit a range of styles, was still employed, but mainly with a 'control group' of adults; with the youngsters, more sophisticated approaches to the problem of obtaining casual speech were attempted. Emphasis was placed on interaction between informants (rather than between informant and interviewer) in double interviews with two close associates, or more importantly, in the 'peer group session'. After contacts with the gangs had developed, quite lengthy group sessions were arranged (with games, films of boxing matches, singing, refreshments, etc) in which each member was equipped with an individual microphone, which would pick up invaluable data from asides, 'interior monologue' and so on, as well as the general interaction.

On the basis of this research, Labov developed a notion that was to be of particular interest to general linguistics at that time: the *variable rule*.[7] 'Rules' in modern linguistics (like 'laws' in philology) are statements of the regularities observed in language.

Probably most rules are 'categorical' – they always apply. For example, a rule

$$\text{indef} \rightarrow \left\{ \begin{array}{l} \text{ən}/ - \text{V} \\ \text{ə} \end{array} \right\}$$

meaning that the indefinite article takes the form *an* before a word beginning with a vowel, and *a* otherwise, is virtually categorical for speakers of English. But where there is variation, which is generally 'structured' (i.e. it is not *free* variation but relates to certain linguistic and/or non-linguistic factors), a variable rule becomes necessary.

Let us illustrate this with an example based on my own observations of British English. The phoneme /t/ is often realized as a glottal stop: for example, *better* is pronounced *be'er* [beʔə]. But a rule written simply as

$$/t/ \rightarrow [ʔ]$$

would be inadequate to express this, for two reasons:

1. Not everybody does this. It is more common among the lower social classes than the higher, and in more casual than in more formal styles; the younger age-groups do it more than the older, and males more than females; and it is more common in some parts of the country than in others. So the rule must be modified to take account of these *non-linguistic* factors:

$$x/t/ \rightarrow [ʔ]$$

where x is a function of class, style, age, sex, and locality: the particular value of x is determined from fuller details about the variation along these several dimensions.

2. It does not occur in every context. At the beginning of words, for example, [ʔ] rarely represents /t/. So the rule has to be expanded in some way to indicate that it applies more commonly in certain *linguistic* environments:

$$x/t/ \rightarrow [ʔ]/ \left\{ \begin{array}{l} 1. - \#C \\ 2. - \#\# \\ 3. - \#V \\ 4. - L \\ 5. \, V - V \end{array} \right\}$$

e.g. *hot bread*
e.g. *why not?*
e.g. *what I like*
e.g. *bottle, petrol, bottom*
e.g. *better*

(This means that: 1. it is commonest at the end of a word where the next word begins with a consonant; 2. next commonest at the end of a word before a pause; 3. then, at the end of a word when the next word begins with a vowel; 4. then, within a word, before /r/, ʌ/l/, or /m/; 5. it is least common within a word between two vowels.)

Details of the relative frequency in each environment will be spelled out; it will also have to be stated that the value of *x* is different for each environment: for instance, middle-class speakers might use [ʔ] in *hot bread* but not in *better*.

A large proportion of this chapter on the development of social and urban dialectology in the USA has been devoted to work carried out by or under the influence of Labov. This is appropriate, since he is the key figure in the history of the subject, both in the USA and, as we shall see in the following chapter, in Britain. Some people might consider that we have strayed out of the territory of dialectology into that of sociolinguistics. But as I stated in Chapter One, there is no clear line between these two subjects, and even if one adopted a fairly narrow definition of dialectology, which restricted it to the study of features peculiar to certain areas, the study of these geographical differences cannot realistically be separated from that of their social distribution.

CHAPTER 7

Social and Urban Dialectology II: Britain

☺☺☺☺☺☺

In this chapter we shall survey a number of British studies comparable to the American ones discussed in Chapter Six.[1] We shall confine our attention to work that would generally be accepted by linguists as falling broadly within the scope of dialectology; this means that, interesting as they are, we shall not concern ourselves with studies such as those of Basil Bernstein, who claimed to have discovered deep-seated differences between members of the middle class and the lower working class in attitudes to and abilities in the use of language; or those of Howard Giles and his associates, who have conducted a number of experiments concerned not with the speakers' variation in performance on specific features but with the hearers' general evaluations of different accents in terms of pleasantness of sound, the speakers' status, and so on.[2] Such works, though obviously of relevance to our subject, belong to sociolinguistics or psycholinguistics rather than to dialectology proper.

Works purporting to describe the dialects of urban areas have been published in Britain for many years. A. J. Ellis's monumental work of 1889 (see Chapter Three), describing the speech of 1,145 localities, includes many towns and cities. For example, his 'District 24' comprises nine varieties, including those of Sheffield, Leeds, Bradford, Huddersfield and Halifax – all of them sizeable industrial towns. But Ellis, though referring to 'a great manufacturing population rejoicing in their dialect', says that 'the *real dialect* is heard in the surrounding villages' (my italics). This clearly implies that though he labelled something 'The Dialect of Bigtown', Ellis did not attempt to give a representative picture of the speech of that locality: he was really only interested in those members of the working class who had retained what he considered the genuine unmodified dialect of the district, such as was more readily heard in the rural areas nearby. The same could be said of most of the articles and books about town dialects published over the following seventy years or so.

Let us briefly examine just three studies, all published towards the end of this period, which are of interest in that all of them depart to some extent from the 'historical' approach of traditional British dialectology (see Chapter Three). Their authors were scholars with a thorough grasp of structural linguistics, so a more modern orientation could be expected – but the concern with 'genuine dialect' can be seen to persist.

Eva Sivertsen's *Cockney Phonology* (1960) has already been referred to in Chapter Four, where we criticized her selection of informants for being restricted to members of the working class with minimal education and social contacts. Her pre-occupation with some sort of 'true' dialect is seen also in the fact that while she notes that there are various styles of Cockney (for example, 'rough Cockney' and 'posh Cockney'), she does not examine the differences between these, preferring to concentrate on 'rough Cockney' and especially on speech produced when the informant was off-guard. She is aware that to abstract certain features from her data and to regard these as 'real Cockney' is a somewhat arbitrary procedure, but consciously decided to proceed in this traditional way. Nevertheless it is a very interesting book: it is an attempt to describe a dialect within the framework of a particular model of modern phonology;[3] and besides describing her informants' speech it gives some attention to opinions they volunteered about speech (for instance, on whether it is important to aim at a 'better' form of speech), and to their varying abilities to detect differences between pronunciations. Especially interesting are Sivertsen's discussions of what is meant by the Cockney 'tone of voice' and of the use of the glottal stop, which she found to be commoner among men and among 'rougher' speakers, i.e. those who come closest to 'real Cockney'. But fascinating though the book is, apart from its concern with descriptive phonology rather than historical phonetics, and the fact that it examines speech in an urban locality, it is not really very far from traditional dialectology.

Much the same could be said of Wolfgang Viereck's work on

the dialect of Gateshead-upon-Tyne,[4] which was also referred to in Chapter Four. Viereck considered that the predominantly working-class character of the town justified a decision to concentrate on 'SED-type' informants. There is much preliminary discussion in the book, about the different ways of defining the phoneme, the town and its inhabitants, and so on. The most interesting and original sections of this are those concerning the influence of Standard English and of 'regional standards' on dialect, and the 'midway forms' that might result. For instance, he suggests that [me:k] for *make* is a midway form resulting from the influence of RP [meɪk] on the genuine dialect form [mɪək]. The main body of the work is a brave attempt at a modern description of the phonology of the traditional Gateshead dialect: the vowel and consonant phonemes and their variant forms, the phonotactics (i.e. combinatory possibilities), the prosodic features, and so on. Very few studies of dialect can have approached this degree of detail in describing phonology,[5] but attention is restricted to a particular type of Gateshead speech.

R. J. Gregg has published a number of studies of Ulster dialects. In 'Scotch-Irish Urban Speech in Ulster' (1964), he presents a detailed description of the phoneme-system of the town of Larne, which reveals several differences of phonemic contrast when compared to RP. This variety, he says, is a 'modified regional standard' – in other words, a form of standard English which is regionally localized. Having described the phoneme-system as it stands, Gregg then compares this with the Scotch-Irish rural dialects of the surrounding area (the main differences appearing to be matters of phoneme incidence), and finally he considers how far the Gaelic previously spoken in this part of Ulster may have influenced both of these. He concludes that rural speakers moving to the town and attempting to speak the standard language have continued to use their repertoire of native sounds, but have re-arranged them for particular words so as to correspond as closely as possible to the sounds of the new variety.

This is a very interesting study, and one which is important for the question of regional standards. But Gregg does concern himself with what he considers to be 'real' Larne rather than with the speech of the population in general. Like the other two studies we have briefly considered, it is only part-way from traditional dialectology towards a 'modern' approach such as both linguists and social scientists would advocate. Synchronic description of the phoneme-system has replaced tracing the historical development of Middle English sounds, and the speech of urban areas has not simply been ignored because its dialect is likely to have been corrupted by contact with others including Standard English; but there has continued to be a concentration on the particular group, usually the working class, which is considered to speak some sort of 'genuine dialect', rather than an examination of the speech of all social classes and their differences. Moreover, little attention has been paid to the problem of variation.

In 1966 J. T. Wright at last specifically challenged the traditional bias of British dialectology.[6] Though he had himself been a fieldworker for *SED*, he pointed out just how unrepresentative of the British population at large is the *SED*'s agricultural-worker informant, and how *SED* proposals for future urban study and also such urban projects as had already been carried out (e.g. Sivertsen) were not a great deal better. He drew attention to the work in America which had shown the importance of studying the speech of all social groups in order both to gain a fuller picture of the speech-patterns of a society and to see the different types of influence for change that various groups might have (which are apparently of at least as much importance as the geographical factors usually concentrated on). He foresaw the importance of the recently-published work of Labov, which had emphasized the need to study the patterns of variation between different forms rather than to label one variant as 'genuine': such an approach produced results which were more representative and also helped linguists to understand the mechanisms and forces behind linguistic change.

Wright said that the dialectologist must acquire some of the sampling techniques developed by social scientists, and he illustrated this by outlining a possible method of sampling with reference to a town such as Leeds. And it was in fact in Leeds that one of the first British urban investigations planned on sound sociological lines was carried out. C. L. Houck[7] employed a 'multi-stage' random sample in order to obtain about 100 informants in the city. The first stage consisted of dividing the map of Leeds into squares of a certain size and population-density; the second of selecting one house at random in each square; the third of choosing the actual informant at random from among those members of the household eligible in terms of age, fitness, being a native-speaker of English, and so on. Houck achieved a 75 per cent success-rate (87 out of 115 randomly-selected informants were actually interviewed), which is good for this type of survey.

Unfortunately, the rest of the operation was not as advanced as this. Houck did seek to investigate phonemic systems rather than historical phonetics, but he set about this by means of a questionnaire which he hoped would elicit large numbers of minimally-contrasting words such as *bill, pill* etc. Some of the questions seem very trivial (e.g. 'A little flying creature with feathers is called a – ' [BIRD]), while others appear most unlikely to produce the desired form (e.g. 'if I took off my shirt and vest, my chest would be – ' [BARED]; 'A man is earnest and full of – ' [ZEAL]). It seems rather naïve that Houck should believe that this very artificial situation would yield 'isolated approximations to *casual speech*' (my italics), though he did also attempt to obtain some more genuinely casual speech by asking informants to relate a funny incident.

The development of a methodology for urban dialect surveys was one of Houck's main objects, but it is a pity that the only linguistic finding that he mentions in his description of the project is that the vowel in '*bud* seemed to indicate that linguistic behaviour in Leeds is a function of socio-economic class'.[8]

Another urban survey on a much larger scale is in one respect similar to Houck's, in that as yet most of its publications have been concerned with methodology rather than with results. *The Tyneside Linguistic Survey*, based at the University of Newcastle, began work in the mid-1960s. It was intended as a long-term project, and much more effort than usual appears to have been devoted to planning and to developing a theoretical framework.[9] One important difference from most other projects is that it is 'a linguistic, not a dialect, survey':[10] what this means is that it is interested in the English spoken by anyone in the area, not just that of native Tynesiders. In order to see what is typical of the area and of certain groups of speakers, and the influence of standard and non-standard upon each other, it is considered necessary not to exclude any type of English speech, however 'untypical' it may be thought. The general aim of TLS is to determine for an urban environment what varieties there are, how frequent each variety is, and what associations between varieties there are – linguistically, socially, spatially and temporally. A key concept is that of *variety space*: a hearer is thought of as locating a variety in a mental variety space, placing it closer to ones to which it is similar, and further away from ones to which it is dissimilar. A full description of the linguistic situation in a town involves not only a representative selection of speakers but also a representative set of dimensions within the variety space. So not only variation in segmental phonology, but also that in morphology, syntax, intonation, and so on must be examined, since there is likely to be *co-variation* between several dimensions – for instance, between intonation and segmental phonology: a 'localized' variant along one of these dimensions may be less likely to co-occur with 'non-localized' variants on the other, but these possibilities have to be built into the model of linguistic behaviour so that the various patterns of association may emerge. A total of 303 'dimensions of the variety space' (in other words, linguistic variables) has been settled on, and 44 'dimensions of the social space'; each dimension divides up the speakers, and the variety space will contain groupings of speakers who are similar in respect of the combination of these divisions.

Publications which detail the findings of TLS (as opposed to discussions of its methodology and conceptual framework) are beginning to appear.[11] Apart from its contributions to the development of methods for urban surveys, which was itself an aim of TLS, the project promises to break new ground by attempting to handle intonation and related prosodic and paralinguistic features, which have generally been neglected by dialectologists.

An urban survey which was not strictly a matter of *British English*, but which is relevant to this chapter in that it did study the social distribution of non-standard features is that of J. C. Wells, reported in *Jamaican Pronunciation in London* (1973). Wells's aim was to see how far Jamaicans who had been born in that country but had migrated to London had adapted their pronunciation of Jamaican Creole (or in some cases, Jamaican Educated English) in the direction of RP or of Cockney. The work is in part traditional and in part sophisticated. Wells's sampling methods and his classification of informants would probably not impress a sociologist. His sample was basically any Jamaican he knew or could contact; the informants were predominantly male, and all were aged between 18 and 42. He divided them as 'arrived in England before/after the age of 20', and by occupation as 'manual/non-manual' (i.e. a social classification based on only one feature, and very simplistic at that). His elicitation methods too were reminiscent of traditional dialectology: he employed a questionnaire to elicit single-word responses e.g. 'Someone who can't see is – ' [BLIND], but also recorded some free speech. But other aspects of Wells's study are more interesting. The most elaborate part is a statistical section, where Wells not only attempts to correlate certain phonological features with sociological ones, but also proposes a measure of the *significance* of these apparent correlations – a question which most works of this type have specifically or tacitly ignored. A particular phenomenon to which Wells draws attention is what he terms *hyperadaptation*, which means that 'a useful and valid rule for adapting one's pronunciation to new geographical or social circumstances is applied too widely'. Thus, for example, the Jamaican Creole pronunciation of *needle* is [niːgl], as compared to RP [niːdl]; the speaker may formulate the rule /gl/→/dl/ – which will produce the more acceptable form of *needle*, but may also result in his pronouncing *eagle* as [iːdl]. This concept could obviously be extended to speakers of other British English varieties who come into contact with RP: Northerners become aware of such correspondences as N [grasp]: RP [grɑːsp] *grasp* or N [bʊlb]: RP [bʌlb] *bulb*, and form some sort of mental rule for adapting their pronunciation – but they sometimes end up with hyperadaptations such as [ɑːspekt] *aspect* or [bʌlɪt] *bullet*.[12]

A study of the speech of Cannock in Staffordshire was undertaken in the late 1960s by C. D. Heath.[13] Though a student of Leeds University, Heath broke away from the *SED* approach. He took 80 randomly-selected speakers, and adopted the reverse of the more usual procedure in that he classified them first on a linguistic basis and then looked for sociological correlations (whereas most studies have first divided speakers into class, sex, age and other groups, and then looked for differences between these groups in terms of linguistic performance[14]). The linguistic breakdown was into six groups: (A) speakers with a two-thirds majority of local features, (B) those with a five per cent majority of local features, (C) those with less than fifty per cent of both Cannock and RP features, (D) those with a five per cent majority of RP features, (E) those with a two-thirds majority of RP features, and (F) those with a majority of features not describable as either Cannock or RP (e.g. a Scots-speaking resident). Obviously these divisions of a continuum from his idea of a 'Cannock accent' at one extreme to RP at the other are arbitrary, and there are questions that could be asked about just what features should be called 'local', what is the total of such out of which one might have two-thirds, and so on; but decisions of this sort have to be taken as a working basis.

Sociological correlations with the above groups then showed up: Group (A), those with the most localized speech, contained men in manual occupations; (B) contained women of similar occupations; (C) and (D) were men and women in non-manual jobs; (E) were people with better jobs and education. Clearly then, local features are more pronounced in the lower than in the higher occupational groups, and are commoner among men than among women. Even women in group (B), the most localized of their sex, were found to make some efforts towards RP, for instance in attempting to differentiate /ʊ/ and /ʌ/.

In 1974 came an important event: Peter Trudgill published the first of a number of British studies to be carried out in a 'Labovian' framework, *The Social Differentiation of English in Norwich*. Trudgill had taken a random sample from the registers of five electoral wards, which were shown to be representative of the city as a whole, eventually interviewing ten informants from each; and since this method only yielded people over 21 he took a further ten from two schools in the city, giving a total sample of 60. He divided his informants into social classes, set up on the basis of six factors, each scored on a six-point scale (0–5): these were occupation, education, and income (like Labov), and also type of housing, locality and father's occupation. The relevance of this last factor in the case of adults may be questioned, and his rating of housing and locality could be criticized as being liable to be arbitrary and subjective. Debatable too is his way of dividing the continuum of social class scores (0–30) into five social classes (Middle Middle, Lower Middle, Upper Working, Middle Working and Lower Working):

this was done on the basis of speakers' performance on a grammatical variable (whether or not the third singular marker occurs in forms such as *he go/he goes*). His lowest class (those with class scores 3–6) was fixed as those who used marker-less forms on over eighty per cent of occasions; his highest (scores 19–30) were those who never did so. The obvious criticism is that in an investigation designed to examine the correlation of linguistic and non-linguistic features, including social class, it seems circular to use linguistic criteria when setting up social classes. However, Trudgill felt that his classes did reflect the general social structure, since the members of each shared certain characteristics: e.g. his MMC were all professional or at least white-collar workers, while the LWC were all unskilled workers, and so on.

The interview was designed very much on Labov's lines: it sought to elicit a range of styles: Casual, Formal, Reading Passage, Word List and Minimal Pairs. Trudgill identified casual speech as Labov had done – on the basis of 'specified contexts + channel cues' (see p. 141); as one method of attempting to get speakers to forget the formality of the situation he asked them to relate a funny incident, thus following Houck. He was concerned, in addition to the grammatical variable referred to above, with sixteen phonological ones (a larger number than Labov): three consonantal ones ('*h*-dropping', /ɪŋ/~/ɪn/, and the use of the glottal stop for /t/), the rest vocalic. The variables were selected largely because previous work on East Anglian phonology suggested that these were likely to be the most interesting features to examine. Scores for classes, styles, sex and age-groups were worked out in much the same way as in the New York survey. In addition to the performance of informants, their evaluations of speech were investigated, by direct questions about Norwich speech and their own, and by a self-evaluation test and a test for 'linguistic insecurity' very much like Labov's.

Many findings were presented in Trudgill's book, of which we can only refer to a few. A nice example of class and style differentiation is provided by the figures for the use of glottal forms to realize /t/: the classes appear in the order LWC – MWC – UWC – LMC – MMC in each style,[15] and each class uses fewer glottal variants as formality increases i.e. the styles are ordered, as expected, Casual – Formal – Reading Passage – Word List. The working classes as a whole use almost one hundred per cent glottal stops in casual speech, but in the most formal word-list style their scores are almost the same as those of the highest class in the least formal style. This clearly suggests that all speakers have the same norm of correctness, but that lower down the social scale this norm is only adhered to in the more 'monitored' styles.

Trudgill makes an interesting suggestion about there being a distinctively Norwich form of speech. This is clearly based on the dialects of Norfolk, which still survive in the surrounding rural areas, but it is becoming increasingly different from these because of the effects both of RP *and* of the speech of London and the Home Counties, which though further removed in geographical distance, have more influence on the speech of the urban centre than does Norfolk dialect.

Interesting claims are also made about the processes involved in such linguistic change. In a separately-published paper based largely on his findings about speakers' evaluations of speech forms (Trudgill, 1972), Trudgill holds that there are important differences between the roles of the sexes in the mechanisms of change. Whereas changes in the direction of RP may be initiated by middle-class women, with whom the standard language enjoys considerable prestige, other changes in a non-standard direction have been introduced by working-class men. Trudgill suggests that there is a 'covert prestige' attached to working-class regional speech: this has desirable connotations of masculinity and toughness,[16] which show up for example in the fact that in the self-evaluation test male speakers tended to claim to use some non-standard features to a greater extent than they actually did.

Possibly the most original part of Trudgill's work is the long and ambitious section[17] devoted to describing the 'Norwich diasystem', a set of rules which he assumes to have some sort of psychological reality for members of the 'Norwich speech community'.[18] His approach owes much to both structural and generative dialectology (see Chapter Eight, 1): he sets up an 'underlying' phonological system, and then has a series of seven different types of rules which are supposed to generate every actually-occurring form, down to quite minute phonetic differences. This proposal can be criticized on several grounds:[19] the basic framework is a model which is obscure to start with; the differences between his types of rules are not always clear and sometimes seem arbitrary; it is difficult to work out how some rules will apply and how certain outputs will be generated and certain others prevented; and the suggestion that this system has been 'internalized' by speakers is very unconvincing. But whatever doubts are entertained about this more theoretical contribution, the descriptive part of Trudgill's work stands: it was the first attempt to apply the Labov paradigm to British data.

Other Labov-type investigations were either in progress at the same time or followed soon afterwards. Many of these have not been published in full, but a collection of papers edited by Trudgill, *Sociolinguistic Patterns in British English* (1978), gives a useful indication of the sort of projects that have been carried out; we can only refer to a few of these here.[20]

G. O. Knowles, based on Leeds University, aimed to describe 'Scouse' (the urban dialect of Liverpool) within a Labovian framework. But he found that the actual identification of the most important variables – the ones which 'give away' a Liverpudlian – was a major problem; as a result, much of his work was directed towards the methodology required for identifying variables and measuring variation. He demonstrated that the 'linear scale' method of treating variation (e.g. dividing pronunciations of words like *sure* into a scale such as [uə-ʊə-oə-ɔə-ɔ:] etc), which is usual in the Labov model, is an oversimplification, both because the divisions are arbitrary and because the variation may be multi-dimensional rather than along a simple scale. Such an approach is even less adequate for dealing with variation in features such as intonation and 'tone of voice' – yet these are often crucial in identifying a speaker's regional origins: even after he has modified all his segmental phonemes in an RP direction, a speaker may be immediately given away as coming from say West Yorkshire or Birmingham or Liverpool by these 'supra-segmental' features. Tone of voice, or 'articulatory setting' – the shape assumed by the whole vocal tract – may well be of more importance than any other feature in this respect, yet it has been neglected by linguists until recent times, though speakers themselves not uncommonly refer to this (albeit in some naïve way) when asked what are the characteristics of the speech of a certain area.[21]

In Belfast, James and Lesley Milroy have worked on three working-class areas, two Protestant and one Catholic (thus ruling out, for the time being, consideration of the social class dimension of variation by concentrating on just one class, but being prepared to recognize status differences between and within these three communities). Informants were approached not on a random sample basis, but through informal contacts, and a quota sample of eight young and eight middle-aged people, equally divided between males and females, was interviewed in each area. In their 1978 paper the Milroys present findings on seven phonological variables, examining scores for style, age, and sex groups in each area. They find evidence of change in progress, and believe that Belfast exhibits a relatively early stage in the development of an urban vernacular, in which a common pattern is that of 'binary choice', i.e. between two variants, of which one is more likely to occur in more casual speech and with particular groups. Belfast communities have close kin and friendship networks, and the Milroys find that the extent to which individuals approximate to a vernacular norm seems to correlate with the extent to which they participate in close-knit networks. The person on the fringe of such a network may look to the wider social group outside his immediate community for speech and behavioural norms. But they believe that the stylistic variation to be observed among working-class Belfast speakers, while showing up some castigated variants, does *not* suggest that middle-class speech serves as a prestige model, and that subjective reaction tests point the same way. This runs counter to common claims and assumptions, and also to most of the findings of other surveys; it will be interesting to see the evidence for it when the Milroys' work (which up to now has mainly been circulated in the form of 'working papers') is published in more detail.

In Glasgow, Ronald K. S. Macauley carried out a study with a sample of 16 adults, 16 fifteen-year-olds, and 16 ten-year-olds, with an equal number of males and females in each group.[22] These informants were chosen so as to give equal numbers in four social class groups, as determined by the occupation of the family breadwinner: in other words, it was a quota sample. Five phonological variables (the vowels in words such as *hit*, *school*, *cap*, and *now*, and the use of the glottal stop for /t/) were examined. One improvement over the 'early Labovian' method of simply noting every instance of the variables in question – which could bias the sample of material towards the variants favoured by the more talkative informants, or those used in particular common words – was that Macauley took for example just the first 40 instances of the (i) variable from the first half of each informant's tape, and the first 40 from the second half; and no more than three examples of a particular word were counted.[23] Macauley found a clear correlation between variation and social class, though several points led him to decide that his Classes III and IV (broadly, the 'working classes') should be grouped together. He also found interesting differences between the sexes (for instance, with his (i) variable, the greater distance between classes for males is between I and II, whereas with females it is between II and III), and between age-groups (the linguistic distance between the social classes appears to increase with age); but there was no systematic difference between two other important social groups in Glasgow, Catholics and Protestants.

Besides working in the Labovian framework, Macauley gave some consideration to the viewpoint of its critics (see Chapter Eight, II), who had claimed that the Labov model produces an artificial impression of differences between groups of speakers. This is because it adds together and averages the scores of individuals who in fact, it is held, form a continuum of linguistic varieties. Macauley found by examining individuals' performances that there certainly was considerable variation within each of his social class groups, in terms of the proportions of the different variants of a variable produced by different individuals, and thus of their total scores; he concluded that linguistic variation is indeed a continuum, just as is social class. But the individual scores did generally follow the social classification of the speakers: in other words, Class II individuals generally fell within a certain range, which was between those of Class I and Class III/IV, rather than it being the case that the Class II average score was a product of some individuals performing like members of Class I and others like Class III/IV.

We shall end this chapter by outlining the study along the lines of Labov and Trudgill which was carried out by the author in West Yorkshire, with the aim of investigating the extent to which features of dialect and/or accent still survive among the general urban population.[24] The conclusions reached on this general question have been discussed briefly in Chapter One above; here we shall describe the general method of investigation,[25] and give just a few examples of specific findings.

Fieldwork was carried out over an eight-week period in 1971. A random sample was drawn from the electoral registers of the three main wool-manufacturing towns, Bradford, Halifax and Huddersfield. The limited time and manpower available made it necessary to examine only natives or long-term residents, and 'outsiders' and other non-respondents reduced the sample actually interviewed to just over 100. This number was almost equally divided between males and females, and contained members of all age-groups from 10+ (this group was randomly selected from comprehensive schools) to 80+, and of five social classes (set up for the purposes of this study on the basis of a total score for categories of education, occupation, income, housing and standard of living). The structured interview sought to elicit speech of several styles distinguished by Labov, so as to be able to describe the 'performance' of informants, and also to get at the feelings people have about the area and its speech, their 'evaluations' of it, by means of direct questions, self-evaluation in respect of alternative pronunciations, and subjective evaluation of tape-recorded passages read by a number of speakers.[26]

A picture of the traditional dialects of the area was extracted from the works of A. J. Ellis, Joseph Wright, the *SED* and other less well-known sources. On the basis of this, and of informal observations, a number of variables (larger than in the investigations of Labov or Trudgill) were chosen for particular study. Most of these were of a phonological nature, and examples of all four types of difference from a structural viewpoint (see Chapter Five above) were included. 'Inventory variables' were whether or not /h/ and /ʌ/ formed part of the phonemic system, whether there was a contrast between /ɛɪ/ and /eː/, and between /ɔʊ/ and /oː/, and whether there were one, two or three contrasting vowels in the sets exemplified by *Shaw – shore – sure*. 'Distribution variables' were /n+tʃ / ∼/n+ʃ / in words like *inch, bench* etc, and final unstressed 'o-type vowel ∼/ə/' in *window, fellow* etc. 'Realization variables' included [ʔ] for /t/ in various environments,[27] and the quality of several long vowels and diphthongs. 'Incidence variables' were /ɑ:/∼/a/ in *grass* etc, /ɪŋ/∼/ɪn/ in -*ing*, /ʊk/∼/u:k/ in *took* etc, and /eɪk/∼/ek/ in *take* etc. A number of commoner grammatical features were also examined as variables, such as the use of /wə/ for standard *was* as well as *were*, and the reduction of the definite article to [t] or more usually [ʔ]. Other non-standard phonological, grammatical, and lexical forms produced by informants were not handled quantitatively, but were nevertheless noted, since they are important for the overall picture of the contemporary dialect or accent.

With most phonological variables the by now familiar patterns of class, style and sex differences emerged in the variation between local variants and a Standard English/RP one: but the extent to which the latter was adopted seemed to depend on whether the 'non-standard' local variant was in some way interpreted as 'substandard'. For instance, '*h*-dropping' is castigated in the schools, whereas the use of /ʊ/ in words where RP has /ʌ/ generally is not: so note the difference between Figures *xxii* and *xxiii* in respect of the overall amount of usage of the non-standard variant, and the amount of style-difference. And the very obvious regional feature (ɑ:∼a) in *grass* etc showed little variation at all: very few speakers had adopted /ɑ:/, almost everyone else clinging to the Northern /a/ *and* insisting that it was 'correct'!

It has been found in several studies of this type that where no awareness of either prestige or stigma seems to exist (and this can be detected for example in evaluation experiments), there are no clear patterns of variation throughout the sample. The situation with (ɑ:∼a) in Yorkshire would support this; another relevant variable was (nch), where /nʃ/ was usual but such use of /ntʃ/ as did occur appeared to be virtually a case of free variation.

With grammatical variables, where the local variant could usually be labelled 'dialect', a slightly different pattern showed up: this variant was largely restricted to the working classes (though these were ranged in the 'usual' order, i.e. III-IV-V), and it rarely occurred outside the conversational styles (i.e. casual and formal speech): it was hardly ever heard in the reading passage or word list.[28]

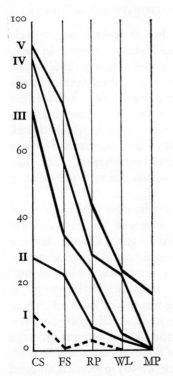

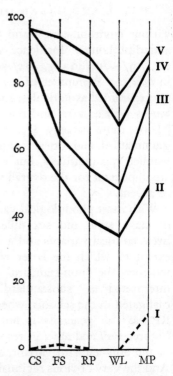

Figure xxii. Class and style graph of (h) in urban West Yorkshire: percentage scores for nonstandard forms (i.e. *h*-dropping).

Figure xxiii. Class and style graph of (ʌ) in urban West Yorkshire: percentage scores for nonstandard forms (i.e. use of [ʊ]).

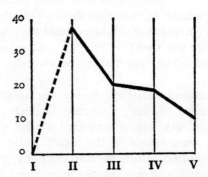

Figure xxiv. Hypercorrection of (ʌ): percentage of 'hypercorrectors' in each social class.

But in a sense more interesting than these 'familiar' patterns are cases where an unusual type of pattern seemed to show up. One more example of this is already before us in Figure *xxiii*, where the minimal pairs scores for (ʌ) seem to present among all classes a sharp reversal of the trend towards more /ʌ/ in more formal styles. In fact there is probably a fairly simple explanation in this case: there is no clear pattern of conditioning by the phonological environment, and nothing in the spelling of words to indicate which have /ʌ/ as opposed to /ʊ/ in RP (unlike (ɑː∼a) in the former respect, and (h) in the latter); so a Northerner attempting to acquire /ʌ/ is sometimes unsure which member, if either, of pairs such as *but – put* or *putt – put* has /ʌ/. These 'deviant' scores in Figure *xxiii* simply reflect the fact that in the very artificial minimal pairs situation more people 'gave up the attempt' than in other contexts where they were not required to concentrate specifically on this problem. This uncertainty over the occurrence of /ʌ/ also shows up in Figure *xxiv*, which refers to *hypercorrection* (i.e. the use of /ʌ/ in 'wrong' words such as *butcher* or *pull*): the graph shows the gross percentage of informants in each class who produced at least one hypercorrect form during the interview: note that Class I, comprising fairly confident /ʌ/-users, produced no hypercorrections, but among the other classes more hypercorrectors are found among the groups that from Figure *xxiii* appear to be more '/ʌ/-conscious' in that they make greater efforts to acquire this feature.

An unexpected reversal of the usual pattern of style differentiation occurred with words such as *book, cook, look, took* etc: see Figure *xxv*. Incidence of the regional /uːk/ variant actually increased in frequency in the more formal styles. We might seek to explain away the very marked increase in the minimal pairs test by saying that in this artificial situation where attention is concentrated on possible differences (in this case between *luck* and *look* etc) informants will strive to produce a distinction even if they would rarely do so in natural speech (compare Figure *xxii*, which shows that almost everybody distinguished *hotter* and *otter* in this situation). But it is noteworthy that a number of speakers who 'already' had a distinction between the two forms in that *luck* was pronounced with /ʌ/ (and *look* in conversational speech with /ʊ/), created an extra difference by using the /uː/ vowel in *look* here. Moreover the /uːk/ variant also increased

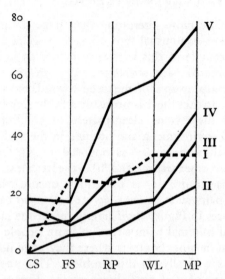

Figure xxv. Class and style graph of (ook) in urban West Yorkshire: percentage scores for non-standard forms (i.e. use of /u:k/).

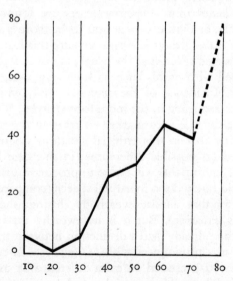

Figure xxvi. Age-group graph of (ook).

in the reading passage and word list, where informants would not be concentrating on finding a difference, and in the evaluation tests there were clear signs that quite a number of people (though a minority) regarded the /u:k/ form as 'correct' in some sense.[29]

Besides the unusual style pattern, Figure *xxv* also reveals a disruption of familiar social class relationships, in that Class I cuts across an otherwise fairly regular array. It is true that Class I was the smallest in the sample, certainly too small to be considered representative (which is why it is indicated by a broken line in Figures *xxii–xxv*) but nevertheless for the great majority of variables this fact did not produce irregularities in the style-class arrays. Now many findings of Labovian surveys have suggested that unusual patterns of style and/or class differentiation result when a linguistic change is in progress, and two facts lead to the conclusion that this is the case with the (ook) variable in West Yorkshire. In the first place, all the examples of /u:k/ in Class I came from one speaker, who was in his seventies; with the small number of informants in this group this was sufficient to bias the results for this class. Secondly, a graph for the overall use during the interview of /u:k/ by age-groups (Figure *xxvi*) indicates that with speakers below the age of 40 this form is rare, but then it 'rises' fairly steeply. (The figures for the 80+ group are not representative, since this group contained only three speakers, all of Class V, but the rise certainly continues.) We may conclude that a change to the use of the 'RP-like' /ʊk/ variant is in progress, and indeed is well advanced: in everyday speech this variant is virtually universal among speakers under the age of 40, and even older speakers show a fairly extensive use of it.[30] But the evidence from the figures for styles (and some of that from the self-evaluation and subjective evaluation tests, which we have not examined in detail here, but which generally in this project supported the findings in respect of performance) suggests that there is not as yet any strong feeling of 'inferiority' about the regional variant: indeed, there is evidence that especially lower down the social scale many people feel it is 'correct'.

In these last two chapters we have looked at examples of a type of dialectology which has gradually moved away from the traditional approach of concentrating on elderly rural speakers. Some earlier scholars would certainly have thought that the sort of speech recently investigated was not as worthy of attention as 'genuine dialect', and some still prefer to concentrate on this, believing that these social-urban studies are not really dialectology. But if dialects are 'different forms of the same language', then these are certainly dialects; and in examining these, 'modern' dialectology has not only produced findings of interest to a wider academic and non-academic audience, it has also drawn nearer to its 'parent' discipline, linguistics. In the last chapter of this book we shall consider two other ways of looking at dialect differences which have brought the study of dialect even closer to 'mainstream linguistics'.

CHAPTER 8

Other Recent Approaches

🔳🔳🔳🔳🔳🔳

I. GENERATIVE DIALECTOLOGY

In 1957 a young American linguist, Noam Chomsky, published a slim volume entitled *Syntactic Structures*, which was to initiate a major revolution in linguistics: in it he argued for a *generative* approach to linguistic description. For the previous thirty years or so structural linguists had largely been concerned with analysing the data they had collected in fieldwork, and then producing a description of this material in terms of phonetics, phonology, morphology and syntax. Chomsky argued that a description of a corpus of observed data in any language is not sufficient; a language is more than a corpus of material – many sentences which have never been uttered before and so are not in a corpus will be grammatical. In fact a speaker is constantly producing, hearing and understanding sentences that have never occurred in precisely that form before; this 'creativity' is perhaps the most essential property of human language, so a complete grammar must account for all the infinite number of possible sentences in a language: it must *generate* all the grammatical sentences and no ungrammatical ones.

A *generative grammar* consists of a set of rules, which are essentially statements of the regularities of the language; applying these rules will produce grammatical sentences, which may or may not have actually occurred in this precise form. A grammar will have several sections or *components*: in a fuller work published in 1965, Chomsky expanded and in some respects reformulated his view of a generative grammar, saying that it would have syntactic, semantic and phonological components. Work on the phonological component, *generative phonology*, had been pioneered by Morris Halle,[1] and later he and Chomsky collaborated in this.[2] Since the greatest number of dialect differences concern phonology, and since most works on generative dialect-ology have concentrated on this area, the discussion here will be similarly restricted. But the same general principles would apply in the case of grammatical differences between dialects.[3]

The job of the phonological component is to specify the phonetic form of sentences generated by the syntactic rules. It does this by means of rules applying in a stated order to the items, which will be represented in an *underlying form*. This is composed of abstract segments referred to as 'systematic phonemes'[4] which are set up to express a relationship between two phonemes such as /eɪ/ and /a/ e.g. *grateful – gratitude*, or /iː/ and /e/ e.g. *serene – serenity*. To give a grossly simplified example: an underlying form might be say /dɪvIn/, and a relevant rule I → $\left\{ \begin{array}{l} aɪ/\text{–}C\# \text{ etc} \\ I \end{array} \right\}$

This means: 'the underlying segment /I/ will be realized as [aɪ] in the environment of a consonant occurring before a word-boundary e.g. [dɪvaɪn] *divine* (and also in certain other environ-ments which will not be detailed here); elsewhere, it will be realized as [ɪ]' e.g. [dɪvɪnɪtɪ] *divinity*.

Where do dialects come into this? The essential fact about dialects is that they are forms of a language which are in many respects similar to each other, but which differ in some respects. How is this fact expressed within the various approaches to dialectology?

The approach of traditional dialectology is to record the data in each dialect, and then essentially to take the similarities for granted and to concentrate on describing the differences between dialects.

Structural dialectology also examines the data of different dialects and describes the systems of elements within each. It then faces a problem: the main tenet of structural linguistics is that elements are defined by their relations to other elements within the system, and therefore it is impossible to equate elements in separate systems. For example, the existence in a dialect of a phoneme labelled /a/ is determined by its contrasts with other phonemes, not just by the fact that it sounds like [a]; if another dialect has a different set of phonemic contrasts, a phoneme labelled /a/ is not comparable to that in the first dialect, even though it too may sound like [a]. Perhaps recognizing that such a strict structural view is untenable in relation to dialects – for in effect it treats two dialects of say, English, as if they were no more similar than one of English and one of Chinese – dialectologists tacitly ignored it. They drew up dia-systems, which aimed to express both the similarities and the differences between the systems of different dialects.

What traditional and structural dialectology have in common is the fact that they both concentrate mainly on the *data* of the different dialects. This is where the approach of generative dialectology is claimed to differ: it focuses not so much on the data, the actual forms, as on the grammars of dialects – the *rules* which generate these forms. (As a related point here, it should be noted that generative grammar is a means only of expressing the facts about a language: it is not concerned with how these facts are discovered. Similarly, generative dialectology is only a way of describing dialect differences: it is not concerned with the 'earlier' major task of dialectology – surveys designed to collect the data to be described.)

If a generative description of phonology consists of a set of ordered rules applying to underlying forms, then clearly two or more such grammars may differ in having different underlying forms *and/or* a different set of rules *and/or* a different order of rules. But linguists of this school hold that when the grammars of different dialects are compared, it is normally the case that they will have the same underlying forms and a majority of the same rules. These two properties will explain one of the essential points about dialects: that they are forms of language similar in many respects. The other point, that though similar they differ in some ways, is explained by the fact that, beside the set of rules common to all dialects, some forms will be generated by:

A. the addition of one or more rules in the grammars of some dialects;
B. the deletion of one or more rules in the grammars of some dialects;
C. a different ordering of the rules in the grammars of different dialects;
D. a 'simplified' form in some dialects of a rule applying in others.

Several works provide detailed exemplification of this approach. An early one is an article by E. Vasiliu, 'Towards a generative phonology of Daco-Rumanian dialects' (1966). Vasiliu set up underlying forms and the rules necessary to generate the actual forms in various dialects; he was then able to classify Rumanian dialects on the basis of which of the set of rules they have, and how these are ordered. His resulting classification into dialects, varieties and subvarieties is in fact very similar to that proposed by traditional dialectologists working on Rumanian, but its basis is held to be more explicit.

B. Newton's *The Generative Interpretation of Dialect* (1972) tackles the situation of the Greek dialects. He states that it is his intention to interpret dialects not as 'a conglomeration of static self-contained systems' (the extreme structuralist position), but as 'the outcome of historical changes acting on an originally uniform language'. So he starts with a set of underlying forms which he sets up as common to all dialects: dialectalization is then introduced by the phonological rules which operate on these: some do not apply in some dialects, some differ in character from one to another; some apply in different orders in the different dialects. As a result, though Greece is a linguistic continuum criss-crossed in all directions by a vast number of isoglosses, it is possible to see five basic groups of dialects emerging, established on the basis of which of nine important phonological rules apply to them, and in which order.

The situation in Greece is unusual in that there is historical documentation of the language and its dialects extending back over two and a half thousand years; we have therefore evidence of many of the actual historical changes which have produced the present-day dialects. But the underlying forms and the rules set up by a generative phonologist like Newton are such as can be established on the basis of internal present-day evidence – such as the phonological alterations within a dialect between different forms of the same word (e.g. [dɪvaɪn] – [dɪvɪn-ɪtɪ]), or cross-dialectal comparisons – rather than on the basis of historical documentation. Thus, though the rules often reflect historical changes, and their ordering often recapitulates the actual temporal sequence of these changes, there may well be some discrepancies between historical fact and synchronic description. But it is the latter which more nearly reflects what the native speaker is aware of: he may know nothing of the history of his language, but he 'knows' in some sense that there is a relation between [dɪvaɪn] and [dɪvɪnɪtɪ], or that Northerners in Britain 'merge' /ʌ/ and /ʊ/.[5]

A book published in the same year as Newton's illustrates the point that a generative description with underlying forms and an ordered set of rules has in principle no connection with a historical study: Gillian Brown's *Phonological Rules and Dialect Variation* (1972) has the subtitle *A Study of the Phonology of Lumasaaba*. This is a language on which there is virtually no historical documentation, but nevertheless Brown was able to relate the dialects through a common set of underlying forms and a set of phonological rules: the correct phonetic realizations for each dialect are generated by specifying which of the rules apply and in what order. The underlying forms are closer to those of the Northern dialects (the three main ones are differentiated by whether or not two particular rules apply); the three Southern dialects all share a set of rules which do not apply in the Northern (and are then differentiated from each other by the order in which a further set of rules apply).

Let us consider some examples of the ways listed above by which different dialectal realizations can be generated from the same underlying forms.

A. *Additional rules*
Let us suppose that words in English such as *cat*, *fact*, etc etc have underlying forms like /kat/, /fakt/ and so on. One way of generating the phonetic forms in British dialects[6] would be by means of a rule such as

$$/a/ \rightarrow \begin{cases} \text{[æ] in RP and dialects} \\ \text{A,B,C} \ldots \\ \text{[a] in other dialects} \end{cases}$$

This rule is in fact an abbreviation of two separate rules for generating two different phonetic forms, so essentially this method of derivation is using different rules for different dialects, and treating these as 'descriptively equal'.

Usually, however, there is good reason for assuming that one dialect form is more basic, and that others can most simply be described as a further step in derivation from this. So for example we might decide that the simplest grammar will contain a rule /a/→[a]. This will be the actually-occurring form in many dialects; but for others a further rule is added which simply makes this a slightly closer vowel: [a]→[æ].[7] The fact that this is a 'late' rule in the grammar would accord with one's intuition that the difference in question is only a matter of detail; to derive [a] and [æ] by means of different underlying segments (which no-one would suggest) would for example run entirely counter to this intuition.

Another example of where an additional rule might be employed in deriving some English dialect forms concerns the set of words including *grass, laugh, bath, dance* etc. From underlying forms such as /gras/, /laf/ etc our rules above will derive [gras], [græs] and so on, forms which do occur in some dialects. But for RP and certain other dialects we would want to add a rule, to be applied at some time *before* that for [a]→[æ], which will lengthen the vowel in certain environments:

$$[a]→[ɑ:]/ - [s,f,\theta,ns] \text{ etc}$$

Here the fact that this is a somewhat 'earlier' rule in the derivation accords with our intuition that the [a/ɑ:] difference is a rather more important one between English dialects than [a/æ].

A particular example of a treatment of dialect differences in terms of 'additional rules' is to be seen in the work of Brown referred to above: the Southern dialects of Lumasaaba all undergo the same basic set of rules as the Northern but they are also subject to an additional three rules.

B. *Deletion of a rule*

It is a well-known fact about German that though the consonants [p,t,k,b,d,g] occur at the beginning and in the middle of words, only [p,t,k] occur at the end. Moreover, it happens that there are alternations between voiced [b] and voiceless [p], and similarly between [d] and [t], and [g] and [k] among forms of the 'same' word: thus [tak] 'day' occurs alongside [tagə] 'days', for example. On the other hand there are pairs of forms such as [dek] 'deck' and [dekə] 'decks', where [k] does not alternate with [g]; and so on. Linguists have suggested that the final consonants of [tak] and [dek] have different underlying forms, /tag/ and /dek/ and that there are phonological rules such as the following:

$$/k/ \rightarrow \quad [k]$$
$$/g/ \rightarrow \left\{ \begin{array}{l} [k]/ - \# \\ [g] \end{array} \right\}$$

This means that underlying /k/ is always realized as [k], whereas underlying /g/ is [k] in word-final position ([tak]), but [g] otherwise ([tagə]).

The above situation applies with most varieties of German, but in some dialects in Northern Switzerland and in Yiddish, this is not the case. In those varieties [b,d,g] *can* occur at the end of words, so that instead of alternations such as [bʊnt] 'band'/ [bʊndə] 'bands' as in most dialects, in Northern Switzerland [bʊnd]/[bʊndə] occurs; instead of [tak]/[tagə], Yiddish has [tog]/ [teg], and so on.[8] Now it is reasonable to say that the grammars of these varieties simply do not contain the rule(s) that devoice /b,d,g/ to [p,t,k] at the end of words. But there is evidence that this rule did exist at an earlier period: the evidence is both external (texts from earlier centuries) and internal (forms in Yiddish such as [avek] 'away', [hant] 'hand', [gelt] 'money', for instance).

Historical evidence is not in itself a reason for including a rule that does not apply at the present time; but it is quite possible that the simplest grammar for German which seeks to generate all the present-day dialect forms will be one which has the devoicing rule applying generally, but then has a relatively 'late' rule applying in the case of certain dialects which deletes most of the effects of the devoicing rule.

c. *Different ordering of rules*
It should be noted that when 'order' is used in this context, it refers to descriptive not historical order. In other words, the order of the rules is that which results in the most natural and economical description of the dialects in question; it does not necessarily correspond to the historical sequence of the appearance of these rules, though it may do (see below).

In his treatment of Greek dialects, Newton has numerous examples of dialects where the data suggests that the same phonological rules exist in their grammars, but that these have different effects because they do not apply in the same order relative to one another. For example,[9] on the island of Rhodes he finds two different forms for the word meaning 'horse-dealer': [alvás] in the South-West, and [aloás] elsewhere. He suggests that the underlying form common to all Greek dialects is /aloɣás/, and that in Rhodes four rules (for which there is ample evidence elsewhere) may apply. In the South-West the order is:

Underlying form		aloɣás
A.	Voiced fricative deletion	aloás
B.	Height dissimilation	aluás
C.	Glide formation	alwás
D.	Consonantality	alvás

In the other Rhodes dialects, which have [aloás] it is *not* the case that rules B–D do not apply: the evidence of other items makes clear that they do, but they apply before rather than after the rule for voiced fricative deletion.

The effect in the case of this example is:

Underlying form		aloɣás	
B.	Height dissimilation	–	(affects only contiguous vowels)
C.	Glide formation	–	(affects only contiguous vowels)
D.	Consonantality	–	(affects only 'glide' consonants)
A.	Voiced fricative deletion	aloás	

Different ordering of the same rules has been found to be an important aspect of dialect difference by others who have produced detailed exemplifications of generative dialectology. Vasiliu in his study of Rumanian found that the traditional major division of the dialects into 'Muntenian' and 'Moldavian' can be explained in terms of the different position of his 'Rule C' which, if it applies at all in Moldavian dialects, occurs in a different order.[10]

In Muntenian dialects the order of rules is A B C D E F . . .
In Moldavian dialects the order of rules is A B E F (C) . . .

Obviously the effect of Rule C will be different if E and F have already applied and thus changed the possible 'inputs' to this rule. Further examples can readily be found in Brown's description of Lumasaaba, where the Southern dialects are differentiated by the order in which a particular set of rules apply.[11]

D. *Simpler form of a rule*

From a synchronic point of view, this is strictly a matter of different rules applying in different dialects – held to be a relatively uncommon phenomenon as compared to those of additional rules or different ordering of the same rules. But these different rules are closely related historically *and* descriptively. A rule applying under specific conditions may either (a) have existed fairly generally at one time, but at a later date have been extended to apply in more contexts in some dialects; or (b) have arisen in one dialect but been reproduced in a less specific form when adopted by another. In either case, the rules as they apply in different dialects at the present time are not unrelated.

Consider the following example. Some English speakers may pronounce word-final /t/ as a glottal stop before another word beginning with a vowel. We could say that they have an (optional) rule of the form:

$$/t/\rightarrow[ʔ]/-\#V$$

Use of [ʔ] for /t/ is becoming commoner in British English, so we could say that more and more speakers have rules such as the above in their grammar. But possibly some of them will misinterpret the data they hear containing glottal stops, and will assume that the rule is: /t/→[ʔ]/ – V. Comparing the two forms of the rule, we see that the latter is 'simpler' i.e. less detailed than the former: the effect of this is that it is applied in a wider range of environments – before vowels *whether or not* a word boundary intervenes. The result is that while the first group may say [ə betə bɪʔ ə bʌtə] 'a better bit of butter', the latter could say [ə beʔə bɪʔ ə bʌʔə]. As noted earlier in this book, evidence from recent British studies suggests that the use of the glottal stop is less common (though increasing) in word-internal position than where a boundary intervenes, and this could be explained by saying that more people at present have the more specific form of the rule, but others are adopting the simpler form.

As has been made clear by the discussion so far, many of the 'rules' formulated by scholars producing generative descriptions of dialect variation look remarkably like the 'laws' a philologist might have deduced as being linguistic changes that have occurred in the historical development of the language.[12] But it must be emphasized that the rules are not established on the basis of historical evidence: this is not available anyway, in the case of most languages, and even where it is, the historical rules and their order are not *assumed* to be 'correct' for a synchronic grammar. (Nor indeed is the general organization, in terms of a common set of underlying forms and many common rules, but with dialect variations handled by differences among the remaining rules, *assumed* to be correct.) The grammar is written on the basis of the internal evidence of the language as it is at the present time, and the preferred grammar will be the set of underlying forms and rules which in terms of criteria of 'generality' and 'naturalness' best handles the present-day alternations and dialect variations. It is held by generativists that the grammar emerging when criteria such as generality and naturalness are adopted will indeed be one which has much of its material common to all dialects and whose rules will largely reflect actual historical changes; in this case, the coincidence of the synchronic with the diachronic, and the way dialect variation is naturally explained as minor differences among a majority of common features, is held to be confirmation of the appropriateness of the grammar.

Adherents of this school of linguistics hold that an important property of any generative grammar is that its *formalization* ensures that it is entirely explicit: it sets out quite clearly all the facts, without leaving anything for the reader to have to deduce for himself. In relation to dialectology, a generative treatment will formalize the essential fact about dialects: that they have much in common but some differences. This is made explicit by deriving different dialects from a common set of underlying forms, applying many rules to all or most of the dialects, and accounting for their differences in terms of one or more rules that are peculiar to them.

Another advantage claimed for generative grammar is that it

is more *powerful* – that it 'explains' more than other types of grammar. A generative treatment of dialects is held to be more powerful than both traditional and structural dialectology. The traditional 'historical' approach revealed at the most the sequence of particular linguistic changes which has resulted in the present-day dialect differences; the generative approach formalizes not only this but also all the consequences for linguistic structure resulting from the different ordering in time of the various changes. The structural approach to dialectology was of course concerned primarily with such differences of linguistic structure, but it is held that generative dialectology is more powerful here too. For instance, (a) it makes it possible to set up a hierarchy among the various dialect differences, in terms of whether the rules concerned are 'early' ones that affect major structural changes and apply to many dialects, or 'late' ones that make relatively superficial changes in just one or two dialects; (b) this in turn makes possible a classification of dialects which groups together those with 'deeper' similarities (in terms of the early rules) and uses the more superficial dissimilarities (produced by later rules) as secondary criteria; (c) the generative description will make clear that identical superficial structures may sometimes result from different rules (reflecting different linguistic changes); and (d) differences of the 'incidence' type may be handled quite naturally in a generative treatment. It will be recalled from Chapter Five that structural dialectology ran into problems with differences of the type where dialects had the same phonemes in their systems but employed different ones in certain peculiar words (e.g. both RP and Yorkshire dialects have /aɪ/ and /iː/ in their systems, but in, say, *night* RP uses /aɪ/ but rural West Yorkshire has /iː/).[13] An article by A. R. Thomas (1967) shows with an example from Welsh how a situation of this type can be handled quite naturally within a generative description. Three Welsh dialects all have /oːɨ/, /oː/ and /uːe/, but select differently in a particular word: thus D_1 [oːɨ], D_2 [oː], D_3 [uːe]. This can be handled by having all three dialects undergo the rules which derive the D_1 form [oːɨ]; the D_2 form [oː] is derived from this by a 'monophthongization' rule, and the D_3 form [uːe] by rules which raise the [oː] element and lower the [ɨ]. These D_2 and D_3 rules are phonologically quite plausible, and moreover they are not set up specifically for these word-sets but are parts of rules which are of more general application.

Though generative dialectology may have some advantages over other methods of description, there remain a number of points on which there is not complete agreement among members of the school, and others where the 'outsider' is far from convinced by the arguments presented.

The underlying forms are one area where different approaches have been adopted by generativists. Some descriptions have set up underlying forms which are either identical with or at least much closer to those of one dialect, with others derived by a sequence of rules that are not required for the 'basic' dialect. For example, in her description of Lumasaaba, Brown has underlying forms which are very close to those of the Northern dialects; Southern dialects are derived by a more complex series of rules. The criteria generally adopted for choosing the basic dialect are 'generality', 'economy' and 'naturalness' in terms of the number and form of the rules required to generate all the dialect forms. Brown says that she also attempted (a) 'to construct a common Lumasaaba that would be neutral between Northern and Southern realizations', and (b) 'to derive Northern from Southern forms'. The former was rejected because 'parity of derivational difficulty between the two realizations could only be achieved by neutral forms that did not resemble any known phonological system, and by long and difficult derivations for both North and South', and the latter because it 'turned out that fewer rules were needed if a Northern form was taken as basic, and that these rules were much more general'. So the decision to derive Southern from Northern forms is justified by the more economical and 'revealing' statement which this method allows.

But as Thomas[14] points out, such criteria could lead one to adopt as basic forms sometimes those of one dialect, sometimes those of another. For example (see above), in deriving the pronunciations in English of words such as *grass, laugh, bath, dance* etc it may be found simplest to take the short vowel form as basic and to have a rule '[a] → [ɑː]/ – [s,f,θ,ns] etc'. In deriving the pronunciations of *cup, love, flood* etc it will almost certainly be simpler to treat the [ʌ] form as basic, and to have the rule '[ʌ] → [ʊ]' in Northern dialects (the reverse would need a statement of environments and many exceptions). But to do this would be to take the Northern dialect as basic in the first case, and the Southern in the second.[15]

The alternative approach to adopting the forms of one dialect as more basic is to set up some more abstract underlying form which is not the same as that of any particular dialect. Again the form in question is held to be arrived at by adopting criteria such as those referred to above: the simplest set of rules for deriving all the dialect forms is possible if we set up this particular underlying form.

The whole idea of a common underlying form for all dialects is one which is superficially attractive, but it leads to considerable problems in certain cases. Perhaps such a form can be set up which does not seem too far-fetched if one is dealing with a language such as Brown was describing, which is spoken by a comparatively small number of people who do not reveal a large range of dialect variation when compared to some European languages. But the suggestion has been made that even with English the underlying forms are common to all dialects, and moreover that these underlying forms persist over long periods of time;[16] the actual forms are produced by a long sequence of rules, which may change from time to time in the various dialects. This proposal was originally made by American linguists; and since American dialects of English generally do not show extreme differences, it may be feasible to set up an underlying form from which they all may be derived without too complicated a set of rules. But if one attempts to do this for British dialects, where there are differences like those referred to in Chapter One between RP and West Yorkshire (e.g. [naɪt]/[niːt] *night*, [faɪt]/[fɛɪt] *fight*, [faɪnd]/[fɪnd] *find*, [naɪðə]/[nɔːðə] *neither*, etc etc), it would be necessary to have underlying forms which are so artificial from a synchronic viewpoint (however closely they and the rules may reflect diachronic developments) that it is difficult to believe they could be anything other than a linguist's plaything.

And the problem is that orthodox generativists maintain that the underlying forms and the rules to derive the actual dialects *are* much more than a linguist's invention: they believe that they have a certain 'reality' in that they are part of the native speaker's *competence,* his intuitive knowledge of the language; and it is this 'knowledge' of the common underlying forms and the rules which enables him to understand speakers of other dialects.

An attempt to produce a description along generative lines for British English is to be found in Trudgill's book on Norwich (1974*a*): see p. 160 above. He tried to account for the differences within Norwich English in terms of a common set of underlying forms and various rules to derive the actually occurring forms – but he admitted that it would be very difficult to produce a 'meaningful' description of this sort for more widely differing British varieties. He claimed that his system 'exists' in the sense that it is part of the native Norwich speaker's competence, and enables him to produce and understand utterances of different varieties within Norwich English (and also to recognize the varieties in question and so 'place' their speakers). If one discounts the claim that a speaker can *produce* examples of all other varieties – the evidence for which appears to be largely anecdotal, and which could be countered by contrary examples – the grounds for supposing that there is a psychologically real shared system are the ability of speakers to understand and 'recognize' those of other varieties. This is a main reason for other generativists wanting a common system for *all* English varieties. But if Trudgill believes the latter is unrealistic (and also, presumably, unnecessary) he must believe that speakers of say RP and West Yorkshire dialects understand each other without sharing a common system – presumably because of familiarity and because there is sufficient similarity between their two different systems (just as speakers of some different languages can understand each other to a certain degree – without sharing a common system). But if it is unnecessary to postulate a common system for two very different dialects of English, is it necessary to believe that all Norwich speakers share the same system?

A final doubt about generative dialectology also concerns the question of dialects having in common the set of underlying forms and a number of the rules. As was noted above, generativists hold that their approach focuses on the grammars of dialects rather than on the data: the starting-point is supposed to be a comparison of the grammars of individual dialects, from which it will appear that they have a great deal in common. This similarity is not simply *assumed* to exist, but it is claimed that grammars of the individual dialects produced independently according to the criteria of economy, naturalness, or whatever, will turn out to be so similar that a common grammar can then be set up. But as A. R. Thomas makes clear,[17] no one has ever done generative dialectology this 'long way round' – they have always started not by writing separate grammars for the dialects and then comparing them, but by producing a grammar with the common set of underlying forms, certain rules common to some dialects, and others peculiar to individual ones, and so on. So in this respect (like several others), the theory of generative grammar must be regarded as 'not proven'.

II. A 'CONTINUUM' OF VARIETIES: THE 'DYNAMIC MODEL'

In Chapter Four it was seen that until around 1960 the problem of variation had been neglected in linguistics. The usual approach in the 'modern' era of the subject (i.e. the present century) had been to view language as something essentially homogeneous. Linguistics was structural: 'a language is a system where everything holds together', said Saussure – and linguists assumed that 'structure' must be equated with 'homogeneity'. They therefore shut their eyes to the differences within a language, and concentrated on an artificially homogeneous object – an individual speaker.[18] Linguists were aware that heterogeneity did exist, but they treated it as if it were merely an uncomfortable but theoretically unimportant fact, which could be left to stylisticians, dialectologists, and other such 'scavengers', whose job was to tidy up the trivial matters on the periphery of linguistics proper.[19]

But since the mid-1960s another viewpoint has been gaining ground. Heterogeneity within a language is so pervasive that linguists have come to accept that this situation is in fact the norm, and that variation should therefore be seen as central rather than peripheral to linguistics. More important, from the work of Labov and his followers it appeared that heterogeneity is not incompatible with regularity and structure: there is 'structured heterogeneity', or patterned variation – within the individual to some extent, but more importantly, within the community. In fact, Labov (a pupil of Weinreich, who had emphasized the importance of structure in the study of dialects: see Chapter Five) suggested that true regularity of linguistic patterns was to be found not in the individual speaker, but in the speech community as a whole. Furthermore, it was realized that this view not only fits the facts 'synchronically' (i.e. for a language at any one point in time), but also makes it possible to relate this to a theory of language change. Ever since Saussure had distinguished between the 'synchronic' and 'diachronic' aspects of language, most linguists had concentrated on the former, and had abstracted an artificial 'static' situation from the variation and on-going change inherent in all languages. It was time now to bring the two axes together again, and variation was seen to be a key issue here.

As variation moved into the centre of linguistics, it was soon realized that such frameworks as had previously been proposed for describing heterogeneity were inadequate. For instance, the idea that there may be 'co-existent systems' within a community (two or more discrete and self-consistent grammatical systems, whose random mutual interference might produce a range of intermediate varieties) was quickly rejected as simplistic, and various more sophisticated models were proposed. That of Labov and his followers was in terms of variable rules: rules with different probabilities of application according to the various linguistic environments and non-linguistic factors such as class, sex, age and style.[20] This model has been referred to as 'quantitative': it attempts to state the relative quantities of different variants in different situations.

The main alternative viewpoint, called 'dynamic' (as opposed to 'quantitative' or 'static') by its adherents because it proposes that variation is simply an aspect of on-going linguistic change, is the subject of this last section of the book. Its relevance to dialectology may initially seem obscure – but dialect differences are of course a matter of variation within a language, and dialectalization is an important aspect of the inter-relation of linguistic variation and change. So this model must be considered in a study of the development of thought about dialect, such as the present volume.

The 'dynamic model' grew out of studies on *creole* languages

(languages which have developed from *pidgins* – 'simplified' varieties adopted as means of communication between speakers of two mutually unintelligible languages. Pidgins have no native speakers; but gradually they may develop into creoles: they are adopted as the native languages of various groups, and consequently expand and acquire all the necessary functions of a natural language). In a situation where a creole is used in the same area as a standard form of the language on which it is based – for example, Krio and English in Sierra Leone; Haitian Creole and French in Haiti; Sranan and English in Surinam; and so on – it has often been found that there are 'intermediate dialects'. Scholars have used the term *basilect* to refer to the 'broadest' form of creole, and *acrolect* for the standard variety; the term *mesolect* has been proposed for a form somewhere between the two. It was suggested that a mesolect results from the mutual interference of the basilect and the acrolect.

In an important paper published in 1971, De Camp[21] argued that the picture was much more complicated than this in a 'post-creole situation' i.e. where there had been an extension of education and some breaking down of a formerly rigid social stratification. Using evidence drawn from his experience with Caribbean creoles, De Camp showed that it was unrealistic to divide varieties into creole and standard (or even into basilect, mesolect and acrolect): there is no sharp cleavage between these forms – rather, there is a *continuum* of varieties between the extreme form of the creole and the standard language. A series of studies by Derek Bickerton on aspects of Guyanese creole developed this view in more detail, and C.-J. N. Bailey embodied these ideas in a wider theory of linguistic variation and change.[22]

There are two essential differences between the 'continuum' view and that of the basilect-mesolect-acrolect. First, it is held to be impossible to divide varieties into three discrete systems – or any number, for that matter. Some of the variable features show more than three variants, some less, and there is no 'bundling of isoglosses', as it were, in respect of these differences. The result is that it is unrealistic to divide varieties into any number of dialects with their own systems – there is simply a continuum of linguistic differences.[23] Second, it is *not* the case that the mesolectal varieties (however many) result from the random mutual interference of the varieties at the ends of this continuum. Rather, it is held that the varieties are related 'dynamically', in that they represent successive stages of development from creole to standard. This is where the synchronic and diachronic axes of linguistics meet: Bickerton has claimed that a synchronic cut across the Guyanese community of today (with individuals ranged between creole and standard) reflects a diachronic cut through 150–200 years of its linguistic history (with progressive development by some speakers towards the standard, while others made less or virtually no 'progress').

Its proponents hold that this model is appropriate not only to post-creole situations, but to any language community. All other approaches to differences within a language have been in terms of *dialects*, which are essentially forms of language shared by a *group* of speakers – whether this is defined geographically, or in terms of social class, sex, age-group or whatever. But this approach puts much greater emphasis on the *individual* – and the term *lect* has been coined for an individual variety of language. Speaking is done by individuals, and probably anyone who has been engaged in detailed fieldwork on any scale – or even anyone who has simply observed the use of language around him – will agree that individuals who have the same sociological characteristics (e.g. sex, age, education, occupation, income etc etc) may nevertheless differ in speech-patterns. Whether this is because of differences in personality, experience, aspirations, or whatever is unimportant for our purposes: the point is that individuals do not all conform to a 'group norm'.[24]

It is when we examine the speech of the individuals in a speech community that we find that there is indeed a continuum of differences. But a Labov-type approach obscures this because it produces *average* scores for speakers in certain (non-linguistic) categories (see p. 142): the result is to give a false impression of discrete 'dialects' rather than a more or less smooth continuum of 'lects'. De Camp pointed out that it would be ridiculous if, when examining socio-economic characteristics which vary gradually within a society, one were to take, say, state-boundaries as natural divisions and then average the socio-economic 'scores' of individuals within each state. But sociolinguists have been doing something very like this when correlating continuously-varying linguistic data to pre-conceived categories of age, education, income etc (instead of correlating such non-linguistic variables to linguistic data, which would be justifiable).

My own research leads me to agree with this point. When investigating urban speech in West Yorkshire (see Chapter Seven), one variable examined was the pronunciation or 'dropping' of *h* in contexts where it would occur in RP. With over a hundred informants altogether, I worked out percentage scores for class, style, and so on. For conversational speech (i.e. 'casual' plus 'formal' styles), there was apparently a clear stratification by social class in the amount of *h*-pronunciation:

I	II	III	IV	V
96	64	43	21	17

But if (a) we examine individuals rather than the group averages, we find that there were the following numbers of informants in each percentage 'band':

0	1–10	11–20	21–30	31–40	41–50	51–60	61–70	71–80	81–90	91–99	100
7	28	13	8	9	4	2	10	6	6	8	5

(b) it is not the case that this continuum can be divided in such a way that the members of each social class fall within a certain range, and members of other classes fall outside this. In fact, the range of individual scores in each class was as follows:

I	II	III	IV	V
81–100	7–100 (40–100)	2–100	0–86	0–80 (0–37)

In the case of Classes II and V the bracketed figures indicate what the range would have been had there not in each case been one individual whose speech was markedly 'status incongruent'.[25] If these two individuals had not formed part of the sample the figures would look more 'regular', but there would still not be 'discrete groups which are relatively unified in their linguistic behaviour'.[26]

On grounds such as these, the whole notion of 'dialect' as a group phenomenon is rejected by Bailey and Bickerton.[27] A dialect is supposed to be a variety shared by a number of speakers, and delimited from other varieties by a bundle of isoglosses of some sort. But in actual fact such a situation is rarely found; instead, there is a continuum of lects (individual varieties). A 'grid' of all possible *isolects* (varieties differing from each other by just a single feature) could be established, covering the whole range of variation within a language. Many of these isolects will be realized by one or more individual speakers using a certain style; some may be (in theory, temporarily) unoccupied.[28]

The various lects are held to be 'implicationally related'. Since the notion of *implicational relations* is crucial to this school of thought, let us start with one or two simple examples of the sort of things that may be implicationally related. In my observation, if a Yorkshireman uses the /ɑ:/ variant in words like *grass*, he will certainly use the /ʌ/ variant in words such as *cut*; but the reverse may not be true – in other words, [kʊt grɑ:s] is most unlikely to occur, but [kʌt gras] is quite possible. So the use of /ɑ:/ in a certain set of words *implies* the use of /ʌ/, but not vice versa. Such implicational relations may hold not only between different variables, as in the above example, but also between different categories of words within the same variable. For example, with the variable incidence of /ɑ:/ and /a/: if one uses /ɑ:/ in *trans-* or *plastic*, one will certainly use it in *grass* (but the reverse need not hold); if one uses /ɑ:/ in *grass*, one will certainly have it in *father* (but not necessarily the reverse); and so on.[29] Even more delicate differences of environment within a variable can be implicationally related: for example, Bailey uses some of the findings of Labov and his colleagues concerning the 'dropping' of word-final [t] from the consonant group [st]: if this occurs in *missed out* i.e. the environment [s+t# V], it will certainly occur in *missed catches* [s+t# C]; if in the latter, then in *mist in the valley* [st# V]; if in this, then in *mist cover* [st# C] – but in no case does the reverse implication hold.

The various lects in a *panlectal grid* (i.e. an array of all the possible lects in a language) are implicationally related to each other: each is essentially an individual grammar – a set of rules – and (since each isolect differs from those 'on either side' in respect of just one rule-difference) any lect implies the set of rules of the lect 'before' it on the continuum. But an essential point about this model is that the lects are held to be related not only synchronically but also historically. This is the 'dynamic' aspect of the model, as contrasted with the 'static' viewpoint of other schools of linguistics.[30]

Essentially, Bailey has proposed a new version of an old theory. The old theory in question is the 'Wave Theory' of Johannes Schmidt, put forward in 1872 to account for resemblances between separate but geographically adjacent branches of the Indo-European family of languages.[31] Schmidt's idea was that a linguistic change spreads outwards from some starting-point like waves on a pond into which a pebble has been tossed. Waves may be of various strengths, and may start at different points – depending on the size of the pebbles and where they were thrown in. The result is that different areas of the pond are affected by different combinations of waves. Similarly, a geographical area is affected by different combinations of isoglosses, and so ends up with various languages and dialects with varying degrees of similarity.

Bailey's modern version of this is that waves of change move, over a period of time, either through geographical space (as Schmidt had suggested) or through *social* space – or both; and they may be slowed down by barriers of either kind i.e. those of age, sex, class, etc, as well as physical geographical features. Changes are of course transmitted by individuals, and at any one time a particular change will have 'passed' certain speakers, but will not yet have reached others. Thus, for example, speaker C (whom a particular change has not yet reached) will differ from speaker A (whom the same change has passed) – and from speaker B (whom the change is just reaching, and who consequently sometimes produces the same output as A, sometimes the same as C). So the model accounts for both interpersonal variation (between A and C) and intrapersonal variation (within B).

Changes such as these are often implicationally related in the sense that a particular wave, say that affecting feature x, will gradually spread to cover the area already affected by the wave relevant to feature w. The result will be that a change in x will imply a prior change in w – but a change in w does not necessarily mean that x will have changed. These implicational relations may again hold either between quite different changes (as in an earlier example it was suggested that a person who changes from saying [gras] to [grɑːs] will already have changed from [kʊt] to [kʌt], but his saying [kʌt] does *not* imply that he also says [grɑːs]), or between different environments of change within the same variable. In fact, it is held that linguistic changes do not affect all examples of a variable at once, but proceed environment by environment; and a change in a particular environment will imply a change in 'heavier-weighted' environments. Thus, for example, it has been seen that my own observations of the spread of the glottal stop in West Yorkshire suggest that it affects word-final environments before word-medial ones – so if a person says [bɪʔə] *bitter*, this implies that he says [bɪʔ ə stʊf] *bit of stuff*, but someone may say the latter but not the former.

Diagrammatically, a simplified picture of the progress of a change is as follows (the symbol '+' is used to indicate that the change has occurred i.e. a 'new' rule is applied; '×' that sometimes the old rule operates, sometimes the new one i.e. there is variation: a speaker sometimes says [gras] and sometimes [grɑːs], for example; and '–' that the change has not yet occurred):

		Environments			
		a	b	c	d
	o	–	–	–	–
Stages of	1	×	–	–	–
change	2	+	×	–	–
	3	+	+	×	–

The 'stages' of change referred to here may be stages of time, but also they may be represented at any one time by different individuals or locations. If it is a matter of locations, these may not always occur in a contiguous area on a map, since changes do not always proceed so regularly.

A more graphic representation of the social or geographical spread of the waves of change is provided by Figure *xxvii*.[32]

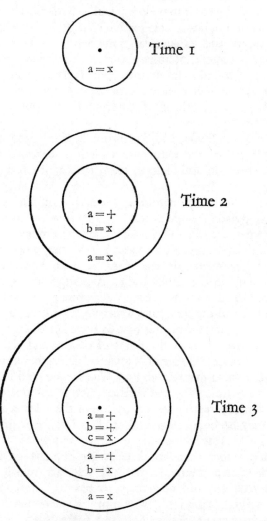

Figure xxvii. Idealized representation of Bailey's 'Wave Model'. (Based on Bailey, 1973*b*.)

From the above table the implicational relations between the environments of change can be seen quite clearly: a 'categorical' change in any environment implies a categorical change in heavier-weighted environments (e.g. at stage 3, + in environment b implies + in environment a), and a variable change in one environment implies a categorical change in heavier-weighted environments and categorical non-change in lighter-weighted ones (e.g. at stage 3, × in environment c implies + in environments a and b and − in environment d). If a change continues long enough it will eventually become generalized, i.e. it will not be limited to certain environments but will apply categorically in all.[33]

The ideas of Bailey and Bickerton in fact constitute a quite different view of the nature of variation, and of the relation between variation and change, from that which had previously been accepted. Labov and his followers had suggested that variation is 'inherent' within any speech community, and that while a linguistic change necessarily involves variation for some time between the old and the new features, the fact that there is variation does *not* necessarily mean that a change is in progress.[34] Bailey and Bickerton on the other hand hold that variation is simply a stage in linguistic change. A change begins by affecting some feature in some restricted environment: what happens is that the old and the new rules alternate for a time, then the new rule becomes categorical. But by this stage the change is affecting another environment at the point of origin, and also the more restricted change has spread 'outwards' from this point; and so on (see the wave diagram above). The earliest and least general changes have time to spread furthest, and at any one point there is, with time, increasing generalization of the rule; eventually the change may become categorical at all points, or it may cease to operate before this happens.

Essentially then there are three stages in a change as it affects any environment at any point: 1. old rule categorical, 2. alternation between old and new rules, 3. new rule categorical. The second stage, 'variation', is simply a developmental phase between two categorical stages, and there is no need for any elaborate device such as 'variable rules' (with attendant difficulties concerning how much the actual speaker is believed to 'know' about the relative probabilities of the rule applying, according to different environments, different social categories, and so on). So what appears, with a 'synchronic cut' across a community to be a situation of inherent variation is in fact the equivalent of a 'diachronic cut' through history, when the variation will be seen as simply a phase in the change from one feature or rule to another.

Variation is thus held to be less of a problem than had been believed. Moreover, it is claimed that there is actually much *less* variation in a community than appears to be the case from the Labovian method of averaging scores for groups of speakers. If *individuals* are examined, and the different linguistic environments are carefully distinguished, it will emerge that most features are categorical, and that alternation between old and new categorical rules (i.e. variation) is much less than had been thought. Bickerton (1973*b*), discussing a feature of Montreal French, shows that when data is examined for individual speakers and specific environments, the amount of variation is 22 per cent; but if environments are lumped together variation appears to be 57 per cent; and if individuals were grouped together the figure would be even higher. So a lot of the 'variation' found in Labov-type studies is in fact an artefact of the method of analysis. Bailey and Bickerton claim that if the percentage of use of a particular variable feature by individual speakers is plotted on a graph, the typical pattern will be an 'S-curve' (see Figure *xxviii*). A curve such as this can be taken as representing a change passing fairly quickly through a population. Speakers with low percentages are those who are just acquiring the new feature; those with high percentages have almost fully acquired it and are getting rid of the old feature. Only relatively few speakers at any one time have middle percentages, i.e. appear to vary between two features without either being dominant.

The 'dynamic model' has not escaped criticism, but this is not the place to enter detailed discussion of the arguments on each side;[35] suffice it to say that while many people find its claims interesting, they feel that further detailed testing is called for. Nor is it appropriate to be concerned here with other questions that have been tackled by the proponents of this model – such as just how much 'knowledge' resides in the 'competence' of native speakers about the various lects in their language (should

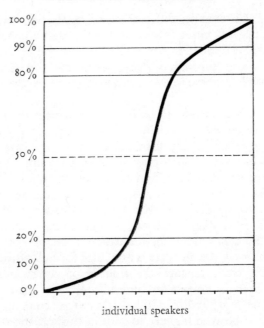

Figure xxviii. The S-curve of linguistic change. (Based on
Bailey, 1973*b* and Bickerton, 1975*a*.)

this be represented by 'polylectal' or 'panlectal' grammars?).
To become involved with such matters would take us too far
from dialectology into general linguistics. It is time to stop.

Indeed, some readers will feel that we have already gone too
far. This chapter has dealt with ideas put forward mainly by
linguists rather than dialectologists; those arguing for the 'dynamic model' even reject the notion of 'dialect' entirely! But we
started out with the broad definition that dialects are 'different
forms of the same language', and both generative dialectology
and the dynamic model are concerned with such. Moreover, the
most 'traditional' dialectology has concentrated on the historical
development of differences within a language – and both these
recent approaches have largely collapsed the synchronic/dia-
chronic dichotomy upheld so fervently by modern linguistics
this century, and have related linguistic differentiation to its
historical context. Though some dialectologists still shy away
from linguistics, a *rapprochement* between the two subjects is

more possible than at any time this century, because linguistic variation – which is essentially what dialectology is concerned with – is now seen by many scholars as central rather than peripheral to linguistics.

Notes

CHAPTER I

1. Trudgill (1974*b*), p. 17.
2. Abercrombie (1951), p. 11. Note that though Abercrombie admits that his 'accentless' definition of RP is really a simplification, and that it is 'really as much an accent as any other', he does not say that Standard English is as much a dialect as any other.
3. This would certainly seem to be implied by Abercrombie: 'a difference in pronunciation alone is not enough to make a different dialect'; Trudgill's definition *could* be taken as allowing some aspects of pronunciation to be matters of dialect.
4. I think 'tone of voice' features would be included here, though relatively little work has been done on such features in this connection.
5. The *r* sound in Berkshire (as also in RP and the majority of regional dialects) is more precisely [ɹ], but [r] is commonly used in fairly 'broad' (i.e. non-detailed) transcriptions.
6. Though of course historically this was the origin of this difference.
7. Though note that more markedly Northern forms are [faðə] *father* and [mastə] *master*.
8. And some people vary between the two (as with '*h*-dropping'): see p. 189.
9. See Catford (1957*a*), Hill (1958).
10. My own findings are that *know* varies between /ɔʊ/ and /oː/ in West Yorkshire.
11. My only doubts about this method of distinguishing accent and dialect concern certain other examples of such distributional differences. Would a difference in words like *clip*, *clash*, *gleam*, *glimpse* etc between [klɪp], [klæʃ], [gliːm], [glɪmps] as in RP and [tlɪp], [tlaʃ], [dliːm], [dlɪmps] as in some regional forms (e.g. West Yorkshire) be accepted as accent? Certainly there is regularity of correspondence: initial velar consonant +/l/ in RP corresponds to initial alveolar consonant +/l/ in other forms, but such pronunciations are associated with 'broad' dialect i.e. they tend to be heard from speakers who would on other grounds be

regarded as differing in *dialect* from RP-speakers (though it has to be admitted that since the difference is barely detectable, and the initial /tl/ and /dl/ combinations do not occur at all in RP, so that there is no possibility of confusion resulting from a substitution of /tl, dl/ for /kl, gl/, some *RP-speakers* do in fact say [tlɪp], [dli:m] etc). Another doubtful case concerns the frequent non-standard pronunciation of words such as *widow, follow, borrow* etc as [wɪdə], [fɒlə], [bɒrə]: the correspondence of RP final unstressed /əʊ/ to non-standard /ə/ is certainly regular, but one suspects that the 'substandard' connotations of /ə/ may lead some people to consider this a matter of dialect.

12. The Northerner may betray himself by applying his rule too regularly – to words like *ass, classic, gas, mass* (lump), *cant, finance, expand, random* etc which exceptionally (there is no obvious basis for this set of exceptions) have a short vowel in the South. RP-speakers also vary between short and long in a number of words, including *elastic, plastic, trans-, -graph*. In the North the exceptions are fewer: there is always a long vowel in *can't*, and most people now have one in *father, master, plaster*.

13. The term 'extreme' is one which has been used to me in this connection when discussing informally the dialect/accent distinction.

14. For a discussion of the various uses of the term 'style', see Crystal and Davy (1969), Chapter One.

15. This use of 'variety' is evident in the classic work on English dialects by A. J. Ellis (1889). An example of the same use in more recent times is Vasiliu (1966).

16. Hill (1958) proposed the term 'tongue' in the same neutral sense that 'variety' has come to have, but this does not appear to have been adopted.

17. See Halliday, McIntosh and Strevens (1966); the particular diagram reproduced here is based on Trudgill (1975*a*), p. 21.

18. See *Linguistic Atlas of Scotland*, (ed. J. Y. Mather and H. H. Speitel), Vol. 1 (1975), p. 7.

19. The lecture-notes taken by a number of Saussure's students were edited and put together after his death, and published as *Cours de Linguistique Générale*. Part IV bears the title 'Geographical Linguistics'.

20. Petyt (1977).

21. See various works referred to in Chapter Three below, for example.

22. In the case of some of the most common regional features it is an interesting possibility that Standard English as a world-wide medium is responsible for their different development in this area:

the presence of /h/ and /ʌ/, and the absence of the /ɛɪ/ – /eː/ and /ɔʊ/ – /oː/ contrasts, are widespread features of the English-speaking world as well as of RP (facts which may be known to many people because of films, broadcasting etc), and in these cases there are signs of the West Yorkshire forms giving way among some or all sections of the population; but with /a/ as opposed to /ɑː/ in *laugh, bath, pass, dance* etc the short vowel is probably the commoner in English generally, and here RP /ɑː/ has made little impression.

CHAPTER 2

1. Initially there were 42, but after two revisions of the questionnaire 40 was the final number.
2. See Keller (1964) and King (1954) for fuller accounts in English of the work of the German school of dialectology.
3. Apparently Gilliéron was fond of saying that Edmont was 'a simple grocer – a grocer I have seen selling his cheese'! (see Scheuermeier, 1932).
4. Scheuermeier (1932): see for example his remarks on the advantages of possessing papers with the appropriate signatures when the police arrived to arrest him 'comme bandit, assassin, espion etc', and of interviewing the informant on his own ground where he feels confident – whatever the inconveniences, e.g. 'la famille va et vient, des importuns se mêlent de nos affairs, la vache fait un veau, la lumière s'éteint . . .'
5. Trudgill includes a fairly extensive list of such publications in the bibliography to his survey paper (1975*b*); the mammoth work by Sever Pop, *La Dialectologie* (1950) is virtually comprehensive up to that date.
6. See Dauzat (1939, 1942, 1955) and Séguy (1973) on the project in general. Séguy's *Atlas linguistique et ethnographique de la Gascogne* (1954–73) is an example of one of the completed regional projects.
7. Atwood (1963) provides a useful overview of the development of American dialectology; (see also McDavid, R. I. and McDavid, V. G., 1956). There are two volumes which make available a selection of articles: Allen and Underwood (1971), and Williamson and Burke (1971).
8. See M. L. Hanley 'Plans for a survey of the dialects of New England' (1930).
9. This is the date when two separate surveys already in progress – of California and Nevada and of the Pacific North West – were merged.

10. See Kurath 'Report of interviews with European scholars' (1930).
11. This 'social' classification of informants will be considered in more detail later: see p. 112.
12. It may be noted that both surveys neglected syntax – as have most of the later projects: modern linguistics as a whole only turned to the problems of syntax in the 1950s.
13. Most other direct surveys have only had a locality-density of less than 5 per cent. That of German-speaking Switzerland (Hotzenköcherle, 1962) is an exception: its 573 localities means a density of about 33 per cent.
14. A further difference between the two great surveys, though not one of method, is referred to below: interpretative works based on the findings of the French survey dealt more with intralinguistic factors (e.g. homonymy and its effects) while those based on German data were more concerned with extralinguistic correlations (e.g. the effect on speech of earlier political and cultural areas).

    It may also be noted that whereas the German work led to the development of an atlas 'school', Gilliéron's atlas (though distributed free to libraries and colleges by the Ministry of Education) did not provoke as much interest as it deserved. Perhaps this difference relates to the different linguistic situations and specifically to the different attitudes to dialect and accent in the two countries: in German-speaking areas local differences are common and respectable among all social groups, while in the French the standard language is dominant – the higher social classes do not use local dialect, and the speech of the lower classes is being affected by the influence of Standard French.
15. Dauzat (1955) says Gilliéron did try to adapt the number of localities in each 'department' to the range of patois which apparently existed. But the maps of the French atlas do suggest a rather 'mechanical' network.
16. If this is not done confusion can result either because the referent of the question is unfamiliar to the informant (see Francis (1959) on the problems arising from a question about bilberries – a fruit unknown in the area of Britain he was investigating), and he may give a word with some similar but not identical referent, or because they are familiar with the word being sought, but use it to mean something slightly different.
17. In this matter too the later regional surveys of France did not adopt Gilliéron's rigid procedure: see Dauzat (1942) 'It is more important to know how people speak in a certain locality than how a certain individual spoke at a particular moment.'
18. Edmont's headlong rush around France led to a number of

criticisms: e.g. that instead of genuine dialect speakers he some-times made do with say the mayor's secretary, whose French had been modified in a Standard direction, and that he worked more often than he should have done in towns rather than villages because it was easier to find lodgings (see Dauzat, 1955).

19. See Séguy (1973) p. 69.
20. See Scheuermeier (1932) p. 104.
21. Well-intentioned local residents often attempt to steer the field-worker to such people: see Scheuermeier (op. cit.) pp. 101–2.
22. The form 'childer' is still heard occasionally in parts of the North of England. It is an example of what was referred to above – dialect preserving an older and 'purer' form: 'child-er-en' in fact contains *two* historical plural formatives (like 'cherub-im-s').
23. A variant of this, adopted in some American works, is to employ large symbols at intervals to indicate universality of usage within a given area.
24. The term *isogloss* is modelled on those used in meteorology: *isotherm*, *isobar* etc. It was coined by a German parson called August Bielenstein, an expert in Lettish and a dialectologist, who not long after Wenker used both the direct and the indirect methods to gather his data.
25. Sources in English giving some particular examples from the German survey are Keller (1964), Viereck (1973).
26. 'In reality, every word has its own particular history' (K. Jaberg, (1908) p. 6). A. Gauchat (1904): 'Are there dialect boundaries?'; Note also G. Paris: 'Il n'y a pas de dialects, les parlers se perdent les uns dans les autres' (1888).
27. Such areas are not always the most conservative, however: Scheuermeier found that quite often the language of the 'last village in an Alpine valley' had been profoundly modified by the development of the tourist industry.
28. It has been found for example that the Mont Blanc range, the highest part of the Alps, has *not* been a linguistic boundary within the Franco-Provençal area.
29. These theories of the German school were widely accepted in the twenties and thirties, but in more recent times serious doubts have been cast on them. For example, opponents have pointed out that signs of the above division of the Rhinelands are to be seen much earlier – even in the findings of prehistoric archaeology. They suggest that the dialect divisions are by no means as recent as had been thought: they may reflect linguistic differences between say the Franks and the Alemannians rather than those between German states of the fifteenth to eighteenth centuries.

30. M. Bartoli and G. Bertoni were the main founders of this school: see Bartoli (1925) and Bartoli and Bertoni (1925), both in Italian. G. Bonfante (1947) presents a very partisan view of the contrasts between the views of the Neogrammarians and the Neolinguists; this paper was written in reply to severe criticisms of Neolinguistics by R. A. Hall (1946: reproduced in Hall's later book in 1963).

31. This example and the following one are taken from Trudgill (1975*b*).

32. Of course, just looking at *England* we could say that the /ʊ/-area (the Northern part, away from the capital and the most populated South East region) is peripheral! Hall (op. cit.) demonstrates how various parts of the Romance language-area are at different times described as peripheral in order to make an example fit the norm.

33. The dialect forms Gilliéron writes as [azã] and [bigey] respectively. See Gilliéron (1910).

CHAPTER 3

1. See p. 84 below for this term used by Joseph Wright.

2. e.g. Wakelin (1972*b*), Chapter Three.

3. One of the earliest publications of the Philological Society, founded in 1842, was R. B. Peacock's *A Glossary of the Dialect of the Hundred of Lonsdale in the County of Lancaster, together with An Essay on some Leading Characteristics of the Dialects Spoken in the Six Northern Counties of England* (1869).

4. Incidentally, during those fifteen years Ellis also produced two books on the pronunciation of Latin and Greek, three on music and one on mathematics; and also five presidential addresses to the Philological Society. This gives a fair indication of the man's industry and range of ability – and also perhaps helps to account for his death in 1890!

5. Ellis did however obtain some data 'from domestic servants and railway porters', and made a number of visits to a teacher-training college in Chelsea, where he interviewed young women 'fresh from the country'.

6. One wonders how much use either the dialect test or the comparative specimen could have been with Hallam's 'illiterate peasants'!

7. *Essays & Studies* (1946): 'A New Survey of English Dialects' – i.e. to supersede that of Ellis.

8. *Notes & Queries* (1870).

9. Introduction to Part III of *Early English Pronunciation*.

10. See Viereck (1970) for an interesting picture of the troubled early history of the Society.

11. *Notes & Queries*, 1879 and 1880.
12. See Viereck (op. cit.).
13. Another consequence of this criterion was that Wright seems to have included some items with written authority which have proved difficult to attest from other sources: see Petyt (1970) pp. 41 and 44 for some otherwise unconfirmed usages included because they occur in *Wuthering Heights*.
14. We may note that early in the period of data-collection Skeat had stressed the importance of saying who used a form and how commonly. He realized in fact that the study of regional dialects cannot be separated from that of class dialects; but this problem was ignored for many years.
15. Dieth (1946).
16. For example, those of Sir James Wilson on the New Forest and Lowland and Central Scots.
17. Brilioth says in his Preface: 'Professor Wright expressed the opinion that in Cumberland, *if anywhere*, I might hope to find a distinct and well-preserved dialect idiom.' (My italics.) See above, on Wright's attitude.
18. Kökeritz (1932) p. xiii.
19. Dieth (op. cit.). Dieth had himself worked in the field of English dialectology for many years. In 1936 he had published *Grammar of the Buchan Dialect*.
20. See Orton (1960): 'traditional vernacular, genuine and old'.
21. The four earlier versions were all tested in the field.
22. Experimental maps were produced quite early, but only occasional ones appeared: e.g. in Orton (1960).
23. On this point see p. 130 below.
24. An example of the latter is to be found in Bailey (1973*b*) p. 86 sq., where an attempt is made to interpret *SED* data in accordance with the 'dynamic' model advocated by Bailey and his followers (see Chapter Eight, II).
25. Research into Ulster dialects is described in G. B. Adams *Ulster Dialects* (1964); see also R. J. Gregg: 'The Scots-Irish dialect boundaries in Ulster', in Wakelin (1972*a*).
26. See p. 21: the dialect/accent distinction discussed in Chapter One was proposed by the *LSS* team.
27. Catford (1957*a*), (1957*b*); and see Chapter Five.
28. For example, Thomas (1964), (1967), (1968).

CHAPTER 4

1. In fact, dialectology, the study of linguistic differences within an

area, has been described as 'the other principal aspect of linguistic investigation', alongside the 'family tree' method of reconstructing the divergent development of languages: see Pulgram (1953) p. 68.

2. This example is of course simplified: dialectologists have often produced a wider range of *narrow* (i.e. more detailed – as contrasted with *broad*) transcriptions of the pronunciations of particular words.

3. This is a true story, told by the woman involved to the author who was doing fieldwork in Halifax. The confusion arose because in Cockney /ʌ/ is realized as [a] (while [æ] realizes /a/), but in Yorkshire [a] is the realization of /a/. Thus:

> *butter* Yks [bʊtə] Ck [batə]
> *batter* Yks [batə] Ck [bætə]

4. In fact Weinreich uses the examples [man] and [mɒn], but since he is *not* talking about the English word *man* (which can have these pronunciations), it is preferable to make this slight change since otherwise the phonemic interpretation becomes more difficult to understand if the reader is thinking in terms of the English system.

5. This is something of an oversimplification: there have been some other approaches e.g. some works have referred to 'co-existent systems' or to 'interference' and 'dialect mixture', and so on.

6. *Free variants* such as these are distinguished from *conditioned variants*; the latter are predictable from their environment, which is said to condition them; for example, the /k/ phoneme has a number of such variants (or 'allophones'): if it is followed by a front vowel, as in *key*, it will have a variant produced further forward on the roof of the mouth; if a back vowel follows, as in *car*, it will have a variant produced further back.

7. Orton (1960). Ellis (1976) notes that as an experiment some Yorkshire towns were included in the *SED* network, but the 'country-oriented' questionnaire was not suitable.

8. W. Viereck: *Phonematische Analyse des Dialekts von Gateshead-upon-Tyne, Co. Durham* (1966).

9. Pickford (op. cit.).

10. Though *LSS* was in fact planned along 'structural' lines even before the call for structural dialectology (see p. 96).

CHAPTER 5

1. Trubetzkoy used the term *function*; I have substituted the one linguists later adopted.

2. Trubetzkoy's term was *etymological distribution*; again, I have substituted the later more commonly accepted one.

3. It may be noted at this point that Trubetzkoy pointed out that comparisons of phoneme inventory, distribution and realization could be extended even to separate languages; but comparisons of incidence essentially concern forms of the same language. He thus anticipated a matter of dispute in the later development of structural dialectology (see below).

4. Though it is interesting to note the brief reference to the importance of structural relations at the start of the chapter on dialect geography in Bloomfield (1933), a work that was a classic of American structural linguistics.

5. Weinreich acknowledged in his first footnote that he drew much of his inspiration from Trubetzkoy's article.

6. Structural dialectology, as will be seen from this chapter, has been almost entirely concerned with phonology. But equally relevant to decisions about dialect divisions could be differences in, say, *grammatical* structure; for example, between areas with a three-term demonstrative system (*this/that/yon*) and those with two terms (*this/that*); those with a simple *you* for second person(s), and those which differentiate as *thou* (singular familiar) versus *you* (singular non-familiar, and plural), or *you* (singular) versus *you all* (plural); and so on.

7. Moulton explains that /$ɔ_2$/ and /$ɔ̃_2$/ cannot be considered shared in the way that /a_4/ is: in the case of /a_4/, the same words in each dialect belong to /a/ and the remaining members of set 4 have /æ/; whereas with /ɔ/ and /ɔ̃/, all items in, say, set 2a have /ɔ/ in LU, but in AP some have /ɔ/ and some have /o/. A different way of establishing and labelling the lexical sets in question might have made this difference clearer.

8. In Britain, the work most clearly in the structural dialectology tradition is that of A. R. Thomas discussed in his paper of 1964, in which he illustrates some aspects of structural dialectology with reference to Welsh. He shows, for instance, how the essential differences between Welsh dialects are those which relate to systems rather than to sounds, and gives examples where *isophones* (isoglosses relating to sound, as distinct from *isolexes*) based on phonemic inventory do not correspond to those based on realization.

An attempt to look structurally at British English accents (rather than dialects) is a paper by J. C. Wells, 1970. He divides differences of accent into systemic (i.e. inventory), distributional, realizational and incidential (though without any acknowledgement that this division goes back to Trubetzkoy), and gives interesting examples of each type. He also attempts to divide the country into regions according to important accentual isoglosses – the result being somewhat reminiscent of Ellis's divisions of British dialects eighty years earlier.

9. The term *system* is here used in the narrower 'British' sense of a set of contrasts at one particular point in structure e.g. the beginning of a word. This is referred to as the *polysystemic* approach as compared with the American *monosystemic* view of an 'overall' set of phonemic contrasts in any variety. Both are of course structural approaches.

10. Moulton (1968).

11. Other relevant references here include Scheuermeier (1932), who makes the distinction between *normalized* and *impressionistic* transcription and shows that as early as the great French survey this problem had been noted: 'Gilliéron a dit: "Envoyez vingt dialectologues dans le même endroit et vous aurez vingt résultats différents".' This was Gilliéron's reason for preferring amateurs such as Edmont – but this was not the complete answer. See also Abercrombie (1954), Ladefoged (1960) and Kohler (1967).

CHAPTER 6

1. Several other 'traditional'-type surveys in urban areas have been carried out. That in Chicago is particularly noteworthy: see Pederson (1976), and other items referred to in that paper.

2. For example 'Hypercorrection in the Lower Middle Class as a factor in linguistic change' (1966*b*); 'The effect of social mobility on linguistic behaviour' (1967); 'The reflection of social processes in linguistic structures' (1968); etc. More references are to be found in Wolfram and Fasold (1964), which is a general introduction to research of the type Labov pioneered.

3. See Labov (op. cit.) p. 64.

4. But note also a suggestion by Trudgill: see p. 160 below.

5. It was reported in Shuy, R. W., W. A. Wolfram and W. K. Riley *Linguistic Correlates of Social Stratification in Detroit Speech* (1968*b*), also published as *The Study of Social Dialects in Detroit* (1968: US Office of Information, Final Report). The sections describing fieldwork were also published separately as (1968*a*).

6. See Wolfram (1969).

7. See in particular the article 'Contraction, deletion, and inherent variability of the English copula' (1969).

CHAPTER 7

1. Since this book will probably have a largely British readership, more individual studies are referred to in this chapter than in Chapter Six, but it is by no means a comprehensive list.
2. Bernstein's work is reported in 'Language and Social Class' (1960), and many other papers published in the following years, and that of Giles in a number of articles beginning with 'Evaluative Reactions to Accents' (1970), and a book by Giles and P. F. Powesland, *Speech Style and Social Evaluation* (1975).
3. That put forward by C. F. Hockett in *A Manual of Phonology* (1955).
4. Viereck (1966).
5. A later paper, 'A Diachronic-Structural Analysis of a Northern English Urban Dialect', (1968) makes clear that Viereck has close links with the traditional historical approach. He attempts a two-dimensional study (i.e. synchronic and diachronic) of aspects of Gateshead dialect. The historical section compares the developments in Gateshead and in Standard English of the Middle English vowel and diphthong phonemes, and offers some interesting conclusions about the results of the influence of a standard language on the incidence of dialect phonemes.
6. 'Urban Dialects: a consideration of method' (1966).
7. See 'Methodology of an Urban Speech Survey' (1968).
8. Ellis (1976) states that Houck's material has undergone further examination after computer programming of both the socio-economic and the phonetic information, and that results will be published. He also notes that the vowel of *bath* etc (as well as that of *bud*) was found to be an important marker.
9. 'The Tyneside Linguistic Survey' by B. M. H. Strang (1968) is a general statement of aims; several later papers, published and unpublished, have been written mainly by the chief researcher, John Pellowe. See especially Pellowe, G. Nixon, B. Strang and V. McNeany (1972), and Pellowe (1976) which also lists other papers.
10. Strang (op. cit.) p. 789. See also p. 95 above (on *LSS*).
11. See Pellowe and Jones (1978), for example.
12. Though in the past linguists did not usually speak of 'rules', Wells's notion of *hyperadaptation* does not appear to me to be essentially different from that of *hypercorrection* – a label which many people have applied to examples such as those just described.
13. This work is reported in an unpublished Leeds University thesis, but it is summarized in Wakelin (1972b) p. 156 and Ellis (1976) p. 98.
14. Most Labov-inspired studies are of this type. The *TLS* appears

from articles such as Pellowe and Jones (1978) to be operating in a manner similar to Heath's: informants' social characteristics are noted, but their linguistic performance is plotted individually, before the common social characteristics of those clustering together linguistically are examined.

15. See Trudgill (op. cit.) pp. 95–96. In fact, on this variable the scores for the two lowest classes, MWC and LWC, are almost identical in all styles; but in three of the four the MWC appears to use slightly fewer glottal forms.

16. Note the similar view expressed by Labov in (1966a) p. 495.

17. See also Trudgill (1973).

18. Labov had also spoken of the 'speech community' of New York, which he held was 'united by a common set of evaluative norms'. For reasons outlined in my own thesis (Petyt, 1977, p. 472 sq.), I find this a very dubious concept.

19. See Bickerton (1975b), for example.

20. I have restricted myself to outlining a number of major completed investigations which could be described as urban dialectology: some of the others, while interesting, are better classed as sociolinguistics or psycholinguistics. Note that Ellis (1976) refers to other projects carried out in Britain, including two dealing with areas of London.

21. Knowles discusses the Scouse tone of voice in his thesis and in the article referred to; so too does Trudgill for Norwich. An article by B. Honikman (1964) and work by J. D. M. Laver (e.g. 1968) brought it to linguists' attention – though it has been referred to in less systematic ways for many years.

22. See Macauley's book *Language, Social Class and Education: A Glasgow Study* (1977), as well as his article in Trudgill (ed.) (1978).

23. This method was earlier employed in the Detroit Survey, where Wolfram (1969) p. 135 took the first 25 examples of a variable from each informant.

24. The investigation is described in full in Petyt (1977). The only part which has yet appeared in print is a paper in Trudgill (ed.) (1978).

25. It is not possible to go into detail here about minor differences of approach and method from previous studies of this type.

26. This last method, employed by Labov (see p. 146 above) had not been tested on British data by Trudgill. See Petyt (1977) p. 397 sq. for a number of doubtful aspects of this approach.

27. See the discussion on p. 149 of this book.

28. Of course, the fact that the written form presented to an informant in these contexts was a standard one must have influenced the

response. But in cases where the non-standard variant was simply a different morphological shape (e.g. [t∼ʔ] for *the*, [wə] for *was*, [ət] for *that*) rather than a different construction, this could be (and was in some instances) substituted for the standard form in a reading passage.

29 It could be held that the spelling had some influence: the written form was presented in the reading passage, word list and self-evaluation test; but one would not perhaps expect the written form to influence readers in a non-standard direction (as written *h* influences them in a standard one).

30 As figures broken down by age, class and style make clear.

CHAPTER 8

1 See Halle (1959) and (1962).
2 See Chomsky (1964), and Chomsky and Halle (1965) and (1968).
3. See Klima (1964) and O'Neil (1968) for examples of papers concerned with generating grammatical differences among dialects.
4. This corresponds to the term 'morphophoneme' earlier used by structural linguists.
5. This is of course *historically* untrue: the North reflects the earlier situation; in the South /ʊ/ has 'split' into /ʌ/ and /ʊ/.
6. I am using 'dialect' throughout this chapter, though we could of course treat some differences as merely 'accent' (see Chapter One).
7. Throughout this outline of generative dialectology I am, for the benefit of those with less technical background in linguistics, using familiar symbols for phonetic and phonemic segments rather than introducing the additional complication of *distinctive features*, as usually employed in generative phonology. Using the latter, the example under discussion would look even simpler, since it would merely be a matter of changing one feature, the degree of 'closeness' of the vowel e.g. [close 4]→[close 3].
8. This example is discussed in Kiparsky (1968) p. 177 and King (1969) p. 46.
9. Newton (op. cit.) p. 65.
10. Vasiliu (op. cit.) pp. 85–8.
11. Brown (op. cit.) p. 156. On ordered rules in general, see also S. Saporta 'Ordered Rules, Dialect Differences, and Historical Processes' (1965).
12. This is the case with generative phonology in general: for example Chomsky and Halle (1968) set up a velar fricative and a Great Vowel Shift rule in their supposedly synchronic description of modern English!

13. Generative phonology does not in fact recognize the relevance of a unit at the level of the phoneme of structural linguistics, but it is not necessary to go into this question here.

14. (op. cit.) p. 190.

15. The objection could also be made that the first case reflects the actual historical development, while the second is counter-historical – though this is strictly irrelevant in a synchronic description.

16. See Chomsky and Halle (1968) pp. x, 54 etc.

17. (op. cit.).

18. This approach is best illustrated in the era of structural linguistics by an important article on phonology by Bernard Bloch (1948): he said that the object of study had to be *a single speaker in a single style on a single occasion*. In the succeeding 'generative' period, Chomsky (1965) said that 'linguistic theory is concerned primarily with an ideal speaker-listener in a completely homogeneous speech-community'.

19. Saussure's 'parole' and Chomsky's 'performance' (though these notions are not exactly alike) both allowed for matters that did not belong to the essential 'langue' or 'competence' respectively.

20. See p. 148. A more developed framework for variable rules was proposed by Sankoff and Cedergren (1976).

21. This was the same scholar whose study of the English of San Francisco was referred to in Chapters Four and Six.

22. See especially Bickerton (1971), (1973*a*), and (1975*a*); and Bailey (1973*a*) and (1973*b*).

23. Note that this notion differs from that of the 'dialect continuum' referred to in Chapter One (e.g. that extending from Northern France to Southern Italy) in that (a) the continuum in this case may be social instead of, or as well as, geographical in its extent; and (b) the continuum is not one of 'dialects', but of individual varieties or 'lects' (see below).

24. Extreme departures from the group 'average' have been termed 'status incongruence' by Labov and his followers. But the present approach would hold that probably *all* individuals within a group exhibit differences.

25. In Class II the individual concerned was a former managing-director and an ex-mayor of Halifax, whose normal speech was more or less that of the stereotype blunt Yorkshireman; he told me that his wife [pleːz amlət əbaːt ɪʔ]. The Class V individual was one of the few cases where the composite social class score concealed certain 'higher' ratings: he was a former clerk who had had grammar school education, but in terms of income, housing

and standard of living he scored very low. Apparently in his case the occupation and education categories were more closely related to his speech.

26. See Trudgill (1974*a*) p. 59, where he says this was the intention of his division of the social class continuum. As evidence contrary to my own, it may be noted that Macauley in his work on Glasgow (see his 1978 paper, p. 137ff) examined individual as well as group scores, with the views of Bickerton and Bailey in mind. He found that there was indeed a continuum of linguistic variation, but that (using his rather crude total scores for a combination of four variables) there was evidence for believing that there *were* three discrete groups with their social dialects (though note that he had started out with the idea that there were *four* social classes).

27. See Bailey (1973*a*) p. 161, (1973*b*) p. 11, and Bickerton (1973*a*) p. 643, for example.

28. The positions on the isolect continuum are really abstract levels, not the fixed locations of actual speakers; and note that it is held that the same individual may on different occasions represent different lects within the 'panlectal grid' (see Bickerton, 1975*a* pp. 116, 203, etc).

29. This example is given in extended form in Bailey (1973*a*) p. 173, but I would not agree that some of his relations hold for British English.

30. The two views are contrasted point by point in Bickerton (1973*b*) and Bailey (1973*b*).

31. See Pulgram (1953) for a useful summary.

32. See Bickerton (1973*b*) p. 43 for a non-hypothetical wave diagram.

33. Obviously the above picture is oversimplified in that it suggests that not only does change affect one environment at a time, but also that variation is only heard in one environment at once. Some of Bickerton's examples (e.g. 1971, p. 476ff) seem to lend support to this view, but in Bailey's fuller work (1973*b*) he suggests that all environments of a rule *may* become variable before the oldest becomes categorical. My own work, say for the change [t]→[ʔ] (if that is indeed the correct interpretation), certainly suggests that there may be variation in several environments at once, though the change may have progressed further in some environments than others.

34. See Weinreich, Labov and Herzog (1968): 'Not all variability and hetereogeneity of language structure involves change, but all change involves variability and heterogeneity.'

35. Several scholars have drawn attention to the problem of 'stagnant' variable rules (see Fasold, 1973): cases where we know that

variation has existed for many years, without there being any clear evidence that a change from an old to a new feature is still in progress e.g. the variation between [θ] and [t] in *th-* words in some American varieties of English, or the '*h*-dropping' in many parts of Britain. A review of Bickerton's book by G. Sankoff (1977), while acknowledging the importance of the work, criticizes him for using his data selectively and illustratively rather than checking each of his hypotheses exhaustively against all his material, and also for not making clear *how* changes occur – do people go through change as individuals, or is it successive age-groups who progress to 'higher' lects? Other scholars feel that Bickerton and Bailey go too far in denying the validity of dialect-groupings (see Macauley, 1978).

Bibliography

This bibliography gives details of all items referred to in the text. The first edition is given in each case.

Abercrombie, D. (1951): RP and local accent. *The Listener*, 6 September.
(1954): The recording of dialect material. *Orbis*, 3.

Adams, G. B. (ed.) (1964): *Ulster Dialects: an introductory symposium*. Belfast: Ulster Folk Museum.

Allen, H. B. & G. N. Underwood (1974): *Readings in American Dialectology*. New York: Appleton-Century-Crofts.

Atkinson, J. C. (1868): *A Glossary of the Cleveland Dialect: explanatory, derivative and critical*. London: J. R. Smith.

Atwood, E. B. (1963): The methods of American dialectology. *Zeitschrift für Mundartforschung*, 30.

Bailey, C.-J. N. (1973a): The patterning of language variation. In: R. W. Bailey & J. L. Robinson (ed.): *Varieties of Present-Day English*. New York: Macmillan.
(1973b): *Variation and Linguistic Theory*. Arlington: Center for Applied Linguistics.

Bailey, C.-J. N. & R. W. Shuy (ed.): *New Ways of Analysing Variation in English*. Washington: Georgetown U.P.

Bartoli, M. G. (1925): *Introduzione alla Neolinguistica*. Geneva: Olschki.

Bartoli, M. G. & G. Bertoni (1925): *Breviario di Neolinguistica*. Modena: Societa tipografica modenese.

Batchelor, T. (1809): *An orthoepical analysis of the English language . . . to which is added a minute and copious analysis of the dialect of Bedfordshire*. London: Didier & Tebbet.

Bernstein, B. (1960): Language and social class. *British Journal of Sociology*, 11.

Bickerton, D. (1971): Inherent variability and variable rules. *Foundations of Language*, 7.
(1973a): The nature of a creole continuum. *Language*, 49.
(1973b): Quantitative versus dynamic paradigms: the case of Montreal 'que'. In: Bailey & Shuy (ed.).

(1975*a*): *The Dynamics of a Creole System*. London: Cambridge U.P.

(1975*b*): Review of Trudgill (1974*a*). *Journal of Linguistics*, 11.

Bloch, B. (1948): A set of postulates for phonemic analysis. *Language*, 24.

Bloomfield, L. (1933): *Language*. New York: Holt.

Bonfante, G. (1947): The Neolinguistic position. *Language*, 23.

Brilioth, B. (1913): *A Grammar of the Dialect of Lorton (Cumberland)*. London: Oxford U.P.

Brook, G. L. (1963): *English Dialects*. London: Deutsch.

Brown, G. (1972): *Phonological Rules and Dialect Variation*. London: Cambridge U.P.

Carr, W. (1824): *Horae Momenta Cravenae or The Craven Dialect*. London: Hurst & Robinson.

Catford, J. C. (1957*a*): The Linguistic Survey of Scotland. *Orbis*, 6.

(1957*b*): Vowel systems of Scots dialects. *Transactions of the Philological Society*.

Chomsky, N. (1957): *Syntactic Structures*. The Hague: Mouton.

(1964): *Current Issues in Linguistic Theory*. The Hague: Mouton.

(1965): *Aspects of the Theory of Syntax*. Cambridge, Mass: MIT Press.

Chomsky, N. & M. Halle (1965): Some controversial questions in phonological theory. *Journal of Linguistics*, 1.

(1968): *The Sound Pattern of English*. New York: Harper & Row.

Cochrane, G. R. (1959): The Australian English vowels as a diasystem. *Word*, 15.

Crystal, D. & D. Davy (1969): *Investigating English Style*. London: Longman.

Dauzat, A. (1939): Un nouvel atlas linguistique de la France. *Le Français Modern*, 7.

(1942): Le nouvel atlas linguistique de la France par régions. *Le Français Modern*, 10.

(1955): La méthode de nouveaux atlas linguistiques de la France. *Orbis*, 4.

De Camp, D. (1958–9): The pronunciation of English in San Francisco. *Orbis*, 7–8.

(1971): Towards a generative analysis of a post-creole continuum. In: D. Hymes (ed.): *Pidginization and Creolization of Languages*. London: Cambridge U.P.

Dieth, E. (1932): *A Grammar of the Buchan Dialect, Aberdeenshire*. Cambridge: Heffer.

(1946): A new survey of English dialects. *Essays & Studies*.

Edmont, E. (1897): *Lexique Saint-Polois*. Saint-Pol: L'Auteur.

(1914–15): *Atlas Linguistique de la Corse*. Paris: Champion.

Ellis, A. J. (1889): *On Early English Pronunciation, Part V: The Existing Phonology of English Dialects*. London: Trübner.

Ellis, S. (1976): Regional, social and economic influences on speech: Leeds University studies. In: Viereck (ed.) (1976).

Fasold, R. W. (1973): The concept of 'earlier-later': more or less correct. In: Bailey & Shuy (ed.).

Fischer, J. L. (1958): Social influences on the choice of a linguistic variant. *Word*, 14.

Francis, W. N. (1959): Some dialect isoglosses in England. *American Speech*, 34.

Gauchat, L. (1904): Gibt es Mundartgrenzen? *Archivum für das Studium der neueren Sprachen*, 11.

Giles, H. (1970): Evaluative reactions to accents. *Educational Review*, 22.

Giles, H. & P. F. Powesland (1975): *Speech Style and Social Evaluation*. London: Academic P.

Gilliéron, J. (1910): Mots en collision: le coq et le chat. *Revue de Philologie Française et de Littérature*, 24.

Gilliéron, J. et E. Edmont (1902–10): *Atlas Linguistique de la France*. Paris: Champion.

Gimson, A. C. (1962): *An Introduction to the Pronunciation of English*. London: Arnold.

Grant, W. (1909): What still remains to be done for Scottish dialects. *The English Association, Leaflet No. 11*.

Gregg, R. J. (1964): Scotch-Irish urban speech in Ulster, In: Adams (ed.). (1972): The Scottish-Irish dialect boundary in Ulster. In: Wakelin (ed.).

Hall, R. A. (1963): *Idealism in Romance Linguistics*. Ithaca: Cornell U.P. (1964): *Introductory Linguistics*. Philadelphia: Chilton.

Halle, M. (1959): *The Sound Pattern of Russian*. The Hague: Mouton. (1962): Phonology in generative grammar. *Word*, 18.

Hanley, M. L. (1930): Plans for a survey of the dialects of New England. *Dialect Notes*, 6.

Hill, T. (1958): Institutional Linguistics. *Orbis*, 7.

Hockett, C. F. (1955): A Manual of Phonology. *Memoir 11 of International Journal of American Linguistics*.

Honikman, B. (1964): Articulatory settings. In: D. Abercrombie et al. (ed.) *In Honour of Daniel Jones*. London: Longman.

Hotzenköcherle, R. (1962–): *Sprachatlas der Deutschen Schweiz*. Bern: Francke.

Houck, C. L. (1968): Methodology of an urban speech survey. *Leeds Studies in English*, NS 11.

Jaberg, K. (1908): *Sprachgeographie*. Aarau: Sauerländer.

Jaberg, K. & J. Jud (1928–40): *Sprach- und Sachatlas Italiens und der Südschweiz*. Zofingen: Ringier.

Keller, R. E. (1964): The use and abuse of dialect surveys: the German example. *Journal of the Lancashire Dialect Society*, 13.

King, K. C. (1954): The study of dialect in Germany. *Journal of the Lancashire Dialect Society*, 3.

King, R. D. (1969): *Historical Linguistics and Generative Grammar*. Englewood Cliffs: Prentice-Hall.

Kiparsky, P. (1968): Linguistic Universals and Linguistic Change. In: E. Bach & R. T. Harms (ed.): *Universals and Linguistic Theory*. New York: Holt, Rinehart & Winston.

Kjederqvist, J. (1903): *The Dialect of Pewsey (Wiltshire)*. London: Philological Society.

Klima, E. S. (1964): Relatedness between grammatical systems. *Language*, 40.

Knowles, G. O. (1978): The nature of phonological variables in Scouse. In: Trudgill (ed.).

Kohler, K. J. (1967): Structural Dialectology. *Zeitschrift für Mundartforschung*, 34.

Kökeritz, H. (1932): *The Phonology of the Suffolk Dialect*, Uppsala: Appelberg.

Kolb, E. (1966): *Phonological Atlas of the Northern Region*. Bern: Francke.

Kurath, H. (1930): Report of interviews with European scholars. *Dialect Notes*, 6.

Kurath, H. et al. (1939): *Handbook of the Linguistic Geography of New England*. Providence: Brown U.P.

(1939–43): *Linguistic Atlas of New England*. Providence: Brown U.P.

Labov, W. (1963): The social motivation of a sound change. *Word*, 19.

(1966a): *The Social Stratification of English in New York City*. Washington: Center for Applied Linguistics.

(1966b): Hypercorrection in the Lower Middle Class as a factor in linguistic change. In: W. Bright (ed.) *Sociolinguistics*. The Hague: Mouton.

(1967): The effect of social mobility on linguistic behavior. In: S. Lieberson (ed.) *Explorations in Sociolinguistics* (= *International Journal of American Linguistics*, 33, 4, 2).

(1968): The reflection of social processes in linguistic structures. In: J. A. Fishman (ed.): *Readings in the Sociology of Language*. The Hague: Mouton.

(1969): Contraction, deletion, and inherent variability of the English copula. *Language*, 45.

Labov, W., P. Cohen, C. Robins, & J. Lewis (1968): *A Study of the Non-standard English of Negro and Puerto Rican Speakers in New York City*. New York: Columbia University.

Ladefoged, P. (1960): The value of phonetic statements. *Language*, 36.

Laver, J. D. M. (1968): Voice quality and indexical information. *British Journal of Disorders of Communication*, 3.

Levine, L. & H. J. Crockett (1967): Speech variation in a piedmont community: postvocalic-r. In: S. Lieberson (ed.) *Explorations in Sociolinguistics* (= *International Journal of American Linguistics*, 33, 4, 2).

McDavid, R. I. (1948): Postvocalic-r in South Carolina: a social analysis. *American Speech*, 23.

McDavid, R. I. & V. G. McDavid (1956): Regional linguistic atlases in the United States. *Orbis*, 5.

McIntosh, A. (1952): *Introduction to a Survey of Scottish Dialects*. Edinburgh: Nelson.

Macauley, R. K. S. (1977): *Language, Social Class, and Education: a Glasgow study*. Edinburgh: Edinburgh U.P.
  (1978): Variation and consistency in Glaswegian English. In: Trudgill (ed.).

Mather, J. Y. & H. H. Speitel (1975–): *The Linguistic Atlas of Scotland*. London: Croom Helm.

Mencken, H. L. (1919): *The American Language*, New York: Knopf.

Milroy, J. & L. Milroy (1978): Belfast: change and variation in an urban vernacular. In: Trudgill (ed.).

Mitzka, W. & L. E. Schmidt (1953–): *Deutsche Wortatlas*. Giessen: Schmitz.

Moulton, W. G. (1960): The short vowel systems of Northern Switzerland: a study in structural dialectology. *Word*, 16.
  (1968): Structural dialectology. *Language*, 44.

Newton, B. (1972): *The Generative Interpretation of Dialect*. London: Cambridge U.P.

O'Neil, W. A. (1968): Transformational dialectology: phonology and syntax. *Zeitschrift für Mundartforschung*, 35.

Orr, J. (1936): *Memorandum* (on a linguistic survey of Scotland). Unpublished, LSS.

Orton, H. (1960): An English dialect survey: Linguistic Atlas of England. *Orbis*, 11.
  (1962): *Survey of English Dialects: Introduction*. Leeds: E. J. Arnold.

Orton, H. et al. (1962–71): *Survey of English Dialects: Basic Material*. Leeds: E. J. Arnold.

Orton, H. & N. Wright (1975): *Word Geography of England*. London: Seminar Press.

Orton, H., S. Sanderson, & J. Widdowson (1978): *Linguistic Atlas of England*. London: Croom Helm.

Paris, G. (1888): Les parlers de France. *Revue des Patois Gallo-Romans*, 2.

Peacock, R. B. (1869): *A Glossary of the Dialect of the Hundred of Lonsdale.* London: Asher.

Pederson, L. (1976): Aims and methods in a Chicago dialect survey. In: Viereck (ed.).

Pellowe, J. (1976): The Tyneside Linguistic Survey: aspects of a developing methodology. In: Viereck (ed.).

Pellowe, J., G. Nixon, B. Strang & V. McNeany (1972): A dynamic modelling of linguistic variation: the urban (Tyneside) linguistic survey. *Lingua,* 30.

Pellowe, J. & V. Jones (1978): On intonational variability in Tyneside speech. In: Trudgill (ed.).

Petyt, K. M. (1970): *Emily Brontë and the Haworth Dialect.* Yorkshire Dialect Society.

(1977): *Dialect and Accent in the Industrial West Riding.* Unpublished Ph.D. thesis, University of Reading.

(1978): Secondary contraction in West Yorkshire negatives. In: Trudgill (ed.).

Pickford, G. R. (1956): American linguistic geography: a sociological appraisal. *Word,* 12.

Pop, S. (1950–1): *La Dialectologie.* Louvain: Gembloux, Duclot.

Pulgram, E. (1953): Family tree, wave theory, and dialectology. *Orbis,* 2.

(1964): Structural comparison, diasystems, and dialectology. *Linguistics,* 4.

Putnam, G. N. & E. M. O'Hern (1955): The Status Significance of an Isolated Urban Dialect. *Language* (Dissertation 53).

Ringgaard, K. (1965): The phonemes of a dialectal area, perceived by phoneticians and by the speakers themselves. *Proceedings of the International Congress of Phonetic Sciences,* V.

Sankoff, G. (1977): Review of Bickerton (1975a). *Journal of Linguistics,* 13.

Sankoff, D. & H. J. Cedergren (1976): The dimensionality of grammatical variation. *Language,* 52.

Saporta, S. (1965): Ordered rules, dialect differences, and historical processes. *Language,* 41.

Saussure, F. de (1916): *Course de Linguistique Générale.* Lausanne: Payot.

Scheuermeier, P. (1932): Observations et expériences personnelles faites au cours de mon enquête. *Bulletin de la Société Linguistique de Paris,* 33.

Schmeller, J. A. (1821): *Die Mundarten Bayerns, grammatisch dargestellt.* Munich: Thienemann.

Séguy, J. (1973): Les atlas linguistiques de la France par régions. *Langue Française,* 18.

(1954–73): *Atlas Linguistique et Ethnographique de la Gascogne.* Toulouse: Institut d'études meridionales.

Shuy, R. W., W. A. Wolfram & W. K. Riley (1968a): *Field Techniques in an Urban Language Study.* Washington: Center for Applied Linguistics.

(1968b): *Linguistic Correlates of Social Stratification in Detroit Speech.* Michigan State University.

Sievers, E. (1876): *Grundzüge der Lautphysiologie.* Leipzig: Breitkopf und Härtel.

Sivertsen, E. (1960): *Cockney Phonology.* Oslo: Oslo U.P.

Skeat, W. W. (1911): *English Dialects.* London: Cambridge U.P.

Speitel, H. H. (1969): An areal typology of isoglosses. *Zeitschrift für Dialektologie und Linguistik,* 1.

Stankiewicz, E. (1957): On discreteness and continuity in structural dialectology. *Word,* 13.

Strang, B. M. H. (1968): The Tyneside Linguistic Survey. *Zeitschrift für Mundartforschung,* 35.

Thomas, A. R. (1964): Some aspects of a structural dialectology. *Transactions of the Honourable Society of Cymmrodorion.*

(1967): Generative phonology in dialectology. *Transactions of the Philological Society.*

(1968): Generative phonology and the statement of morphophonological variants in Welsh dialects. *Zeitschrift für Mundartforschung,* 35.

(1973): *The Linguistic Geography of Wales.* Cardiff: University of Wales P.

Trubetzkoy, N. S. (1931): Phonologie et géographie linguistique. *Transactions du Cercle Linguistique de Prague,* 4.

Trudgill, P. J. (1972): Sex, covert prestige, and linguistic change in the urban British English of Norwich. *Language and Society,* 1.

(1973): Phonological rules and sociolinguistic variation in Norwich English. In: Bailey & Shuy (ed.).

(1974a): *The Social Differentiation of English in Norwich.* London: Cambridge U.P.

(1974b): *Sociolinguistics.* Harmondsworth: Penguin.

(1975a): *Accent, Dialect, and the School.* London: Arnold.

(1975b): Linguistic geography and geographical linguistics. *Progress in Geography,* 7.

(ed.) (1978): *Sociolinguistic Patterns in British English.* London: Arnold.

Vasiliu, E. (1966): Towards a generative phonology of Daco-Rumanian dialects. *Journal of Linguistics,* 2.

Viereck, W. (1966): *Phonematische Analyse des Dialekts von Gateshead-upon-Tyne, Co. Durham.* Hamburg: Cram, de Gruyter.

(1968): A diachronic-structural analysis of a Northern English urban dialect. *Leeds Studies in English*, NS 11.

(1970): The English Dialect Society and its Dictionary. *Transactions of the Yorkshire Dialect Society*, LXX.

(1973): The growth and present state of dialectology. *Journal of English Linguistics*, 7.

(ed.) (1976): *Sprachliches Handeln-Soziales Verhalten*. Munich: Fink.

Wakelin, M. F. (ed.) (1972a): *Patterns in the Folk Speech of the British Isles*. London: Athlone.

(1972b): *English Dialects*. London: Athlone.

Weinreich, U. (1954): Is a structural dialectology possible? *Word*, 10.

Weinreich, U., W. Labov & M. I. Herzog (1968): Empirical Foundations for a theory of language change. In: W. P. Lehmann & Y. Malkiel (ed.): *Directions for Historical Linguistics*. Austin: Texas U.P.

Wells, J. C. (1970): Local accents in England and Wales. *Journal of Linguistics*, 6.

(1973): *Jamaican Pronunciation in London*. Oxford: Blackwell.

Williamson, J. V. & V. M. Burke (1971): *A Various Language: Perspectives on American Dialects*. New York: Holt, Rinehart & Winston.

Winteler, J. (1876): *Die Kerenzer Mundart des Kantons Glarus*. Leipzig.

Wolfram, W. A. (1969): *A Sociolinguistic Description of Detroit Negro Speech*. Washington: Center for Applied Linguistics.

Wolfram, W. A. & R. W. Fasold (1974): *The Study of Social Dialects in American English*. Englewood Cliffs: Prentice-Hall.

Wrede, F. (continued by W. Mitzka) (1926–56): *Deutsche Sprachatlas*. Marburg: Elwert.

Wright, J. (1892): *A Grammar of the Dialect of Windhill in the West Riding of Yorkshire*. London: Kegan Paul, Trench, Trübner.

(ed.) (1898–1905): *English Dialect Dictionary*. London: Frowde.

(1905): *The English Dialect Grammar*. London: Frowde (as appendix to *EDD*).

Wright, J. T. (1966): Urban Dialects: a consideration of method. *Zeitschrift für Mundartforschung*, 33.

Phonetic Symbols

When using English examples, I have generally adopted the system of transcription employed in one of the best-known British works of reference on pronunciation: A. C. Gimson: *An Introduction to the Pronunciation of English.*

For the variety known as RP (Received Pronunciation), Gimson uses the following set of symbols (with the exception of [ɪ] and [ʊ], all are taken from the International Phonetic Alphabet):

Symbol	*Phonetic description*	*Key-word in* RP
CONSONANTS		
p	Voiceless bilabial plosive	*p*ole
b	Voiced bilabial plosive	*b*owl
t	Voiceless alveolar plosive	*t*oll
d	Voiced alveolar plosive	*d*ole
k	Voiceless velar plosive	*c*oal
g	Voiced velar plosive	*g*oal
ʔ	Glottal plosive	tha*t* chair
f	Voiceless labiodental fricative	*f*eel
v	Voiced labiodental fricative	*v*eal
θ	Voiceless dental fricative	*th*igh
ð	Voiced dental fricative	*th*y
s	Voiceless alveolar fricative	*s*eal
z	Voiced alveolar fricative	*z*eal
ʃ	Voiceless palato-alveolar fricative	*sh*ip
ʒ	Voiced palato-alveolar fricative	*g*igolo
h	Voiceless glottal fricative	*h*eal
tʃ	Voiceless palato-alveolar affricate	*ch*ap
dʒ	Voiced palato-alveolar affricate	*J*ap
m	Voiced bilabial nasal	*m*ight
n	Voiced alveolar nasal	*n*ight
ŋ	Voiced velar nasal	ki*ng*
l	Voiced alveolar lateral continuant	*l*ip
r	Voiced post-alveolar approximant[1]	*r*ip

Symbol	Phonetic description	Key-word in RP
j	Voiced palatal approximant	*y*et
w	Voiced labial-velar approximant	*w*et

VOWELS

i:	Long close front unrounded	b*ea*d
u:	Long close back rounded	b*oo*ed
ɑ:	Long open back/central unrounded	b*ar*d
ɔ:	Long mid back rounded	p*aw*ed
ɜ:	Long mid central unrounded	b*ir*d
ɪ	Short close front[2] unrounded	b*i*d
e	Short mid front unrounded	b*e*d
æ	Short open[3] front unrounded	b*a*d
ɒ	Short open back rounded	p*o*d
ʊ	Short close[4] back rounded	h*oo*d
ʌ	Short half-open central unrounded	b*u*d
ə	Short mid central unrounded	butt*er*

DIPHTHONGS — In each case, a glide starting in the position of the first vowel symbol and moving in the direction of that of the second.

eɪ		p*ai*d
aɪ		p*ie*d
ɔɪ		c*oi*n
ʊɪ		r*ui*n
əʊ		l*oa*d
ɑʊ		l*ou*d
ɪə		b*ea*rd
ɛə		b*are*d
ɔə[5]		b*ore*d
ʊə		m*oore*d

1	[ɹ] would be a more precise symbol for this sound ([r] generally indicates a rolled sound), but [r] is commonly used because it is easier to write.
2	Less close and front than [i:].
3	Less open than [a] (see below).
4	Less close and back than [u:].
5	Many speakers of RP nowadays extend [ɔ:] to all words where others have this diphthong.

For other varieties of English, consonants pose few problems, and the above symbols are used, with more or less the same values. With vowels, where the sound in question is not markedly different from one in RP, the same symbol is used. Where I wish to draw attention to a difference, I follow Gimson's practice of using the symbol from the IPA which stands for the 'idealized' vowel position which is closest to that of the actual vowel in the variety being transcribed. For instance, when Gimson uses the symbol [e] for RP *bed* etc, he does not imply that the sound in question is precisely 'front half-close' (as specified in the IPA); rather, as his detailed descriptions make clear, the vowel is most commonly somewhere between 'front half-close' [e] and 'front half-open' [ɛ] but tends to be nearer to the former. Similarly, [ɑ:] in *bard* is 'somewhat nearer to [ɑ] than to [a]': i.e. more 'back open' than 'front open'.

The following additional symbols have been used:

ɛ   More open than [e]
a   More open than [æ]
a: More front than [ɑ:]
e: Long pure vowel (i.e. not diphthongized), nearer to [e] than
     to [ɛ]
o: Long pure vowel (i.e. not diphthongized), nearer to [o] than
     to [ɔ]

Diphthongs such as [ɛɪ], [ɑɪ], [ɛʊ], [ɔʊ], [oʊ], [aʊ], [eə] etc, are symbolized on the same principle: e.g. [ɛɪ] has a more open starting-point than RP [eɪ], but glides towards the same end-point; [ɔʊ] starts at a backer and more open starting-point than RP [əʊ], but glides in the same direction; and so on.

A number of 'modifiers' are employed, where I wish to indicate a more precise phonetic quality:

ˌ (under vowel symbol):	tongue lowered e.g. [e̞], a vowel more open than 'ideal' [e], but not sufficiently open to be symbolized [ɛ].
ˆ (over vowel symbol):	tongue raised e.g. [ɛ̂], closer than [ɛ], but nearer to this than to [e].
˙ (over vowel symbol):	tongue retracted e.g. [à], less front than [a], but closer to this than to [ɑ].
ˇ and ¯ (over vowel symbol):	shortness and length respectively. These symbols are more commonly employed by philologists; modern linguists use [:] after a vowel symbol to indicate length

and do not symbolize shortness, but I have found it necessary to adopt ˘ occasionally.

ʰ (after consonant symbol): aspirated release.

When other languages are referred to, a few extra symbols have been required:

x   Voiceless velar fricative
ɣ   Voiced velar fricative
i   Close central unrounded vowel
¨   (over vowel symbol): centralized e.g. [ë] is centralized [e]

In this last case, the above ˘ symbol could have been employed, but where examples are drawn directly from other works (either on English or on some other language), I have often left the transcription unchanged; certain symbols may be employed in a manner slightly different from what is described above, but these differences should not cause any difficulty for the reader.

Finally, it should be noted that square brackets [ ], indicating phonetic transcription, have been employed throughout except when I wish to emphasize that a difference of phonemic system is involved, when the usual slants // have been adopted; also that ♯ indicates a word-boundary.

Indexes

Index of Names

🈂🈂🈂🈂🈂🈂

Index of Topics

🆂🆂🆂🆂🆂🆂